DATE DUE

D1159598

Communicating Change

SERIES EDITOR

BARRIE DALE
UMIST

Communicating Change

Bill Quirke

McGRAW-HILL BOOK COMPANY
London · New York · St Louis · San Francisco · Auckland
Bogotá · Caracas · Lisbon · Madrid . Mexico · Milan
Montreal · New Delhi · Panama · Paris · San Juan
São Paulo · Singapore · Sydney · Tokyo · Toronto

Published by
McGRAW-HILL Book Company Europe
Shoppenhangers Road, Maidenhead, Berkshire SL6 2QL, England
Telephone: 01628 23432
Fax: 01628 770224

British Library Cataloguing in Publication Data
Quirke, Bill
　　Communicating Change. – (Quality in
　　Action Series)
　　I. Title II. Series
　　658.45

　　ISBN 0-07-707941-8

Library of Congress Cataloging-in-Publication Data
Quirke, Bill
　　　　Communicating change/Bill Quirke.
　　　　　p. cm. – (Quality in action)
　　　　Includes index.
　　　　ISBN 0-07-707941-8
　　　　1. Communication in management. 2. Organizational change.
　　I. Series. II. Series: McGraw-Hill quality in action series.
　　HD.30.3.Q57 1995
　　658.4'5–dc20　　　　　　　　　　　　　　　　　　　94-29585
　　　　　　　　　　　　　　　　　　　　　　　　　　　　　CIP

12345 BL 98765

Typeset by BookEns Ltd., Royston, Herts.
Printed and bound in Great Britain by Biddles Ltd, Guildford, Surrey.

**From the fruit of his lips a man is filled with good
things, as surely as the work of his hands rewards him**
Proverbs 12:14

*This book is dedicated to my wife Briony, my mother Ann,
and to my brother Tom, who got me started in the first place.*

*My special thanks to Sarah Langsford
for typing the manuscript.*

Contents

Series Preface

Quality is regarded by most producers, customers and consumers as more important than ever before in their manufacturing, service and purchasing strategies. If you doubt this just think of the unsatisfactory examples of quality you have personally experienced, the bad feelings it gave you, the resulting actions you took and the people you told about the experience and the outcome. The concept of Total Quality Management (TQM) is increasingly being adopted by organizations as the means of satisfying the needs and expectations of their customers.

Total quality management has been practised by the major Japanese manufacturing companies for the last 30 or so years. Their commitment to continuous and company-wide quality improvement has provided them with the foundation by which they have been able to capture markets the world over. In response to this competitive pressure Western manufacturing companies, first in America and then Europe started to embrace the TQM ethic; this was followed by commercial and service-type organizations. The superior performing Western organizations have now some 15 or so years of operating experience of TQM.

Total quality management is a subject and management philosophy in which there appears to be an unquenchable thirst for knowledge, despite the considerable volume of published material. The objective of this major 'Quality in Action' book series is to help satisfy this need and fill what we believe are gaps in the existing range of current books. It is also obvious from the arguments advanced from some quarters that there is still a lack of understanding of TQM and what it is about. Hopefully the books in the series will help to improve the level of understanding.

McGraw-Hill has already published books by three of the best known and internationally respected quality management experts – Crosby, Feigenbaum and Juran. The 'Quality in Action' series will build upon the work of these three men; this in itself will be a challenge.

I was honoured when asked by McGraw-Hill to be the 'Quality in Action' book series editor. I have personally been involved in industrially based TQM research for the last twelve or so years and from this experience believe I am well placed to identify the aspects of TQM which need to be addressed by new books on the subject.

The prime focus of the series is management and the texts have been prepared from this standpoint. However, undergraduate and postgraduate students will also find the books of considerable benefit in understanding the concept, principles, elements and practices of TQM, the associated quality management systems, tools and techniques, the means of introducing, developing and sustaining TQM and the associated difficulties.

One objective of the series is to provide some general TQM reading as guidance for management in introducing, developing and sustaining a process of continuous and company-wide quality improvement. It will focus on manufacturing, commercial and service situations. We are looking for recognized writers (academics, consultants and practitioners) who will be able to address the subject from a European perspective. The books appearing on this theme will not duplicate already published material, rather they will build upon, enhance and develop the TQM wisdom and address the subject from a new perspective. A second objective is to provide texts on aspects of TQM not adequately covered by current books. For example, TQM and human resources, sustaining TQM, TQM: corporate culture and organizational change, partnership sourcing, TQM and business strategy. It is likely that the authors of these books will be from disciplines (e.g. accounting, economic, psychology, human resources) not traditionally associated with quality management. A third objective is to provide texts which deal with quality management systems, tools and techniques in a practical 'how-to' manner.

My commitment to this series is that I am prepared to allocate time from my considerable research, teaching and advisory activities in order to ensure that it meets and hopefully exceeds the needs and expectations of our readers.

B. G. Dale, Series Editor

About the Series Editor

Dr Barrie Dale is Reader and Director of the UMIST Quality Management Centre. The Centre is involved in three major activities: research into Total Quality Management (TQM); the Centre houses the Ford Motor Company Northern Regional Centre for training suppliers in Statistical Process Control; and the operation of a Total Quality Management Multi-Company Teaching Programme involving, at any one time, eight collaborators from a variety of industrial and business environments. He also coordinates the Bowater Corrugated Division Total Quality Performance Multi-Institute Teaching Programme. Dr Dale is also a Non-Executive Director of Manchester Circuit Ltd, a company specializing in the manufacture of high technology and complex printed circuits boards.

He is co-editor of the *International Journal of Quality and Reliability Management*, now in its eleventh volume. Dr Dale is co-author of *Managing Quality, Quality Costing, Quality Improvement Through Standards, Total Quality and Human Resources: An Executive Guide* and *The Road to Quality* and has published over 180 papers on the subject of quality management. Dr Dale has also led four missions to Japan of European executives to study the application of TQM in major Japanese manufacturing organizations.

Preface

Competition is so fierce today, and businesses face threats from so many and so diverse quarters, that the energies and ideas of their people are vital to survival and success.

Effective communication has been recognized as the prime factor in making much needed change happen inside organizations – yet while business has changed out of all recognition in the last 20 years, employee satisfaction with communication over the same period has barely shifted.

Ask anyone who works inside an organization what they think of its internal communication and they are likely to lambaste it as poor. Employees claim that no one listens to either their complaints or their ideas; managers claim that when they ask their people for input they get no response.

Yet there has probably never been more attention paid to communication in organizations, no greater realization of its importance, no greater activity in terms of roadshows, videos, newsletters and electronic mail. Most organizations acknowledge that they need not just good but great communication between their people if they are to survive and thrive. Large amounts of time, energy and money are being poured into the communication process, without the expected return on investment. We are using yesterday's communication approaches to meet tomorrow's demands, and they are not delivering what organizations need.

This book comes out of a number of years spent with colleagues and clients asking the same question, 'How can we improve communication?', and the realization that everyone seems to have a different interpretation of what communication is, what job it is supposed to do, and what constitutes an improvement.

This book is aimed at those who want to improve communication among their people:

- leaders who want their companies to be more effective and more competitive
- senior managers who want to speed up the rate of change in their organizations
- managers involved in change initiatives
- communication directors trying to educate their colleagues about communication
- operations directors trying to educate their colleagues about the realities of the business.

Directors in the same organization, trade the word 'communication' meaning something quite different by it, knowing that they somehow disagree, but being unable to pinpoint just how. One aim of this book is to provide a framework for a more informed and productive approach.

Internal communication strategy is often based on the desire to satisfy what it is that employees want from communication. One of the constants of life seems to be that employees believe communication inside their organization is poor. Pursuing their happiness is not always the best way to make improvements.

This book aims to provide a different framework for agreeing what communication is needed, and a structure for developing and implementing an internal communication strategy. It is based on the view that communication is a means to an end – the success of the organization, and that it should be based upon, and serve, the business strategy. The link between the business strategy and the communication strategy depends on three things:

- the business's structure and stage of development
- the external pressures on the business to change
- how the business competes to gain and keep customers.

This book takes a practical look at the Catch 22s that dog communication, provides a framework for identifying the right communication strategy to match an organization's business strategy, and gives insights into how to make a new strategy work or to identify where a current strategy is failing.

KEY CHAPTERS

1. Communicating in a world of change

This chapter describes the changes facing organizations, the fundamental shift in roles and relationships between people at work, and the need to tap into their thinking, energy and creativity to develop a competitive edge. It also describes some of the underlying attitudes that get in the way of effective communication.

2. The business of communication

This chapter argues that a communication strategy should support the business strategy, and provides a new framework for identifying the role of communication inside the organization. This argues that a communication strategy should be based on three factors: the stage of development the organization has reached; the external pressures on an organization to change; and the competitive offer that it makes to the customer. The next three chapters examine each of these factors in turn.

3. Structure, identity and values

Internal communication strategy is usually approached from the viewpoint of the senior manager who wants to get a message across, or starts with deciding what it is that the employee would like to know.

This chapter takes a different approach – it argues that organizations wrongly adopt ideas and approaches designed for other, different organizations, in different markets, at different stages of development and with different strategies. It argues that communication strategies are often developed in isolation from the business strategy. It also looks at what kind of communication is needed at different stages of an organization's development, and what are the characteristics of communication at each stage. This allows the reader to check whether the characteristics of his or her own organization match its stage of development, or whether there is a mismatch.

Finally, it examines the effect of corporate identity on employees' loyalty, and describes the increasing importance of shared values on aligning employee energies.

4. Communicating for change

This chapter addresses the most frequent and pressing question faced by senior managers: 'How do I get my people to change – and fast?'

Almost every organization is facing fundamental changes in the number and type of people it will employ, the markets in which it operates and the technology it is trying to master. Senior managers need their staff to embrace and adapt to change, but are becoming increasingly frustrated at the slow pace of this change. The chapter argues that some of the pain managers feel is self-inflicted, and is directly caused by their approach to communication. It also describes typical reactions to change, the seeds of sabotage and apparent resistance, and presents a model for developing a communication strategy, ways of avoiding communication collisions, and using communication to create greater involvement in, and ownership of, change.

5. Customers and quality

In order to compete, businesses need to be close to their customers, and to provide them with the quality they require and will pay for. This chapter looks at creating greater customer orientation within organizations, and highlights the schizophrenia that employees experience, which can undermine customer service initiatives. It outlines the kind of communication needed for a quality organization, and the different ways in which communication can be organized to help serve different types of customer. It also describes different ways of organizing communication depending upon different competitive strategies.

6. Using internal research to create change

Internal research is the first step to developing a strategy, on the basis that if you don't know what the problem is, you don't have a solution. This chapter discusses how to organize an internal research project, alerts the reader to the pitfalls, outlines different ways of interpreting data, using tracking research to change behaviour, and how to conduct feedback to participants in research exercises.

7. Communicating in teams

Putting people together in teams is a growing way of pooling complementary strengths and sharing expertise. Individuals are increasingly becoming members of a number of different teams, some temporary, some more permanent, demanding different ways of working together. This chapter looks at the challenges of using communication to get teams to work more effectively together. It looks particularly at the problems of team briefing as a vehicle for communication, and suggests new models of team meetings, with a description of the different roles of team leaders and the skills required. It discusses the barriers to getting the most out of teams, tactics for overcoming these, and ways of organizing team meetings laterally as well as vertically.

8. Orchestrating communication

Complexity is confusing communication. Information overload is frustrating employees at a time when control of communication media and technology is shifting from the producers of information to the consumers. There is so much change under way within organizations that the old model of managing communication is no longer up to the task.

In the past the only limit to producing and distributing information seemed to be the number of trees left for the production of paper. Today, the real limited resource is time, which needs careful management. This chapter argues that a new communication contract is needed between the employee and the manager, and a new drive for collaboration rather than competition is needed between internal communicators.

One of the long-running arguments in organizations is over the most appropriate 'home' for the communication function – should it be the responsibility of Personnel, Public Affairs, Marketing or Operations? Should the corporate centre, in London or New York, be able to communicate to employees at a local divisional depot? This chapter provides a framework for resolving the debate, which is not based on the personal ambitions of managers, or on the gladiatorial competition between decentralized division and corporate centre.

It also looks at the increasing clutter of communication, the competition between communicators and argues the need for greater coordination between internal communicators.

Acknowledgements

Andy Leaf

Jaffer Lokhandvala

Geoff Nightingale

Stephen Quirke

Charlotte Grobien

Viv Taylor

Caroline Marland

Stella Beaumont

Mandy Wright

Leonie Hull

Caroline Good

Richard Bloomfield

Paul Lloyd

Peter Agertoft

Debbie Standish

Alistair Cheyne

Karen Myers

David Bernstein

Richard Eyre

John Mumford

Simon Barrow

Steve Pain

Bob Hodges

Don Hughes

Bob Watson

Sue Hurley

Bob Keen

Charles Laughton Scott

Sandie Palmer

Brenda McAll

Adrian Seward

Communicating in a world of change

W hile high-tech companies are proudly outlining the information super-highway of tomorrow, most organizations today risk finding themselves down a communication cul-de-sac.

The pace of change in most organizations is rapidly increasing. In search of a distinctive competitive edge, in an ever-changing marketplace, managers need to meet rising expectations among customers, while beating the tactics of competitors. To compete through better quality, cost effectiveness and customer service, managers need to create motivation and commitment among their employees. They need to respond both to the changing way people want to be managed, and to what they want out of their jobs. No wonder managers feel under stress.

As product life cycles shorten, and competitors catch up, success will depend on the speed of response to external change. This has brought internal communication to the fore.

Most organizations recognize the need for good communication with their people. Over the last few years, that battle has largely been won. What still remains is a lack of understanding of what communication is, and the role it has to play within organizations. Managers want, and organizations need, more from communication than before.

While there is a common agreement that effective communication is a vital part of change, and can help tap into employees' energies and ideas, companies are not getting what they need from their internal communication. In every organization, people seem to believe that communication could be better. There is general agreement that it could and should be improved, but that improvement seems difficult to achieve.

While there may be a general agreement that communication is important, that consensus masks very different perceptions of why it is important, what is its role and how it can help the organization succeed.

People look at communication differently, have different definitions and mean different things – but the one thing they all have in common is frustration. The nature and the role of internal communication is changing, driven by the changes taking place both outside and within organizations. The world has changed, people have changed – and the way internal communication is managed has to change with them. Internal communication is still largely based on assumptions which are no longer true, is designed to do a job which is no longer needed, and is managed in a way that is outdated.

To understand how communication should be helping you, and how you should be using it, it is necessary to understand how change is affecting you.

WHAT'S CHANGING

- The balance of power between supplier and customer is shifting.
- Organizations are reducing in size and restructuring.
- Employee values are changing.
- The roles of the employee and the manager are changing.
- Relationships within the business are becoming more complex.

The balance of power between supplier and customer is shifting

There is a fundamental shift in the balance of power that has existed between customer and supplier. With greater choice available, consumers are becoming more fickle and more demanding. Most consumers of goods and services now have a wide range of potential suppliers, both local and international, from which to choose. The balance of power is shifting increasingly towards the customer, and the customer is learning to enjoy and exercise that power.

Henry Ford may have offered 'any colour, as long as it is black', but once a supplier starts offering a range of options it is only a matter of time before the customer starts asking for options which do not currently exist, or configuring the most desirable option and asking the supplier to provide it.

Information is a virus that creates freedom ... because revolutions occur when people become aware of alternatives (Wriston, 1991).

Customers are becoming increasingly sophisticated and informed. They will inevitably become more discerning, more demanding and will have higher expectations. Customer care and service, which a few years ago was seen as a competitive edge, has now become standard, and the quest now is to provide the customer with additional value in a distinctive way that creates loyalty and prompts them to tell their friends.

Organizations are reducing in size and restructuring

The basis of competition has changed over the past 20 years, and businesses have been driven into untraditional areas in search of a competitive advantage.

For decades firms in almost every sphere of activity sought 'economies of scale' – manufacturing or distributing goods in ever larger volumes lowers the unit cost, so that a firm becomes more efficient as it grows bigger. However, even big businesses now see themselves as ungainly elephants, oversized and unresponsive to their marketplaces.

Factory automation is making it possible to produce goods cheaply in much smaller volumes. The decreasing price of computers is enabling smaller firms to automate administrative tasks in ways that were available only to large firms in the past. Quality techniques are being applied almost everywhere by big and small firms alike, eliminating variation in the quality of many products and creating higher expectations among customers.

As the advantages of size diminish, so the costs of size are becoming obvious. Many large firms are scrambling to reduce these, scrapping layers of middle managers, cutting overheads and reorganizing themselves into 'federations' of autonomous business units – trying to become more like their smaller rivals.

Information technology is driving change in the structure of organizations, in the same way as the automation of manufacturing processes led to the reduction in manual workforces.

Most of the banks have been downsizing. Building societies and insurance companies are widely expected to follow the trend.

Part of the downsizing is the result of questioning what value is added by tiers of managers, with the discovery that tiers are useful for an organization based on a philosophy of command and control, not the flat responsive structures needed today:

> ... when a company focuses its data processing capacity on producing information ... it becomes clear that both the number of management levels and the number of managers can be sharply cut. The reason is straightforward: it turns out that whole layers of management neither make decisions nor lead. Instead their main, if not their only, function is to serve as 'relays' – human boosters for the faint, and focused signals that pass for communication in the traditional pre-information organisation (Drucker, 1991).

With shopfloor manning levels cut to the bone by years of scrutiny and reorganization, businesses are looking to reduce management levels to lower costs and improve service. In March 1994, BT announced that it was reducing the number of senior management by 30 directors below board level. Over the last two years, 5000 middle managers and 900 senior managers have left as management levels have been cut from 12 to 6.

Part of this exercise has been carried out in pursuit of cost reduction, but it is also being done to increase responsiveness. Speed of decision making is a competitive advantage, and layers of management are seen as slowing down this process.

During the course of its reduction programme to date, IBM has moved 30 000 people from overhead positions to areas where they can actively add value to the customer, such as sales and system engineering.

As the drive for cost reduction and creating greater value for money increases, people will be moved into areas that bring them into contact with customers, and traditional central management and support jobs will cease to exist.

W.H. Smith announced the axing of 950 positions and the elimination of two management levels in its shops. To increase both customer service and productivity, new roles of 'customer service leaders' were created to put more people into the shops to help and advise customers. This is another example of how companies are not just reducing numbers of staff, but redeploying them into customer-facing positions.

Employee values are changing

The traditional distinctions are breaking down as companies become more and more closely involved with their customers and suppliers, with greater collaboration and interdependence.

The traditional definition of the employee is also changing. Work life is becoming more complex, driven by the need for more effective cost management by the employer, the need to cater for the varying demands of the customer and the aspirations and needs of the employee.

Key timers, outsourced functions, networkers, flexiworkers, subcontractors, interim managers, franchisees and telecommuters are all alternatives to the traditional employer/employee relationship.

Having focused for so long on blue-collar productivity, and with the greater proportion of the workforce now being white-collar, businesses now have to look to increasing white-collar productivity to improve profit. This will mean greater accountability for white-collar workers, and more pressure on their time and emotional energy.

Employees may not be willing to supply more of their time and emotional energy. The flattening of corporate structures and the wholesale reduction of management levels means the breaking of the bonds of corporate loyalty. With flatter structures there are fewer opportunities for promotion in any case, and so middle managers seek motivators other than promotion prospects.

The drive towards flexible working, and contracting part-time staff, as a way of reducing the salary bill, has a strong effect on employees' willingness to give 'emotional labour'.

Employees report that the old feeling of being part of a community is being lost, as management's apparent concern is with cost reduction and exacting a full day's work for whatever pay is provided. Employees point to the appeal for their loyalty, commitment and energy made by their managers, while in the next breath these same managers are referring them to the small print of their employment contracts.

People seem to have a need to feel part of a greater whole, a team, a company, and that feeling of belonging can rapidly be eroded by a neglect of the relationship and too great an insistence on the small print in the contract. Employees may recognize that the days of all being part of one happy family are gone, but they do not believe that the only other alternative is to become merely a cog in an uncaring machine.

To keep customers, companies have to keep improving the product and the service they supply. Service and customer satisfaction depend on the commitment and 'emotional labour' of employees. Companies with high-profile values attract and retain people who give high productivity and high quality work. Employees will not give that emotional labour to an organization which does not share their values, and whose highest calling is apparently only to increase the return to shareholders.

With the growth in the debate about quality of life, the decrease in the concept of the 'corporate man', the decline of the nuclear family as the traditional model for family life and the increase in jobs for women in the workplace, there is a redefinition in what people want from their work lives.

As career paths lose their certainty and companies' futures grow less predictable, people can at least be in charge of their own professional lives.

More and more professionals are passing up jobs with glamour and prestige in favour of those that give them greater control over their own activities and direction.

A Gallup poll published in September 1993 showed that people would rather have more time for things that are important in their lives and accept less money. People want more control over their lives and are becoming less tolerant of corporate pressures.

The roles of the employee and the manager are changing

Formal and informal communication is shifting from the vertical to the horizontal, from the line management chain of command to networks of colleagues, suppliers, collaborators and customers. The focus on customers, greater cross-department cooperation, Business Process Re-engineering and Total Quality means that the spotlight is increasingly on links that run laterally across the organization. These are usually between people of similar rank and status, with no line power over each other, and so rely more on collaboration and cooperation. Increasingly then communication – especially informal communication – runs laterally between equals, while the formal channels run vertically, between people of different status.

The traditional reliance on position, title and authority is increasingly misplaced. When organizations want people who will think about what they are doing and come up with better ways of doing it, it is not credible to back up a managerial instruction with 'Do it, because I say so'.

As people begin to work more as teams of equal status, dealing in ideas and information, the organization will operate more collegiately, like an academic faculty. The shift in titles away from manager to variants such as team leader, coordinator, etc. shows the closing of the gap between the manager and the managed.

The changing role of the manager

If hierarchical power is diminishing, and the manager may well be the person least familiar with the details of his or her people's work, how then does he or she add value? The value of the manager will be in building bridges between areas where collaboration is needed, networking and facilitating rather than dictating. Managing will be less about exercising power and more about building relationships, helping people to identify issues and assisting teams to work together in more creative ways to solve problems.

The drive to internal alliances and cross-departmental cooperation puts a greater onus on how well people are able to get along with each other. Cross-department collaboration means greater interdependency, and greater sharing of objectives and problems. The ability to negotiate and problem-solve becomes vital when you do not have power to dictate, and when you cannot say 'That's your problem, not mine'.

Rosabeth Moss Kanter (1991) highlights the new role of the manager:

> Executives must be able to juggle a set of constituencies rather than control a set of subordinates.
>
> They have to bargain, negotiate, and sell instead of making unilateral decisions and issuing commands. The kind of power achieved through a network of stakeholders is very different from the kind of power managers wield in a traditional bureaucracy.
>
> The new way gets more done, but it also takes more time.

Relationships within the business are becoming more complex

While organizations may be shrinking in terms of numbers, and layers may be being removed, life inside is becoming more complex. The organization chart of a company may nominally reflect the lines of accountability, but it rarely reflects the lines of communication and day-to-day dealing.

Confronted with change on every front, the typical organization will have strategic action teams, cross-functional task forces, supplier quality groups and new product development project teams galore. With an increasing sense of meeting and communication overload, managers rush between meetings, getting their 'real' work done in the early morning or late evening when the phones are not ringing. Most of these will, by definition, operate across functional and departmental lines, and managers will simultaneously be members of a number of teams, to which they may owe more allegiance than their nominal line supervisor, and which operate outside the formal chain of command.

All of these activities, and the informal networks they create, share influence and information. Attempting to control communication formally becomes increasingly ineffective. Organizations may want employees who will use their initiative and creativity to solve a problem and who will stretch themselves to help the customer. However, encouraged to speak up, and exercise their initiative, employees are now far more challenging of authority and far more likely to interrogate the rationales for decisions.

Some managers perceive that they are losing power as information and authority flows through other networks, not exclusively down the line management chain. The markets they operate in, and the technology they use, will probably have shifted significantly during a manager's rise up the organization, so managers may well not be familiar with, or understand, the work being done by the people who report to them. Managers may well know less than their subordinates, and may be tempted to control what information they do have to protect their power.

The central skill in managing today's organization has gone from 'telling the troops' to fostering and facilitating communication. This means bringing the same respect and disciplines to communicating with the employee as are brought to communicating with the customer. It is as much a question of attitude as of technique, and often the attitude undermines the technique.

In 1985, MORI found that 1 in 3 working people felt they could do more work without much effort, but 53 per cent believed management was more interested in giving its point of view than in listening to what employees had to say.

The responses of shopfloor workers in the MORI poll demonstrate a continuing deterioration in communication. In 1975 56 per cent of them had described themselves as fully or fairly well informed. Ten years later, that figure had fallen to just 37 per cent.

A 1990 KPMG/CBI study showed that 65 per cent of British managers felt their communication was very good, good or adequate. However, in 1991 the Price Waterhouse/Cranfield School of Management report found managers reluctant to communicate with employees on financial and strategic issues:

> Managers seem to concentrate on feeding themselves and each other with information, neglecting the important task of taking their staff and organisation with them.

Overall, British managers are clearly more satisfied with communication in their organizations than their employees are. This is a satisfaction which is being challenged daily. Any organization today is likely to be facing at least one of the following pressures:

- A new managing director is appointed with the mandate to re-energize the business and give strong leadership.
- A new competitive strategy calls for a fundamental change in attitudes and behaviour.
- A re-examination of the roles of the divisions and the corporate centre calls for a restructuring of the organization.
- A shift in the environment, either regulatory or competitive, redefines what is needed from employees.
- The adoption of a change initiative, such as Business Process Re-engineering or TQM, calls for employees' understanding of the initiative's aims and a change in attitudes and behaviours.
- A shift in strategy involves restructuring, downsizing, cost improvement, divestiture of non-core businesses and acquisition of new businesses.

Any and all of the above will call for careful management of communication. Each will demand a different kind of communication, will involve different processes and will require different roles of those involved in managing communication. However, each will be fundamentally affected by the unconscious attitudes and assumptions inside the organization.

MORI's research shows that, for all the millions spent on internal communication over the past 20 years, employee satisfaction with it has barely improved. This is a reflection of some of the assumptions and attitudes that hold back communication, and undermine well-intentioned initiatives to improve it.

WE DISAGREE MORE THAN WE THINK

Organizations accept that good communication is important. From there, paths diverge. Different members of the management team have different views. The word 'communication' is traded around the boardroom table, but hides the divergence of values, definitions and agendas. While there is a natural tendency to believe that everyone is in agreement, it is more likely that, unbeknown to each other, each board member has a significantly different perception of communication issues.

Communication is soft and separate

The dilemma faced by organizations is that while internal communication is central to success, managers tend to regard it as peripheral, or as an optional 'bolt on' to their real job. It is something to be done when there is time and leisure, or something to be delegated to the communications department. Most managers will readily agree that communication is a good thing and terribly important. However, that readiness is usually followed by a strong desire to get back to the real job of running a business. There is a low level of understanding of what communication involves and little commitment to getting it right.

While there is general agreement that communication is the responsibility of the line manager, it is usually the communications manager who has to stimulate line managers into improving. There is usually a low level of perception on the line manager's side that communication demonstrably impacts the business.

Communication equals information

There is a belief that communication is a question of mechanics and a focus on delivering messages. This usually shows up as a desire to build the chief executive a bigger megaphone, on his assumption that if people are not doing what he wants them to, it is because they cannot hear him. Typically, this involves shopping for new media and imitating the technology employed by another organization, without the spirit that made it work.

Similarly, attention is paid to pumping out news of new developments which may interest the board, but which are not relevant or interesting to the people being addressed. Information is based on what managers believe should interest employees, not on what employees actually want to know.

Communication is seen as an event, not a process

When there are redundancies, or a drive to cut costs, or when a new strategy is launched, senior managers feel there should be a communication programme to get the message across. Once that need has passed and the programme is completed, it is business as usual, and communication wanes.

Unfortunately, there is a belief among management that employee communication is something that can be turned on and off like a tap, at will. Managers say 'We did a lot of internal communication until we had to cut back on costs'. This leaves employees with the clear message that internal communication is a low priority. Therefore it is not surprising that when an internal communication programme is revived, its credibility is seriously damaged from the start, since it is seen as a whim of management.

Telling the troops

Senior management often translates communication simply as 'telling'. There tends to be an in-built assumption that the right to communicate lies with those at the top of the organization.

Most employee communications is like sending people their New Year's resolutions through the post and expecting them to keep them.

The production line mentality

Decisions are taken at senior levels, then passed down the line to the internal communicators to be packaged and distributed as well and as appropriately as possible. There is little consideration of how communication issues should affect and shape decisions themselves, and the process of communication is a reactive and a limited one. The internal communications manager may depend on receiving the minutes of the board meeting to begin the communication process, and may well be unaware of the issues behind decisions and the extent and nature of debate of other options. The minutes set the process going, and the agenda largely determines the content of the minutes. In one organization, it was a director's secretary who drew up the agenda – she effectively was, without knowing it, setting the communication strategy for the business.

There is a manufacturing and production mentality underlying communication: an assembly line, in which discrete messages are produced by the specialists, crafted, packaged and sent out, relegating the communication function, at worst, to the dispatch department.

If a production mentality underlies communication, so too do the assumptions of a hierarchical approach, where importance depends on rank, and information becomes a badge of status and a means of exercising power.

The hierarchical mentality

The drive to get closer to the market and closer to the customer is turning organizations upside down. There is a shift away from the values of the traditional hierarchical pyramid organization of the past. Unfortunately, it is impossible to simply overlay a customer-focused culture on the practices of the production-focused past.

An organization of the past was typically inward-focused, where managers were secure in their jobs and steadily progressed up the career ladder in a flight from the customer. In this kind of organization, managers gave orders and checked on the progress of employees. They issued dictats and expected compliance.

Though organizational structures may have flattened, the hierarchical mentality is still alive and well.

At the outset of change, the board goes away for a three-day off-site retreat. They are the best informed, the most strategically minded and take the long-term view. When the change has been decided they come back to present the future to their employees. Employees, who are least well informed, least involved in the background thinking and critical to the strategy's success, get only a two-hour slide presentation, after which they are expected to be enthusiastically committed.

The role of internal communication in this model is that of pushing information down to the troops rather than listening to staff. Passing down information has been largely limited to communicating the company's stance on particular issues, rather than providing context for decisions, or responding to issues raised by employees. Communication tends to be, in short, a product crafted to the satisfaction of the supplier, rather than necessarily of value to the internal customer.

Megaphone management

Companies reviewing their communications spend too much time deciding what it is they want to say, and what are the core messages that they want their employees to receive. While it is important to be clear what the messages are, this is only one side of the equation. Companies do not spend enough time trying to understand how their employees *listen* to the messages. Without an understanding of employees' listening, companies, however efficient their dissemination of information, are only in control of half the communication equation. Employees 'decode' all communication they receive, listening for the 'real' message.

How people listen depends on the organization's culture. In the public sector, for example, there is an acute sensitivity to 'business speak' – and the suspicion that it shows a betrayal of old values. Culture 'refracts' communication. You may say one thing – but people hear another. If you do not know how your employees listen, you are not in control of your communication.

Boxitis

The greatest cause of employee cynicism and resistance is a lack of cohesiveness within the company – either the right hand doesn't know what the left hand is doing or, worse, the right hand is actively fighting the left hand.

The typical relationship between departments is one of a box mentality and turf protectiveness. The strategic direction of the company is broken up into smaller functional tasks, and each function gets its own piece of the picture. Without remembering the whole picture, functions and factions inevitably start competing with each other.

With all the best intentions in the world, the organization pulls itself apart pursuing different objectives. This leads inevitably to mixed messages and conflicting priorities.

Internal communication is usually taken up on too narrow a front, and is a victim of this organizational disease of 'boxitis'. Employees look for signals of what really lies behind management's exhortations, and take their cue from management's behaviour – not its words. Inconsistent signals usually convince sceptical employees to believe the worst, and the grapevine kills management initiatives. Those inconsistent signals are an almost inevitable product of the structuring of organizations into functional boxes, and the assignment of communication to its own functional box.

THE COMMUNICATION MISMATCH

For the kind of responsive, creative and innovative culture businesses need to foster, new communication channels are needed. The majority of existing channels are designed for effective downward communication, and are wrong for the strong upward and horizontal communication that a quality culture demands.

Managing a company's culture is becoming increasingly important as the very nature of work is changing. Increasingly, the 'inner market' – all those working in and comprising the company – are becoming 'knowledge workers' and independent professionals, whose behaviour often cannot be directly monitored or evaluated.

This means a far greater challenge for managers. Hierarchical power can no longer be relied on to deliver dictates from the top. The central skill which will be vital to managing any organization in the future will be the ability to foster and facilitate communication within it. As the effectiveness of formal controls diminishes, and the importance of line power decreases, the importance of managing the culture as a means of keeping the organization together and on course will become paramount.

Often companies are fighting their pasts, their traditions, their no-longer relevant assumptions about the business environment. The culture that they have built up simply will not allow them to be innovative and change direction. Most companies are not in control of their culture; their culture is in control of them.

If your internal communications and actions are directed at making changes in attitude and behaviour, or in getting people to start doing things differently, you have to start at the very top. It is with the top management and the chief executive that responsibility lies for strategy formulation, for identifying the need for cultural change and for pursuing this change. If the top team is not clearly united behind its mission and the policies it sets, its behaviour will always act powerfully and silently to undermine the mission.

Once you have achieved alignment and consensus among the senior management team you are far more likely to achieve it at levels lower down through the company. What often stands in the way of achieving this is a mental barrier, and an attitude that undermines communication. While the example of Japanese companies' success has been qualified by their more recent problems, one quote about attitudes has a chilling relevance to communication:

> We are going to win, and the industrial west is going to lose out. There is nothing you can do about it, because the reasons for your failure are within yourselves. With your bosses doing the thinking while the workers wield the screwdrivers, you are convinced that this is the right way to run a business. For you the essence of management is getting the ideas out of the heads of the bosses and into the heads of the labour.
>
> The survival of firms today is so hazardous in an increasingly unpredictable environment that their day to day existence depends on the day to day mobilisation of every ounce of intelligence. For us, the core of management is

the art of mobilising and putting together the intellectual resources of all employees in the service of the firm.

Because we have measured better than you the scope of new technological and economic challenges, we know that the intelligence of a handful of technocrats, however brilliant they may be, is no longer enough to take them up with a real chance of success.

Only by drawing on the combined brainpower of all its employees can a firm face up to the turbulence and constraints of today's environment.

The kind of organization envisaged here needs free flows of information, with the internal relationships that encourage thinking and welcome the exchange of ideas. This quote from Matsushita highlights precisely the need for a different model of communication, while underlining the prevailing current use of communication, to get management thinking into workers' minds.

There is a cultural deregulation going on, where cultural barriers to the free flow of the currency of ideas are being challenged and dismantled. The shift is to an organization where ideas, rather than information, are the currency.

If everyone agrees that communication is a good thing, and yet attitudes underlying it are so at odds, how did the mismatch arise in the first place? Chapter 2 looks at reasons for the mismatch, and ways of getting out of it.

The business of communication

T he debate about internal communication has traditionally revolved around what it is that employees need. Today, the greater urgency is felt by senior managers, who want communication to give them what they need to make the business succeed.

An internal communication strategy should support the business strategy, and should help an organization to compete more effectively. It should take into account how the business has chosen to serve its customers, the stability or volatility in its environment, and internal as well as external pressures on it to change.

An employee communications strategy will be different for different types of organizations, and needs to be based on an awareness of the business gaps which communication is designed to bridge.

A chief executive trying to create change will want a flow of ideas, suggestions and feedback. Communication should help to create that flow, but the organization may find that it has to use communication practices which suppress precisely what is needed. Senior managers face a dilemma: how to get people to speak up, when they have been trained to keep their heads down. The kind of organization that is now needed in order to compete may be being blocked by precisely the communication structures, practices and style that have existed for years.

This chapter looks at the role of communication in the past, then looks at the requirements for communication for the organizations of the future. In particular, it examines the production focus behind communication, the different perception of the role of the employee, and the danger of having too internal a focus that ignores the market and the business strategy.

Imagine three different organizations – a car manufacturer, an insurance company and an advertising agency. A team from each is gathered in separate rooms to discuss communication. Each knows they could be doing better and all are nagged by the feeling that they are not getting communication right.

In each organization, the teams begin to discuss how they could improve communication. Some are interested in using satellite broadcasting to get the message across and to bypass the delays of middle management. Another talks of greater empowerment and managers walking the job. The discussion turns towards the prevailing low morale and lack of direction of managers, while noting that more junior levels are happy enough, but are leaving the office as soon as possible in the evenings.

Although the conversations about which communication tactics and tools to adopt will probably be quite similar, the business challenges they face will be completely different.

THE CAR MANUFACTURER

After years of focusing on the excellence of the car they produce, dealers now observe that they make little profit on the sale of a car. Customers are wily enough to shop around, and rival dealers are happy to best the last offer. In the future it looks as though profit will come from the servicing of cars and from the sale of spare parts, as well as through the sale of related items like financing and insurance.

Whereas in the past both the job of the manufacturer, and that of the dealer as part of the distribution chain, was to take the cars the factory wanted to make and push them out to the customer, the game has now changed. Now the aim is to hang onto the customer over his or her lifetime, to build a relationship and to provide responsive service. The sale of the car is just the opening of the relationship; it is what happens afterwards that will produce profit. That means getting to know the customer, following up to find any sources of irritation and feeding that information back up the line to the manufacturer.

From being an outlet for cars, a dealership has to become an inlet for communication from the customer.

However, there is a problem. Traditionally, communication, like a river, flows one way, from the manufacturer to the dealer. Feeding information from the customer back into the system runs against the current. There is a customer complaints department to handle comment from customers and to act as a baffle to deaden the voice of the customer internally.

On the sales side there are well developed means of communication, regular meetings and flows of information. All these have grown to serve the *former* purpose of the business – to 'move the metal' down the distribution chain to the customer. In that conception of the business, the customer took the car, handed over a slice of profit and, hopefully, went away quietly. Service departments were the price you paid to keep the customer happy, and if there were any comebacks there was always a complaints department to handle them.

Those attitudes have long since changed, but the communication practices based on them have not followed suit. The majority of the manufacturer's communication is with the sales side of the dealership, and the focus is on sales and moving units. It is the service department in the dealership which has the greatest contact with the customer after the initial sale. Service people have some feed into the manufacturer on service issues, but there are few formal channels inside to connect service to marketing and product planning.

THE INSURANCE COMPANY

Long established, and having evolved in a stable market, this business has a loyal workforce occupied with processing large amounts of paper and complying with procedures proven over years of practice.

The company has three divisions, each operating in a separate part of the market and all under different names. Each division operates independently, having been split from the corporate body some years before. A corporate identity review resulted in each division adopting the group name as a prefix to their own, although they operate autonomously.

Recent changes in competition are causing ripples through the company. Car insurance in particular has changed as customers have been able to go direct to competitors and get lower premiums and better, faster service. The new strategy calls for greater responsiveness to customers while increasing the efficiency of operations internally, providing faster service to internal customers and colleagues and reducing costs in the process.

Staff already believe they provide a good service and that they have been doing a good job for years. Dedication to their traditional customer is a value they hold dear. Their business strategy of focusing on a more selective customer base, with lower processing costs and lower claims, seems to them to be discrimination, dropping the loyal customers of the past to chase the more profitable customers of the future. The emphasis on customer service, within cost, seems to be attacking the traditional values of the past.

The strategy of offering customers a one-stop service where they can buy all types of insurance at once calls for greater cooperation between the divisions and a reorganization of processes to reflect the customer's needs rather than the company's operational priorities. However, employees tend to identify with their own individual businesses, and this loyalty is reinforcing a parochial focus and hindering cooperation.

THE ADVERTISING AGENCY

Chastened by the recession, and with the value of share options having long since declined, the agency, composed of a string of acquisitions in related services, now has to organize itself better to serve clients across Europe.

While there is a holding group at the centre, the strategy has always been to run the group as a loose federation of like-minded agencies and to allow each to continue its specialist strengths in its local market. Now, however, falling revenue within the group, and a sober assessment of the acquisitions made over the years, have prompted senior management to try to realize some of the benefits of being part of a group, and to take advantage of the synergy they claim by cross-selling to their client base. This means creating a greater sense of being part of a network among member companies and creating greater cooperation between country offices, especially where they are handling multinational client accounts.

These three organizations have different markets, and different ways of serving the customer. They have different strategies, and the attitudes that hold them back will be different. They are structured differently, have different attitudes towards the balance of central and local control, different ways of managing their corporate identities, and are at different ages and stages of evolution.

How should the teams within each organization be looking at using internal communication to support the business strategy?

EVOLUTION AND DEVELOPMENT

In a stable market, slow and methodological organizations that consistently follow established successful procedures thrive. Adopting internal procedures that run counter to this methodical approach may actually endanger a company's survival. Adopting communication processes which do not fit the stable, hierarchical organization detract from its success and breed dissatisfaction and diversions.

Large organizations vary, from the conglomerate, such as a GEC or a BTR, usually run by an entrepreneurial individual with clear goals and strategy, to the sleeping giant, resting on its laurels with little clear direction or leadership, and stagnating in bureaucracy. Businesses can range from the established market-leading Goliath to the flexible and opportunistic David – each of which will need, and adopt, a quite different focus on its communication strategy.

An organization which is dominant in its market and is old and well established, such as a major general insurance company or a commercial bank, may be able to retain its old communication practices. In a stable market, the inclination will be to maintain existing practices, and communication will centre on keeping people happily doing the same job they have always done.

Discussion about the quality of communication will stem from concerns about employee morale. Attitude surveys will be used to test for levels of employee satisfaction, and consultation procedures will exist to give employees a voice and an opportunity for contact with senior management. Employees will welcome the regular 'royal visits' of senior management, and will support long-service award ceremonies and read newsletters specially designed for retired members of the company who are invited in annually for the chairman's drinks party. The focus of communication will be on reinforcing a reassuring feeling of belonging within the organization.

While the market remains stable, and a company's competitive position is unassailed, there is some argument for maintaining the paternalism and welfare model of communication, rather than pursuing empowering communication in a culture that does not welcome it, and in a market where there is no pressure to change.

A large organization, such as Pilkington or Allied Domecq, may suddenly have to face a hostile environment, to fight off takeover attempts. Suddenly the focus of communication will be on enlisting employee support in resisting the unwelcome bid, as with the Rowntree response to Nestlé. Internal communication will be articulating the values shared by everyone within the organization, and providing information about the business environment, competitive and regulatory pressures, imminent threats and their possible consequences.

In a flexible and adaptive corporation, attention is focused on staying tuned to the environment, responding quickly to new demands and being able to change direction swiftly. Here communication will concentrate on focusing employees' attention on the world outside. It will make people aware of competitive pressures and the organization's need to achieve a competitive advantage. Communication will feed in information about markets and customers, and levels of customer satisfaction, quality and service will be tracked and reported.

The organizations described above could be separate companies operating in different markets, or competitors choosing different routes to the customer in the same market. They could also be the same organization at different times in its history and at different stages of development.

Drucker argues that the primary resource of the post-capitalist society will be knowledge, not capital, and that the manufacturing productivity revolution is over. Now it is the productivity of non-manual workers that matters. The various classes of the old capitalist society are being replaced by just two: knowledge workers and service workers.

The flow of ideas, information and knowledge around such organizations will be crucial to success. The role of communication as the process by which this flow is achieved is central to the management of the organization. However, it is still viewed through the filters of the past, when it meant the dissemination of information and the announcement of decisions 'top down' through the organization.

What do organizations need?

Organizations have to master the basics of communication and lay the foundations of information channels before building more advanced approaches.

Organizations are evolving in terms of where they are going, their strategy, and what is required of their people and of communication. Any communication strategy developed today will need revisiting tomorrow, and the review of communication should be a continual process rather than an occasional event. Although there is less conflict between, and more overlap of, what organizations and employees want from communication, there is a more productive way of coming at communication.

While there are doubtless organizations already exploring the use of holorams to project the chairman into the homes of employees, and of virtual reality to take new employees on an induction tour of the business, others are wondering whether to refurbish the noticeboard in the factory canteen.

Behind these debates will be some assumptions about what is required of employees to make the business strategy succeed. Is the focus on getting information to people so that they are at least aware of what is going on before they read it in the papers? Do employees need to have a full understanding of the strategy, the rationale for it, and its implications? Or having established that, is the real challenge to engage them in advocating it to colleagues and customers, and to become involved in implementing the chosen strategy? Or, having managed to bring employees with them so far, are the management team now looking for a new degree of commitment and 'emotional labour'?

Traditionally, the organization and the employee have wanted a range of different things from communication, some of which overlapped, some of which conflicted. Areas of overlap might be information on the direction of the company, its progress and well-being, and announcements of upcoming developments. Areas of conflict might be access to information which was commercially and competitively sensitive or price sensitive and so restricted by Stock Exchange rules.

What a company wanted its people to know might well differ from what employees wanted, or felt they needed, to know. The process of communication then involved an implicit negotiation between the two agendas, to agree a middle ground. Internal research might show that employees wanted more information on other parts of the business than had at first occurred to their managers, and that would be made available. Employees might have wanted advance warning of the precise number of any threatened redundancies, and a compromise would be reached.

What do employees want?

People need:

- a job with reasonable pay and conditions;
- security with a predictable and fair working environment;
- a sense of belonging both to an immediate work group and identification with the organization as a whole;
- involvement and recognition, and the opportunity to contribute knowledge and skills and be rewarded for it.

Employees need to have a clear picture of the overall direction and ambitions of the company. Each employee should have a clear sense of where he or she fits in and how he or she contributes to the company's goals. As individuals, we have some basic questions about our work life, such as:

- What is my job?
- How am I doing?
- How secure is my job?
- Where is this taking me?

People need adequate answers to these before they start wanting answers to wider concerns:

- Where are we going?
- How are we doing?
- How can I help?

DIFFERING DEFINITIONS OF COMMUNICATION

For an organization to be successful, people need a sense of belonging to it, and to feel a sense of pride and excitement in what the business does. They need to be informed about its activities, and clear about its direction. There needs to be trust in management, and confidence in the leadership. To create this, communication needs to happen at a number of levels (see Fig. 2.1):

- People need to understand the overall vision, mission and direction of the organization as a whole.
- They need to feel part of a community and to have a sense of identification with, and belonging to, the organization.
- They need to understand the objectives of other departments in the organization, and how theirs fits in with others.
- They need to understand, be clear about and get feedback on their department's purpose and objectives.
- They need to understand, be clear about and get feedback on their team's objectives.
- They need to understand and get feedback on their own objectives and performance, and have a sense of where they are going in life.

Levels of communication

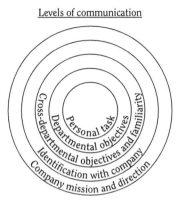

FIGURE 2.1 **People need communication at a number of levels, and all levels need to be addressed**

For any number of people discussing communication within an organization, there will be at least the same number of different definitions of the word 'communication', and different mental pictures of what communication looks like. 'Good' or 'bad' assessments of communication can range from the lack of specific information on a production line set-up procedure to the failure of the MD to return a greeting in the car park. It can mean anything and everything. One of the reasons, it seems, why audits of communication almost always produce unsatisfactory news is that people cluster current complaints and dissatisfactions under the heading of 'bad communication'.

From the employee's point of view, he or she is receiving communication from the organization in whatever its dealings may be with him or her – not just those items which are formally labelled 'employee communication'. Since one could be forgiven therefore for thinking that everything is employee communication, it is useful to have a model which can act as a comb to disentangle some of these intertwined strands.

Discussion between colleagues about improving communication is often based on two different definitions. One may want simply to pass clear messages to nominated individuals in an appropriate and coherent format via a reliable channel. The other may wish that senior management would be more open with staff about future plans, and to generate a more lively and enthusiastic meeting of minds between various grades of managers and staff.

Here is a working distinction between two clearly different aspects of communication within an organization – information and relationship. An organization needs both the climate and the supportive attitude that encourages communication, and the mechanisms and channels that allow for the flow of communication.

Information: what do I need to know, analyse and interpret?
Relationship: how do I feel about the people around me, how am I valued and what is the extent of my goodwill to put myself, my thinking and my effort into going further?

Typical examples of information would include:
- instructions
- availability of information needed to do the job
- management information
- activity reports
- notification of changes in procedures
- alerts to new developments with customers
- telephone directories
- organization charts
- health and safety directives
- update meetings
- product factsheets
- call reports.

Issues concerning relationship might include:
- the purpose and direction of the business
- opportunity to contribute
- management style

- sharing common values
- acknowledgement of role
- perception of, and relationship with colleagues.

From product to relationship

There is a clear evolution in the concept and practice of communication, which is following the development from a product focus to a customer and service focus within business. Traditionally, the role of communication would focus on some of the following:

- the announcement of management conclusions;
- the working of management thinking into messages which are then efficiently distributed via communication channels;
- ensuring consistency of information and making messages readily comprehensible and easy to disseminate.

Additional objectives

The additional objectives communication has now to fulfil include:

- the stimulation of thinking, participation and ideas;
- the networking of know-how and learning across the organization;
- the involvement of all employees in improving processes;
- the identification of ways of providing additional value to customers;
- the expansion of what all employees believe is possible.

Communication is mirroring the evolution from product to service to relationship focus within organizations dealing with an increasing number of changing stakeholders.

The shift can also be seen in the movement away from the use of a limited number of one-way distribution channels – memos, announcements, noticeboards, issued from behind the closed door of the manager's office – to the proliferation of interactive communication channels, such as company meetings, management forums, speak-up lines, videoconferencing, satellite broadcasting, electronic mail and conference databases.

The role of communication is shifting, and shifting rapidly, because lessons being learned about customers, and about processes within the organization, are being applied to it. It is difficult, for example, to communicate the need for greater two-way dialogue with customers to improve quality and competitiveness simply by broadcasting it over the firm's public address system. This may well be a first approach, but at some point the mismatch between the message and the medium will become embarrassingly apparent.

So as organizations are forced to shift from product-out to market-in, communication will have to follow suit, first to provide the 'nervous system' of the new organization, and secondly, so as not to be clearly out of step with the avowed drive for quality, and itself being a source of conflicting messages.

Since even product superiority is no guarantee of competitive edge, the culture of the organization, and how people interrelate, is increasingly seen as a way of differentiating service in a way that others cannot easily match. As people become familiar with principles of quality, process improvement and customer value, they will need to approach communication as a process that needs management and continuous improvement.

The contract between employer and employee

Any consideration of communication is affected by the relationship between the employer and the employee, and is based on assumptions about the role of the employee and the job he or she is expected to do.

Issues of communication bring out basic philosophies about the nature of individuals. McGregor (1960) developed Theory X and Theory Y to illustrate two widely differing views of human nature and the management of people. One argues that people want to be involved and contribute; the other that people will shirk unless they are carefully watched and disciplined. Managers who seem determined not to communicate with their staff may simply be operating on the unconscious belief that people have to be carefully controlled.

People are not blank sheets of paper on which management can inscribe their thinking, nor are they passive recipients of messages which attach themselves uniformly to the brain. We still operate day-to-day on a mechanistic approach to people and a production-oriented notion of communication. Messages are crafted and honed, refined through draft after draft, and then distributed to the consumer via various channels of communication.

Through the good agencies of organizations such as the Industrial Society, the understanding of the need for at least some form of communication with employees was established. Their argument was that, for any organization to operate efficiently and profitably, commitment from its employees was vital. However, that commitment would be difficult to achieve unless people understood the importance of their contribution. People could only give their best when they fully understood and appreciated how their role fitted into the organization.

However, even this understanding of communication tended to be crudely translated within an industrial context as 'an informed worker is a happy and productive worker'. Communication could be seen as a means of ensuring informed compliance with instructions.

While some older, production-oriented organizations in mature markets were establishing cascade briefings as a way of passing on information, others were discovering that they needed more from their people than simple compliance, however well informed they might be, and however well instructions were put in context.

The Industrial Revolution brought with it an implicit contract of work that fitted employees to the demands of the production machinery. The asset was the machine, and the worker was fitted in around it. The feudal working relationship of an agricultural society was changed to what Thomas Carlyle called 'the cash nexus' – the employer paid for the 'muscular labour' of the employee, and there was no relationship or obligation beyond that.

The rise of information technology, from the 1960s onwards, shifted the focus to purchasing the 'intellectual labour' – thinking and processing information – of employees. The 1980s and the 1990s have been a quest to tap into the *emotional* labour of employees, not just their physical and intellectual labour.

The drive has become to engage the thought, creativity, energy and commitment of employees, which involves a significant shift in the basis of the employer/employee relationship and changes totally the assumptions on which communication is based and the job it is intended to do. However, in almost any organization today there are a mixture of these three views of work and workers, which continually clash and frustrate. Debates about communication are actually debates about the nature of the contract with those who work in the organization, and stem from an underlying belief about the nature of the work and the rights of the workers.

THE AIM OF COMMUNICATION TODAY

The aim of communication for strategic advantage should be to align attitudes, share knowledge and manage information. The metaphors for communication for the future have less to do with the chief at the top of the mountain shouting down through a corporate megaphone, and more to do with the air traffic controller, the switchboard operator and the wiring diagram.

From top down to networking

If you look at the career path of a typical manager, it starts off on day one with no authority and no familiarity with the business issues.

As managers progress up the organization they get a better insight in day-to-day issues while gaining a degree of authority to make things happen. They promise that when they get to the top they will change all the nonsenses and inequities that they have seen during their time.

However, by the time they reach the top of the organization it has moved on, and the market, the technology and the skills have changed. Managers may have gained a lot of authority to make change happen, but they have lost the familiarity with day-to-day issues about what actually needs to change. They may well no longer be part of the informal networking and grapevine that kept them in touch with what was really going on. Staff members are more careful about what they say, and more conscious of putting a foot wrong. Although managers now have more power to make change happen, they know less about the specifics of what needs to change.

The role of communication becomes not the top-down dissemination of management thinking, but the bottom-up means of connecting those who know the specifics of what needs to be improved to those who have the authority to make changes happen.

Choosing a communication strategy that supports the business strategy depends on having a clear sense of where the organization needs to be, and where it is currently. This begins not with an audit of internal communication but with:

- a clear view of the market;
- a clear choice of how the organization has chosen to compete in serving its customers;
- an understanding of the external pressures for change, what type of change it is, and the urgency for, and speed of, change involved;
- an understanding of the organization's development to date, and its current stage of development;
- the next stage of development to which the organization needs to move.

Communication tends to grow and change as the organization develops, and the role it is expected to play will differ between organizations which are of different ages, in different industries, at different stages of development and of a different competitive positioning, even in the same market.

Not only will communication strategy need to be developed to complement the organization's culture, its market, its stage of development, it will also increasingly need to reflect what it is that the organization has chosen to emphasize as its competitive edge.

Organizations choose to serve customers in a particular way, and organize themselves internally to serve in that way. How communication is organized depends upon the chosen customer approach.

How the organization has chosen to compete in serving its customers

Different people buy products and services in different ways. Within a single product or service area, different customers show different values and priorities. Someone who spends time browsing in thrift shops for bargains may purchase expensive fashion items, buy a cheap car to get around and then spend as much again on an expensive car stereo to give high-quality sound.

When compact disc players were launched, a number of people attracted to the technology, the sound quality or the cachet of being first in the street to own one bought them. Others waited until the technology was proven, the range of CDs availability widened, the range of products increased and the price fell. They were concerned about whether the new machine was compatible with their existing tape and vinyl disc players, and were anxious to discover which of the range of products and features available were best suited to their needs.

Most people, however, waited until CD players were bundled into stacker units with cassette decks, tuners and turntables, with a host of features at a cheap price, before buying, often on appearance rather than sound quality.

At each of those three stages, different suppliers appealed to different customers' motivation, from the audio boutique where CD sound quality was agonizedly compared to traditional vinyl played on a good turntable, to a high-discount, out-of-town warehouse where they piled audio towers high in industrial racking and threw in a free cassette at the check-out.

Any company adopts a competitive positioning in terms of the value it offers for the money it charges. But it also chooses to cater to a particular type of customer, and to that customer's particular balance of price, value and quality.

To the early adopters of new technologies and products, who spend time looking at alternatives, delving into features and benefits, new, different and unusual products are the most attractive. These are the people who bought the first CD players, the first Walkmans, the first Swatches, the first laptop computers, and who are already scanning articles on virtual reality home entertainment. A company focusing on these customers has to lead in new product development and innovation.

The superstore shopper may be more concerned about price and convenience, and less disposed to investigate too closely the ins and outs of the product – they want to get it cheaply and without fuss. They will be less concerned about a specific brand or will not be attracted to a premium service or product. They will shop for bargains, buy retail goods at discount factory outlets and use mail order for convenience and savings. The company that serves these customers focuses on being well-organized, efficient and convenient.

Some customers are more concerned with obtaining precisely what they want or need, whatever the inconvenience it might involve. They do not mind waiting for what they want, or paying more for it, just as long as it does the job precisely as required. They value a product or service according to how closely it appears to be designed just for them. These people require a company to focus on closeness to the customer.

Today's customers have a definition of value that includes convenience of purchase, after-sales service, dependability and so on. In the past, customers judged the value of a product or service on the basis of some combination of quality and price. However, as customers see more choice they become choosier, and their list of criteria lengthens.

Organizations cannot be all things to all people, and while choice proliferates, companies focus selectively on what they will offer and how they will go about providing it. Michael Tracey and Fred Weissema (1993) have highlighted the need to choose a customer discipline, predominantly in one of the following categories:

- Operational efficiency
- Closeness to the customer
- Product leadership.

Operational efficiency
Operational efficiency means providing customers with reliable products or

services at competitive prices and delivered with minimum difficulty or inconvenience.

Companies pursuing operational efficiency minimize overhead costs, eliminate intermediate steps in the service or production process, reduce costs and increase the effectiveness of business processes across functional and departmental boundaries. They continually refine the process from order entry through to product or service delivery, they will have adopted just-in-time inventory systems and use information systems to measure the timing of component parts of the process.

DHL is typical of this kind of operational efficiency company, using a bus to pick up parcels and using the time between pick-up and airport to document the package and enter it into the system.

Closeness to the customer

Closeness to the customer means segmenting and targeting markets precisely and then tailoring offerings to match them. Knowledge of the customer and flexibility in their operations allows companies to fulfil particular requests, or to tailor individual products. They build long-term customer loyalty and look at the customer's lifetime value to the company, not the value of any single transaction.

Employees try to ensure that each customer gets exactly what he or she really wants. Salespeople spend time with a customer to become familiar with their needs and objectives and to assess which product or service will solve a problem, or add value.

Product leadership

Sony, Apple and Microsoft are good examples of companies offering leading edge products, and which aim to produce a continuous stream of innovative products and services. This takes creativity of ideas, applicability of those ideas and speed in getting them to market.

The job that communication has to do will differ according to which of these routes an organization chooses to follow.

A company has to choose a competitive positioning that takes into account its capabilities and culture as well as competitive strengths. There may well be a gap between the route the organization chooses to take, and the capabilities and attitudes that prevail internally. While communication can be organized to support the chosen positioning, there are likely to be other organizational issues that may undermine the strategy.

Types of change

Some changes are triggered by a sudden or unexpected *event*: the threat of a takeover; the introduction by a competitor of a much superior product; a regulatory change; or the restructuring of the organization. These may have a significant impact, but are essentially 'lurches'. They require swift but not continual adaptation, and may be followed by periods of relative calm.

Others are driven by a larger *process* of change or evolution in the marketplace: the convergence of banks, building societies and insurance companies in the provision of financial services; the increasing overlap between computing and telecommunications; or the drive of consumer electronics hardware manufacturers to acquire software developers. Here, change is likely to be continual, with little respite and fresh changes landing on the desk each morning.

Companies are affected by the degree of urgency to change, as well as the speed at which they have to make change happen. The privatization of the water industry, for example, demanded changes in attitudes and practices among staff, but there was time to plan a process that helped to explain the need for change and provide the skills to make change happen. The successive deregulation of the electricity industry has allowed the evolution of a change strategy geared to each stage of deregulation. These situations could afford a much slower change process, and the involvement and education of people within the organization, taking the time to cope with reactions and minimizing resistance.

A personal computer company faced with the collapse of the unit price in its market, and having to produce innovative products and dramatically reduce its cost base, while its market share spirals downwards, has less room for manoeuvre and has to change fast. Such a crisis might call for rapid action, a centrally developed plan of action and minimal involvement of others. The risk of failure in the market might override the risk of alienating and offending staff.

Stages of development

Organizations are conditioned by their past, and their ability to respond to present challenges may be driven as much by this as by current pressures on them from their environment.

The ability of an organization to respond to external pressures also depends on its internal condition. It is cold comfort to be told you need to be lean, mean, swift and responsive, when you have slowly become comfortably corpulent over the preceding decades.

Organizations begin from a set of circumstances and ambitions which change over time. They go through periods of change, and develop to meet differing circumstances. From their youth to their maturity they will go through stages of development, as the thrusting maverick of yesterday becomes today's elder statesman of industry. Developing a strategy for communication means assessing where an organization is on that path, what problems are forcing it to develop further and how communication should be used to help it reach the next stage.

Communication is a means to an end, and to arrive at the best strategy you first have to start with the business strategy and define the end. What kind of company do you want your communication to support? The communication strategy supports the business strategy. To arrive at the best strategy for internal communication, organizations need to answer a number of questions about their external focus:

● What are we offering to customers, and what do we regard as our competitive edge?
● What kind of organization do we need to be, and how should we be operating?
● What are we now?

- What stage of development have we reached?
- What pressures do we face from our environment?
- How swiftly do we need to change, and continue to change?

The three factors of stage of development, type of change and competitive positioning are all intertwined. Chapters 3, 4 and 5 look at each separately and examine the options and issues within each.

Structure,
identity and values

I n any organization's attempt to tap the emotional labour of its people, who an employee identifies with, and how they feel about their employer and the product or service they provide, is vital. As businesses decentralize, and devolve responsibility, the values employees share become the prime guide for setting priorities and making decisions.

Issues of how an organization should structure itself are intertwined with issues of identification. A choice of a particular structure will cut across existing loyalties and create new ones. While the planners may be tempted to go back to the organizational drawing board, they should also be aware of the implications in terms of relationships and loyalties.

STRUCTURE AND STAGE OF DEVELOPMENT

In office after office, across the country, the same photocopied quotations appear. A manager may have on his wall the quote from Machiavelli:

> ... there is nothing more difficult to take in hand, more perilous to conduct or more uncertain in its success than to take the lead in the introduction of a new order of things, because the innovator has for enemies all those who have done well under the old conditions and only lukewarm defenders in those who may do well under the new.

The more junior among us will have the quotation from Petronius Arbiter, to the effect that every time we looked as though we were making progress they reorganized us.

The structuring and restructuring of an organization is like the equivalent of an insomniac trying to find a comfortable position in which to drop off to sleep. Any structure announced this month will be changed again next month, as the management restlessly try to solve their problems by shifting the organizational charts around, and as the organization swings pendulum-like from centralization to decentralization. The implication is that there is no perfect solution, and that we merely oscillate between imperfect alternatives.

However, organizations do not simply swing from one state to another, but go through a development path in which they shift to meet changes in their environment. Normally, the change in the structure is an attempt to find a solution to a problem. The structure that once served to solve an earlier problem has now become a problem in its own right.

In periods of calm environments and stable markets, an organization might stay at any one stage for an indefinite amount of time, only being pushed onwards by problems arising out of a developing mismatch between how it operates and what it is trying to achieve.

Figure 3.1 shows the stages of development a company might go through. The first stages will be instantly recognizable – a company grows, needs to organize itself and, feeling too hidebound, divides into smaller units to recapture lost vigour. The last two stages will be less familiar – central coordination and networking.

Businesses that decentralized in the recent past are discovering that the baby almost went out with the bathwater. Autonomy in some decentralized units turned into something closer to a unilateral declaration of independence. Now there is a renewed attempt to regain the advantages of size in areas such as centralized purchasing, IT strategy and human resources. This is not a move back to centralization but to greater coordination, in an attempt to stay close to the market and take advantage of any internal synergies that exist.

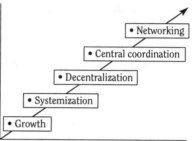

Stages of development

FIGURE 3.1   Organizations grow and change through different stages of development

One of the questions that should lead to an internal communication strategy is: Where is the organization currently on this development path, and what is the prevailing management style? The challenge is to identify those communication practices which conspire to keep in place the constrictions of an outgrown structure and style, and to change them into practices that will enable the organization to respond better to its environment.

Bulldog Chemicals plc

Bulldog Chemicals is a large British plc, with a number of businesses serving the chemicals market. While successful in its home market and expanding rapidly abroad, it does not rank among the foremost of the global chemical companies. The organization is currently shifting from being a successful British-based international organization to being a global marketeer of bulk and speciality chemicals.

It has recently been restructured into a number of divisions, formed from the component businesses of the plc. The thinking behind the restructuring has been to set up each of these divisions as a company in its own right with its own bottom line and its own clear means of tracking performance. It is felt that the restructuring will allow divisions the latitude to respond quickly to their own markets, and ensure that each division is providing an adequate return on its investment.

The restructuring is intended to enable closer monitoring of financial investments and resources, and a clearer focus to planning. For the division heads, this allows a clearer strategy on how they will serve their customers.

The bulk chemicals division will use greater efficiency of production, more responsive service and more convenient delivery to differentiate what are seen as commodities by customers and to give them an edge over competitors.

The speciality chemicals division intends to build its reputation as a leader in creating innovative products. It will invest heavily in research and development, decrease the time it takes to develop products and get them to market faster.

The agrochemicals division's aim is to get close to both its end-customers and its distributors. It is reorganizing itself into market and customer groups and is supplying greater levels of technical advice and agricultural and business development support to all customers.

While each division feels independent to pursue whatever means it sees fit, there is still the implicit expectation at the centre that they trade and deal with each other wherever possible to keep maximum revenue within the group.

Following the restructuring, each division has developed its own identity, all bearing a family resemblance to the original. While the group name was well known to businesses and consumers alike, it was felt to hamper the independence and cloud the individuality of the new divisions.

While each division is trying to build an individual culture to help it perform, there is still a strong influence from the old prevailing culture not just of the division but of the plc. While the division heads can communicate with their own people, the group corporate centre still communicates with division employees. Pension arrangements are still retained by the centre, and regular communication about employee benefits are also sent from the centre, reinforcing old loyalties to the old corporate brand. These are in conflict with some of the messages within the individual divisions, and are seen to undermine the attempt to create a strong distinctive local identity.

Managers within the divisions have welcomed the message that they are being freed from corporate shackles to run the business and do what they know best. However, it becomes clear that once the gospel of decentralization starts, it rapidly takes hold. The creation of a separate division brand leads to the proliferation of other separate brands within each division, 'Logo mania' begins as individual areas try to create their own distinctive identities, and even the stationery cupboard ends up with its own logo and strap line.

Individual units within the division itself argue that they should be stand-alone, and that, freed from the overheads of corporate management, they should not now have to pay for the overhead of a divisional management tier. Greater accountability for cost and results creates greater sensitivity to carrying apparently unproductive management overheads. Individual units argue that they should focus on their own local interests, rather than funding development initiatives elsewhere in the division.

The three divisions differ in their share of the old plc's traditional values. The speciality chemicals division is most comfortable with the old core values, while agrochemicals is attempting to shift its culture away from the old values. The bulk chemicals division has enthusiastically embraced the need to pull away from traditional values, but its independence of thought is occasionally seen by the other divisions and by the centre as fomenting rebellion.

Meanwhile, at the bottom layers of each organization people see only continuity of the old, as they continue to work on the same site as they always did, and the proud Bulldog logo still appears on their wage slips and on the group newspaper.

The restructuring reflects a number of different hopes and ambitions among the leadership group. The chairman hopes for greater transparency and a better return on investment, while the division heads hope that they will have greater freedom to make changes and to shift from being a product-focused hierarchical organization to a more market-led customer-focused business.

In the event, the organization becomes a twisted hybrid, with some of the divisions being customer-focused while others unconsciously retain their former hierarchical, production-focused and centralist approach to life. This is no surprise in a period of transition, where people are learning new attitudes and new skills. However, where individuals are unaware that they still apply the values of the past in pursuit of a strategy for the future, there is conflict.

This case study illustrates a number of the issues that underlie a company's stage of development.

- What is the intention behind the restructuring?
- Who should employees identify with?
- What is the best use of corporate identity?
- What are the values that people share?
- What is the role of communication?
- Who should be communicating, and how should communication be managed?

In the above example there is little agreement between the various players on the answers to these questions. Communication intended for a new stage of development is firmly anchored in a previous phase and is dragging the organization backwards.

One lesson to be drawn from this is that communication has to match the company's stage of development. There are different characteristics of communication which suit each stage (see Fig. 3.2), and it is likely that an organization at one stage is managing its communication based on an earlier stage. Organizations are caught in the anarchic practices of their youth, or are stuck with a communication structure like a zimmer frame that slows them up and condemns them to premature senility.

The following section looks at each stage of a company's progress, and the typical characteristics of communication for each.

Growth

Two partners found a company based on a good idea – as Apple Computers and Ben & Jerry's started. They have a good idea they think they can

Stage of development
and communication style

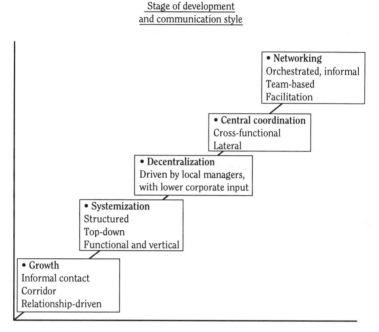

FIGURE 3.2   Communication has different characteristics at each stage of development

exploit, they may be technological wizards, escapees from the restrictions of a large corporation, and want simply to get on with the business. They spend all their time working on the new product, and hire in friends and colleagues with similar attitudes and passions. They talk all the time, and communication happens informally, with little distinction between work and play.

The company knows how well it is doing – the product works well, and distributors are agreeing to stock it. Colleagues use flipcharts in the coffee area and whiteboards in the meeting room to discuss developments and exchange ideas. People who join the company are attracted to its dynamism, excited by the product and reflect the attitudes and values of the founders.

As the business prospers, and the number of people in the

organization grows, the problems begin. The dependence on informality, and the assumption that communication will simply happen by osmosis, becomes a vulnerability. The shift to a new factory to cope with the increasing flow of orders demands more systemization of procedures. Informal communication which depends on frequent contact and interaction between colleagues starts to fail. People are now on different sites and working on specialized functions, so individual pictures of how the company is doing become fragmented.

Few people have a clear and complete picture, and confusion begins as the lack of managerial experience outside the technical areas and the concentration on entrepreneurial drive to the neglect of management systems begins to tell.

The founders acknowledge that they do not have the necessary management skills, and bring in a more rounded and experienced business manager to provide structure and direction for the business.

Systemization

Clear roles, responsibilities and accountabilities are established, and the business is organized around a functional structure. Communication becomes focused on the function, and becomes more formal and impersonal. Contact and meetings happen within the department, but departments have little contact with each other. The overall business picture is neglected for a clear picture of the function's role and purpose, and communication shifts away from relationships toward task-focused information.

Whereas in the past managers in each area all had a say in the direction of the company, now it is the new business manager and the executive team who decide strategy and set direction. Middle managers now have less power and less say, and are expected to fulfil specialist functional responsibilities within a framework set for them by the leadership.

As the company continues to grow, enjoying a period of relative stability, the tension between the senior management group and its staff increases. Middle managers feel they are weighed down with policies and practices developed by the management centre, and that centralized approaches do not fit with different local parts of the business. The leadership is seen to be less in touch with the customers, while those at the sharp end feel they are the ones better placed to know what is really good for the company. While they may acknowledge the need for consistent standards and procedures across the business, they increasingly pursue their own initiatives tailored to local needs.

Communication tends to be about the local unit or division, to the exclusion of other parts of the business. Team meetings stress the performance of the business unit, and corporate news and messages are filtered out as uninteresting or irrelevant. Newsletters for the unit spring up, and new individual logos are developed.

Lower-level managers start to push for greater autonomy, and the business begins to allow greater delegation of responsibility, while talking more of local empowerment. At this time of tension and internal competition, the senior management response is to resist the temptation to reassert authority, and actually to delegate greater responsibility to the divisional managers, the factory production directors and the market sector sales managers.

Decentralization

Senior managers in the division are allowed to get on with the job, reporting regularly to the centre on progress against agreed budgets. Managers at the centre maintain a hands-off approach, and focus on identifying opportunities which can be rolled out across the divisions.

Communication at the unit level aims specifically to foster strong identification with the unit. Open days are held for employees' families, and social events are subsidized for employees to get to know each other. Long-service awards are presented by local management.

Communication from the centre tends to be only occasional, the Christmas letter from the chairman, or the employee annual report during the financial reporting season. Senior managers visiting the divisional locations see only the senior management team, and the feeling of the centre being the corporate 'them' grows, as the centre implicitly assigns ownership of the employees' loyalty and allegiance to local management.

This stage of greater delegation allows increased closeness to the customer and faster responsiveness to the market. Employees can see who they are working for, and greater identification and loyalty makes for greater motivation and productivity.

Problems begin when divisional managers are seen to be going too far in their local initiatives and disregarding the interests of the organization as a whole. The division heads begin to act as barons, and there is muttering at the centre about their fiefdoms. One divisional head refuses to use a fellow division's manufacturing capability, preferring to use a competitor. Another runs an advertising and press campaign that cuts across corporate identity guidelines. What started as healthy decentralization now seems to be toppling into fragmentation, and managers at the centre worry that the benefits of being a single organization are being lost.

In their own defence, unit managers begin to quote the chairman's speeches on the desirability of operational autonomy, and argue about the nature of the strategic framework within which that autonomy is supposed to be exercised. Pressing on with their local objectives, operational managers initiate projects within their own fiefdoms without thinking of coordinating with the rest of the organization.

Autonomy then creates a parochial attitude and an unwillingness to sacrifice local interests and benefits for the good of the business as a whole. Employees focus on local issues and priorities, and do not appreciate the wider picture. Internal familiarity with other divisions decreases, and the opinion of other divisions' effectiveness declines at the same rate. Internal competition increases, and divisions are found to be reinventing wheel after wheel.

Individual divisions hold separate management conferences and have individual newsletters. Divisions' successes are highlighted against the perceived failure of sister divisions, and sensitivity grows among 'scapegoat' loss-making, or high-investment business units. Some divisional managers feel that colleagues at other divisions are getting away with murder, and begin complaining of growing separatism. There is little communication between the divisions, and managers see their careers progressing within their division, rather than within the group.

Central coordination

In a bid to maximize the benefits of having divisions within the same group, a bid is made at the centre to halt the fragmentation. Decentralized units are merged into product or market sector groups, and more formalized planning and review procedures are established. Return on capital invested becomes an important criterion used in allocating funds, and each group has to compete for, and justify, the allocation of corporate funds.

Corporate function staff are increased at the centre to develop and implement company-wide programmes of control and review for line managers. Some technical functions, such as information technology, are centralized at headquarters, while daily operating decisions remain decentralized. Centralized purchasing is adopted to take advantage of group negotiating muscle and bulk discounts.

Consistent processes for selection and recruitment are established. Group-wide management training programmes are created, and managers from across the divisions are brought together for induction and development programmes.

The corporate centre reasserts its ownership of employees, and standard contracts, terms and conditions are introduced across the group. Share options, employee share ownership and company-wide profit sharing are used to encourage identity with the firm as a whole. An employee annual report is designed to make the financial workings of the business more easily accessible to the workforce.

Communication is coordinated more strongly from the centre. A cascade briefing system from the group chief executive down is adopted to ensure that employees in the units are fully aware of corporate messages. Corporate videos are regularly distributed, and a weekly press clipping service is established to keep everyone up-to-date on any developments affecting the group.

Annual conferences are staged for the management teams of all the divisions to come together. A corporate identity manual is circulated detailing corporate guidelines and outlawing any deviant abuse of the logo in the units. A corporate newspaper is created, and an electronic mail service helps to link separate sites together. Job openings within the group are advertised on noticeboards and circulated in the mail. The group corporate logo now features prominently on internal communications, and local newsletters are phased out in favour of locally tailored editions of the group newsletter.

All of these new coordination systems prove useful for achieving growth through more effective allocation of a company's limited resources. They prompt field managers to look beyond the needs of their local units and to feel part of a greater whole. Employees still identify with their local units, but are bolstered by the security of being part of a financially strong group and by the kudos of working for a well-known corporate name that their friends recognize from the advertising campaign.

Managers retain much of their local decision-making responsibility, but spend more time accounting for, and explaining, decisions to the centre. The proliferation of functional staff at the centre and the increase in initiatives on all fronts sponsored by the centre, starts to erode the time that managers have to do their jobs. Lines of communication become entangled, as functional managers at the centre bypass the operational line management chain and go direct to their dotted line, functional, reportees in the units with requests for information, market statistics and progress reports on initiatives. Local management team colleagues complain of conflicting instructions, competing claims on their time and lack of coordination between functions at the centre.

Bureaucracy overload

The increasing number of systems and programmes begins to exceed its usefulness, and the initiatives begin to seem a diversion from the day-to-day business of serving the customer. The choice is forced between serving the external customer and supplying the internal customer at the centre with reports, information and updates.

As the message to become market-led spreads down the company, and corporate standards of quality are pursued, local managers become increasingly disenchanted with functional managers at the centre pulling rank to force them to do things at the expense of the customer. Since those at the centre are not familiar with day-to-day operational pressures and local pressures, their requests inevitably appear insensitive and untimely. At the centre, functional staff are equally exasperated at local managers' lack of responsiveness, grudging compliance with requests and lack of understanding of pressures and demands put on the corporate centre.

Parties on all sides complain of a deluge of paper, and criticize the bureaucracy that has grown. One man's bureaucracy being another man's system, the apparent consensus on the bureaucratic overload masks the fact that bureaucracy is the word that each side gives to the other's system, and conceals the lack of shared objectives and definitions of value.

Established managers are able to build up a shadow network of informal contacts, and can get things done by using relationships and contacts rather than following what they perceive as increasingly cumbersome procedures. It is common for managers to use these informal networks to make up for the shortcomings of the formal structures and systems. Part of the intention behind bringing managers together on induction and training programmes is to create relationships that will smooth the rough edges of the organization. When cooperation between divisions is needed, people will do favours for each other and put themselves out for the sake of the relationship.

When the perceived bureaucracy goes too far, the informal process assumes greater power and importance, as managers use it to bypass the frustrations of the system. Managers take pride in knowing who to contact and what strings to pull. This can work well to get things done to meet tight customer deadlines, but it can also act to bypass official lines of communication to thwart a management initiative for change.

Whether you were on the distribution list for the important reports used to be an indicator of status and influence; now it is which task forces you are part of, and which meetings you attend. Status and influence now come from which formal and informal networks you belong to, and may have little to do with your actual title and position in the hierarchy.

The canny manager has always created cooperation, traded favours and channelled information as a way of getting things done. This has usually been the informal way needed to make the formal channels work. Now, as the formal structure fades away, the informal becomes the necessary way of operating. Getting things done demands the ability to communicate across networks, to enlist support and to form temporary coalitions around specific issues.

Animals have two kinds of skeletons: the endo skeleton which humans have, an internal framework of bone on which everything else is hung, and an exo skeleton, like that of insects, which acts as a shell that contains everything else. The formal structure of organizations has been more like an exo skeleton - an attempt to contain activity within the organization. The formal organization was created to manage relatively simple and standardized approaches to a narrow range of predictable problems. As complexity increases, the organization chart will become an endo skeleton - a framework around which informal lines of reporting, communication and cooperation centre.

Networking

Once the organization, and the markets it serves, have grown too complex for regimented systems, formal procedures and controls are seen as too inadequate to manage the complexity of the organization. There is a need to use more of the informal power of relationships to make the organization work. Faced with the erosion of their hierarchical power, and having line power only over people below them in any case, managers start to consciously farm their networks and engineer informal contacts.

Working with their teams, managers help them to identify the networks of influential colleagues whose help and support is needed. Departments who are critical to their success are identified, and their people are invited to sit in on meetings, updates and presentations to gain some understanding of different perspectives, pressures and priorities.

Breakfasts and lunches are hosted to allow people within departments that rarely meet formally to get together, in the expectation that contact will create greater familiarity, a higher rating of each other's effectiveness and greater cooperation.

The move to managing a network, rather than a hierarchy, requires a more flexible approach to management. The focus is on solving problems quickly through bringing together teams from across functions. Teams are assembled to meet a particular problem, and may be disbanded again once the problem has been addressed.

Communication centres on establishing networks as a means of creating cooperation and sharing knowledge. Conferences of key managers are frequently held to focus on major problem issues. Business forums are held to keep people up-to-date on industry issues, customer plans and activities in other divisions. Senior managers tour the units to listen to employees in informal sessions, and upward feedback is seen as vital to progress.

People who need to cooperate with each other are brought together both for social occasions and to discuss business issues. The aim is to create contact and familiarity and so increase trust and develop relationships. Managers from areas across the organization are brought together at off-site sessions and are trained in behavioural skills for better teamwork and resolving conflict.

Communication is organized across the network as well as within units. Forums are held in which colleagues from different divisions present and discuss solutions to common problems. Functional networks are established, so that professionals who do not share the same reporting lines can come together to discuss relevant technical and professional issues. Electronic discussion databases allow them to continue debates and pool views, approaches and experience despite geographical separation.

Matching communication to stage of development

The perception that communication is poor is often a reflection that the organization is experiencing a problem that will force it to the next stage of development. A young partnership complaining of poor communication may be signalling the need to move from growth to systemization; the corporate banking division of a commercial bank's complaint that communication is poor may be a signal that the overload of perceived bureaucracy demands a shift to greater networking.

Simply reacting to the cry that communication is poor by introducing more and better techniques can actually worsen the situation, for example spending time with the young partnership addressing interpersonal problems and differences in personal styles and differences in values, to the neglect of getting some basic channels installed to help the flow and availability of necessary information.

Similarly, the communication pains of an organization that is suffering from a perceived overload of bureaucracy are unlikely to be soothed by the introduction of structured brief updates of colleagues' activities – something which the young growth company might use to good effect.

In organizations that are pursuing decentralization, there is often a robust debate as to who is responsible for what communication. Managers of corporate communication at headquarters compete with operational managers in the divisions for the attention and loyalty of the employee.

It is often difficult for the centre and the division to agree their respective roles, and this can be because they have no common framework for coming at the debate. Is the business moving from a systemized, centrally managed to a more decentralized style? If so, the local manager will have primacy, with the support and consultation of the centre. Has the organization moved on from decentralization to greater central coordination? In this case the centre will have a greater role in creating the sense of corporate belonging, and in the education of each division about the others' activities.

A US-based multinational pharmaceutical company found itself moving from centralization to greater decentralization. This was a strongly centralized organization, with a well known monolithic brand and leading research and development at world headquarters. Dominant in its markets, and innovative in product development, the organization's successful history had bred a degree of paternalism and the strong aim to reproduce the success it had created in the USA in individual national markets.

Now, individual country operations were calling for the greater tailoring of products to the individual requirements of their markets. In competitive local markets, customers disliked being supplied with standardized packs and doses which had been developed to suit the supplier's desire for efficient long-run production. Local customers demanded different sizes, different packaging, different delivery, timing and conditions. There was increased pressure on margins created by the lower prices which could be charged locally. This in turn demanded increased productivity from employees.

However, in an attempt to ensure that individual national markets did not invent their own wheels, a European management structure was created to provide greater linkage between individual markets, to help pool expertise and to develop national centres of excellence.

The shift towards greater responsiveness to local markets was reflected in the shift in the management of communication. Formerly, communication was managed from a well staffed and professional department at the centre. Communication followed from the centre, and materials were produced centrally for local managers to use with their people. There had always been some grumbling about the inappropriateness of some of the language used and about the insensitivity to local national pride. However, feeling that they had to implement what was sent out, busy managers were glad of whatever help they could get.

Now, a shift towards greater decentralization meant that the central department served local operations as a centre of expertise and advice, rather than as the providers of packages for local implementation. Communication managers at the centre liaised with in-country communications departments which now had their own national communication managers.

The corporate hub was responsible for worldwide communication on policy, issues, research and development and environmental concerns, and for informing countries about each others' developments and activities. It provided the countries' communication departments with communication media – video/audio briefing packs which were to be adapted and tailored to local needs.

In the division of communication responsibility, the national subsidiary was responsible for local communication, for creating face-to-face communication forums and for developing team meetings. The international communication responsibility was focused on providing tools, promoting awareness and communication about the global organization, and for communication about the brand.

The move from decentralization to greater central coordination can be seen in an organization like Apple. Apple Computers is an organization which enjoyed fast growth on the back of an innovative product and the missionary zeal of its people. Spread over a campus of buildings in California, it had a background of being strongly decentralized. The culture of the independent 'empowered' employee, interfacing enthusiastically with his or her machine, reinforced a natural antipathy towards central direction and control.

However, with the need to become a more serious contender in both the personal and business markets, there was a need to act as a globally coordinated player for the local implementation of a global strategy. Added to this, the need to reduce selling prices to become more competitive had had a serious effect on the gross margin of products, calling for a significant reduction in the cost base and a shift in attitude from free spending to belt-tightening. The drive was now for thinking globally and acting locally.

The decentralized style of the past had to give way to a greater degree of central coordination. The existing communication practices and procedures were based on a decentralized style, and to continue to use them would have resulted in reinforcing the old style.

The business strategy, and the demands of the market, have a great impact on the structure and organization of a company. However, the issue of employees' identification and loyalty, sometimes a greater influencer of success, is often left to sort itself out, without conscious management.

The earlier case of Bulldog Chemicals plc raised a number of other questions:

- Who should employees identify with?
- What is the best use of corporate identity?
- What are the values that people share?

Who should employees identify with?

In organizations with divisions, departments or business units there is usually the hidden issue of who the employee should identify with. There are debates on centralization and decentralization, autonomy within guidelines and the value of operating brands versus the group brand.

Heads of divisions do not want any interference from headquarters, and want their staff to concentrate on the division. They resent communication that bypasses them and anything that dilutes the employee's strength of allegiance to them.

This is replayed within each further division and sub-division – managers do not want their people to be told that they are a proud part of a multinational conglomerate; they consider it much more productive for employees to feel a close-knit part of a leading Yorkshire fuel oil wholesaler. The glossy newsletters from New York are quietly binned, after news items are copied over into the locally desktop-published Yorkshire Fuel Oil Bulletin.

Identification with the organization

In the argument about employee loyalty and corporate identity there are two main questions to be asked:

1 How far can the loyalty of the employee be stretched?
2 Where does the business strategy require the focus of employee loyalty to be?

The loyalty of employees and their identification are not infinitely extendible. Employees can identify with their team and usually with two levels above that – whether by region or function. They may also be able to identify with a national office, such as the UK or France, and, depending on their level in the organization, on a European region.

Typically, people identify with their immediate team, department and company. But their identification is also influenced by their location, the familiarity of the brand or company name and their profession.

Customers and employees may know a company by the name it has always had, and do not look at the small print on the letterhead or the sign on the gate, which reads, 'another division of Global Co'. Global Co. is a large, financially sound and diversified group, and lends the reassurance of size and the security that the company will not disappear overnight.

Where the company or even the group name is a consumer brand, like Esso or Boots, people can identify strongly with their own area and then with the group, bypassing the division of which they may be part.

The way people describe themselves to outsiders differs from their description of themselves to insiders. With outsiders, the tendency is to start with the handle that will make sense more quickly in a conversation. A geologist with BP may say, 'I work for BP', but if he works for a firm that people are unlikely to have heard of, he may say, 'I'm a geologist'.

Where companies have had a history of being bought and sold, it can actually help that employees have never developed an allegiance to the parent company and can find comfort and reassurance in identifying with their local employer.

There is a finite amount of stretching that can be done with identification. I may identify with my local branch, and see myself as part of a regional network, but if we are bought by a Belgian group I might not be able to stretch to being a Brussels man, and may revert instead to a purely local focus.

Corporate identity

The corporate identity depends on the nature of the group and the role of the centre, and whether individual brands or businesses are merely being held in a portfolio, with no opportunity and little need for contact between them.

Organizations fall into two groups, the monoliths and the federations.

The *monolith* is a group which has a strong single identity shared by its divisions (e.g. BP, Boots, BUPA, the Automobile Association). Employees in each of the divisions will have a strong loyalty to the name, which will be constantly on show in advertising campaigns and on the High Street.

The *federation* is more likely to be a portfolio of businesses, each with its own identity, held by a Hanson or a Tomkins, known by the City but probably not by the consumer. Each of the businesses operates autonomously within an agreed framework, and employees within each of the businesses may well never have heard of the final owner and may never need to.

Managing corporate identity involves a careful balancing of the identification of consumers, employees and shareholders, each of whom has quite different needs.

At the corporate centre of a federation, there will be little desire to communicate directly with the plants or offices of one of its businesses. That will be the province of local management, and there will be seen to be little benefit for employees in knowing that they are, ultimately, part of a larger whole.

However, at the head office of a company like Marks and Spencer it will be important for customers and staff at any one of the network of stores to identify with the values of the whole, since consistency and reliability form the core of what customers are offered at whichever store they happen to visit. Similarly, the essence of McDonalds offer has been consistent standards wherever you go, so there is an obvious advantage in employees feeling part of the whole of McDonalds, its approaches and values.

However, a customer looking for a pub may be more interested in one with quaint individuality, rather than the uniformity of a chain. Should the bar staff feel part of the King's Head, or part of the pubs division of Whitbread? Perhaps managers may feel happier as part of the Whitbread group, seeing exciting diversification into other retail ventures offering a range of career opportunities?

In an organization which is a federation, and in which the business strategy is to present a local brand to the consumer, the focus may be on encouraging employees to identify strongly with their local unit. BET, for example, is a conglomerate which owns a number of well-known brands such as Initial. Within Initial there are component companies, which have joined through acquisition and whose employees are likely to identify with a company that was acquired. It is entirely possible that they may identify strongly with the Initial name, since it is so well known and successful. When BET presented itself as a corporate brand, with a new identity strongly attached to its divisional brands, and with strongly BET branded advertising, the question could be asked: With whom was the employee supposed to identify?

When a management team bought out Cadbury Typhoo and renamed it Premier Brands, it was very keen to create a new sense of values and urgency among the workforce as a way of realizing the potential of the management buyout. However, for some time after the introduction of the new identity and the new brand, employees still went out at lunchtime to rejoin their old colleagues on the Bourneville site at the Cadbury social club and to continue hearing the Cadbury news. They were still, in their own minds and to all intents and purposes, Cadbury people. For them, little seemed to have changed and they were still effectively employees of the old company, subscribing to all its values and absorbing messages of continuity rather than the need for radical change.

There is increasing reason to revisit issues of corporate identity and identification. While in the past it made sense for people to keep a strong local focus, things have changed.

As takeovers threatened large groups who owned well-known brands but who were themselves not well known, it became important to create a higher profile by transferring familiarity with the brand to familiarity with the owner. Allied Domecq was one of the first to start attaching a corporate sign-off to advertising of any of its brands, and today the Cadbury 'tear-off strip' appears in the same way on its advertising.

The threat from without, prompted a change in the balance of brand and corporate identities. A similar threat will prompt a rebalancing of identity for employees.

While managers have always encouraged a local focus on the business unit and the job at hand, they have found that it can backfire. The pressures of change and the lack of security can force individuals to focus first and foremost on themselves, their family and their team mates. They do not want to know the wider picture, and they lose sight of any context to their job. This tends to fragment the company, and works against internal cooperation and understanding at the very time that the business strategy calls for it. While the business strategy may declare 'think global and act local', local employees' focus is local and they think parochial.

In the absence of a predetermined context, people supply their own against which they make interpretations. They see their organization cutting costs and view it as a sign of impending redundancies. They get a visit from the chairman one day and a visit from the managing director the next, and they feel their branch is being sized up for closure.

The dilemma in which managers will increasingly find themselves is that their staff may not have felt a need to know more about their environment, beyond questions of job security, but unless they know more they will not be able to bring the right context to the work they are being asked to do.

As companies look more closely at using flexible workforces, and mixing and matching full- and part-timers, the problem will get worse. Part-timers see the job as only a part of their lives, which has to fit in with other commitments. They will probably, by definition, be working short and irregular hours, and it may not be easy to pull them together in one place as a group. They may also be reluctant to stay behind or come back into the workplace after hours. Yet they will increasingly come to represent their company to the customer, and it is vital that they understand what is going on.

In an increasingly international and fragmented organization there is a need to develop a framework of understanding and communication between different parts of the company and to promote a strong corporate identity. In highly decentralized companies, corporate culture, and particularly the sense of shared values and a common identity, will often serve as 'corporate glue' to hold the organization together (see Fig. 3.3).

Within a unified hierarchy, corporate values are taken for granted, and everyone unconsciously holds them in common. Once there is a breakdown

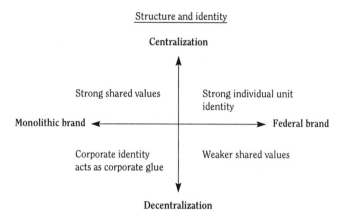

FIGURE 3.3 Shared identity and values offsets the fragmentation of decentralization

into smaller units, that unconscious asset is lost. Little attention is usually paid to that loss, and people cast around to find what are the new cultural rules. Individual units left to their own devices turn inwards, and identify with their local leaders and priorities, to the (at times) aggressive exclusion of others within their corporate family.

There are a host of forces lowering the horizons of employees and attacking the bonds of identification that used to bind people together. The drive to get closer to the customer, in smaller, more responsive units, in increasingly complex environments, while employees look to their own security, all conspire to increase fragmentation. As businesses try to contain this fragmentation, they will find that they have to pay more attention to the values they share and the way they identify with each other. In times of change, when divisive forces are at work, values and relationships form the glue that holds things together.

Corporate identity and the power of the brand

A monolithic brand acts as an 'eggshell' of identity, holding everything together. Even where internal communication is not fulfilling its objectives, external communication of brand values will serve to reinforce internal corporate values and hold the employees together, keeping at bay the usual process of fragmentation.

Common values and common meaning hold people together. An organization can decentralize, using common values as a 'corporate glue', if people identify with the same brand or corporate identity.

When an organization's divisions do not share the same brand they lose the benefit of this corporate glue, and different brand names and different corporate identities begin to erode the glue that held them together. Employees look for signals to try to understand how values have shifted and by what rules people are now playing. Individual units adopt their own mission statements which, while they give a clear focus to their own people, can signal conflicting priorities with their colleagues in other divisions.

Organizations considering decentralization can draw two lessons from this:

1 The fragmentation of people's loyalties can be avoided by strengthening the identification with the corporate brand.
2 Those organizations who already have a strong monolithic brand will have an advantage over those with a federal brand.

The importance of shared values, both among colleagues and with customers, is growing. Increasingly, the trend is away from simply a transaction with a customer, to a lifetime relationship with a customer. The drive among suppliers then is to build increased levels of relationship with, and loyalty among, their customers.

The seller's desire for deeper relationships is reciprocated by the customer's desire for a relationship with a trusted supplier. The customer wants someone who provides not only a product or a service, but also advice on how to make the most appropriate decision. As life becomes more complicated, the number of suppliers vying for a customer's trade increases, and the number of products offered proliferates amid more confusing technical information, there is a crying need for someone to make it all simple and understandable again.

People are looking for long-term partnerships with a trusted and authoritative partner who shares their values and makes sense of the complexity around them.

The customer is increasingly interested in looking at the internal workings and values of an organization, if he or she is to have a long-term relationship with, and commitment to, it. The student boycott of Barclays because of its South African involvement was the beginning of a process that will not be limited to student activists. Today, companies take pains to communicate about their environmental activities, on recycled paper. Tomorrow, they will publish the names of their partners, and how their operations are helping the community. It will not be enough to be a good corporate citizen; they will also need to be an active member of their community.

A good brand name, and a good business reputation, have always given a corporate endorsement to a product or service. Increasingly, consumers will be interested in using their money not simply to ensure a satisfying purchase, but to vote for the supplier. While this has been called 'point of purchase politics', and not every consumer will be as politically active, there is an increasing drive to see the supplier in terms of its activities and its values. This has been seen clearly over the past few years in the growing consciousness of a supplier's environmental record, and now with companies like the Body Shop and Ben & Jerry's, the record of its suppliers and partners.

Customers are extending the range of criteria by which they judge the suppliers or partners with whom they choose to do business. American supermarkets provide a wealth of information to consumers to allow them to make an intelligent, informed decision about purchases. The demand is for more information, not simply about the product but now also about the company that produces it. Customers judge a supplier not according to the higher standards within that supplier's industry but by the standards of service they have learned from dealing with other industries. You have to meet and beat not the best in your field, but the best in any field.

The importance of customers seeing their values reflected in the supplier they choose has already been seen to some degree in the focus on environmental awareness, the growing sales of dolphin-friendly tuna and of ethical unit trusts. Now, says an *Economist* article of June 1993:

> ... will come the era of corporate image, in which consumers will increasingly make purchases on the basis of a firm's whole role in society: how it treats employees, shareholders and local neighbourhoods. This is not just about being politically correct; it entails conveying a complete image as Sony has done with innovation.

Organizations which seem exciting in the external market also seem to attract and motivate employees. The Body Shop, Virgin and Apple Computers are all entrepreneurial start-ups, which have grown by responding to demand, initially in the consumer marketplaces. However, they are seen to have not simply a focus on profit, but on championing the customer and having a wider vision of what can be achieved through doing business.

This may reflect a change in the age profile of employees and reflect on babyboomer values. People simply may not buy into the profit motive or financial success alone, and do not leap out of bed in the morning galvanized by the thought of increasing shareholder value. In all the companies above, a strong external profile feeds back internally and gives a sense of worth to employees. In the future, then, will a strong internal sense of mission require a high profile externally and a greater sense of external contribution to society?

One company that seems to embody the close link between company values, employee values and customer values is Ben & Jerry's Ice Cream in the USA. Ben & Jerry's has used its external communication to foster pride among employees that they work for a company known not only for great ice cream, but also for its alternative approach to business. Ben & Jerry's describes itself as a 'business that wants to do business differently', and one that intends to turn 'values into value'.

Ben & Jerry's was formed in 1978 by two superannuated hippies, who have now turned tie-dyed clothes into their corporate uniform. It practices what it calls 'caring capitalism', in which it helps communities and makes profits by making great ice cream. It has a mission statement with three equally significant parts: an economic statement which reflects profit and shareholder returns; a product statement which reflects excellence of the product; and a community statement which reflects its belief that companies should pay back into the communities from which they draw their support.

Ben & Jerry's gives 7.5 per cent of its pre-tax profits to various causes in the community, and uses its partnership with selected suppliers to support their causes. Suppliers who employ the homeless or dependent are candidates to become partners, and Ben & Jerry's believes in using trade, not aid, to support areas in need of development.

Like the Body Shop, Ben & Jerry's uses its trading activity both as a tool to help others develop and as a platform for raising awareness about issues and concerns. The company is very upfront about its values, and uses its business as a platform for creating greater political activity. It supports what has been called 'point of purchase politics' – that people can use their spending power to make a difference in their community. Visitors to their showpiece factory in Vermont are encouraged, for example, to use a telephone to register their names for information about children's welfare and to lobby their representatives on legislation going through Congress.

Posters show the delegation of employees who had gone to spend time on an Indian reservation in an area destined to be flooded to provide hydro-electric power that will in turn be bought by Vermont. The resulting protest advert was written by the employees and was published by Ben & Jerry's with its full support.

Ben & Jerry's is very visible in terms of its involvement with communities. The company obviously has highly active external communications and a wealth of activities in supporting community events, concerts and giving away free ice cream wherever it is called for. One day each year it gives away free ice cream nationwide. The company found that such activity engendered a lot of goodwill which helped offset the high price of its super-premium product and earned it a lot of press coverage and free publicity.

It also orchestrated a grass roots campaign when Pilsbury's Häagen-Dazs allegedly pressured distributors not to take Ben & Jerry's product.

The campaign, built around the slogan 'What's the doughboy afraid of?', brought Pilsbury to an out-of-court settlement and a hands-off agreement. However, Ben & Jerry's is no longer the David to Pilsbury's Goliath. In many markets they share first and second position, and market shares are broadly similar. The main difference is that Ben & Jerry's sees itself as a business that does business differently, and by pursuing its community and social responsibilities sees profit as a by-product of sticking to its values. It also seems to be in the vanguard of combining work and fun, to tap employees' enthusiasm and energy or to offset the potential boredom of the production line.

Organizations elsewhere are already finding that pulling scattered groups of employees together has to become a more social event. To reinforce identification with the organization, and to cope with logistical difficulties, communication takes place as part of an evening, breakfast or lunch event, only part of which will be about work. The need to create relationships between different groups across the organization, and the need for an informal atmosphere in which it is safe to raise issues and make suggestions will call for updates over drinks and nibbles.

At the Waterbury factory, things look like a circus from the outside. Around the simple core of the manufacturing lines they have built a tour and merchandising operation. The grounds are filled with gaily painted chairs and tables, banners hang over the covered walkway and a large picture of the planet Earth surmounts the factory front. In a small field in front of the factory two Vermont cows, with characteristic black and white markings, peacefully graze.

In their own production area, shifts of 60 employees are kept entertained by the Joy Gang whose task is to find out how to make the work fun. This is done in a variety of ways, by providing music throughout the shift, or providing good lunches, or on some occasions having a masseur come in to provide back massages.

First Direct similarly sets out to create an atmosphere of fun, and both it and Ben & Jerry's have theme days, when people arrive in fancy dress – Elvis lookalikes at Ben & Jerry's, schoolboys and schoolgirls at First Direct.

Sharing values

The importance of shared values is increasingly being felt by those companies trying to create change. What people hold as important, and the beliefs they hold dear, act as the mental programming which guides their decision-making and determines how they act.

AT&T has merged with NCR, to combine their individual expertise in computing and communications in a single product offering. Their close attention to articulating values as a guiding framework is an instrumental part of merging and getting all business units to work closely together for better results.

Levi Strauss, the jeans makers, now has an aspirations statement, which managers are charged with turning into reality. This expresses not just what it is that people have to do, but how they should be doing it. Chief executive Bob Haas believes that 'the truly successful enterprise of the future will have soul. You can't energize people or earn their support, unless the organization they are committed to has soul.'

In times of change, the net of shared values keeps people together and acts as the glue that prevents things falling apart. While there may be no specific instructions or procedures to help people react to specific situations, they have an idea of what the organization feels is important and an idea of what it is appropriate to do.

As organizations devolve authority to the person closest to the customer, getting common approaches and consistent decisions cannot be achieved by providing rules and procedures – there will never be enough to cover individual situations. Shared values and beliefs will be the main way of ensuring common approaches.

This is easier where people have a strong identification with the product and with the values behind it. Employees in the early days of Apple Computers were renowned for the fervour they felt for the proprietary technology. They identified closely with the users of the Apple machines, and wanted to share new developments with them, as a tool for liberating their creativity.

The *Guardian* and *Observer* newspapers are also prime examples of focusing on the needs and values of their customers. This is a business which has to produce papers seven days a week, to juggle the different jobs of gathering stories by journalists, selling space in the advertising department and feeding this into a complex production and distribution process.

The newspaper industry itself has been going through major change, first prompted by Rupert Murdoch's breaking of the old print union practices and the move to Wapping. The fierce competition, the introduction of new titles and the proliferation of newspaper sections has made this a fiercely contested market. Getting the newspaper out is challenge enough on a day-to-day basis. Coping with the longer-term structural shifts in the industry is all the more challenging. Planning for, and managing the introduction of, electronic input processes that do away with centuries-old processes of movable type printing presents a major challenge in managing change and complexity.

In 1993, the *Guardian* acquired the Sunday newspaper, the *Observer*, after fierce speculation in the press and competition from other would-be purchasers. Shortly before its acquisition, the *Observer* was described in the London *Evening Standard* as 'being on its deathbed' – six months later it had been revitalized and was voted 'Newspaper of the Year'.

There was the challenge of integrating the new newspaper using existing resources, without letting the eye stray from the success of the *Guardian*. In terms of advertising, the volume of advertising being processed almost tripled in a six-month period, putting stress on all concerned. What acted as a net to hold together the organization was the sense of shared values and identification with the product.

People within the *Guardian* identify closely with the product and its values. The paper was founded in 1821, as a 'newspaper in the liberal interest', sparked by a sense of outrage at the Peterloo massacre in Manchester, when peaceful protesters at a public meeting were killed by charging cavalry who were trying to break up the demonstration. The *Guardian*'s progress since then has been striking the correct balance of staying faithful to its founder's vision while adapting to the changes in its environment. What has kept it from becoming irrelevant and stuck in the past, or from abandoning the values on which it was founded, has been feedback from its readers and the shared values within the organization.

The *Guardian* in particular has pursued a strategy of product leadership, pursuing innovations in the newspaper while sticking close to its readers and hanging on to its traditional values. It has been a major success story over the last couple of years. The advertising industry attributed its success to 'brilliant, radical and successful product development', and it was named 'Newspaper of the Year' in 1992 and 'Medium of the Year' in 1993.

The marketing success of the newspaper is attributed to staying close to readers. All developments are tested and are responses to continual feedback from readers. On the editorial side, readers tend to identify strongly with individual journalists, and any wrong note that they sound in the newspaper rapidly brings response from readers.

The paper's traditional values have been to be questioning and challenging. Journalists would describe it as hard-hitting, well written, witty and irreverent. The advertising salespeople mirror the customers they serve in values and outlook, and they identify strongly with the attitudes and values that the newspaper espouses. They would also probably describe both their readers and themselves as witty, irreverent and questioning.

The acquisition of the *Observer* in 1993 highlighted the importance both of shared values and of the importance of the brand. The *Guardian* and the *Observer* were seen as similar in the values they espoused and the readers they served, both by themselves and by those well-wishers hoping for a marriage of the two titles.

While the besetting sin of acquisitions is often the rolling in of the conqueror's management tanks, the integration of the *Observer* and the *Guardian* provides a number of lessons in how to bring people together more successfully.

The *Observer* is a separate title, with an identity and style distinct from those of the *Guardian*. The two titles are also separate editorially, though they share the same commercial, production and support departments. It was in these areas that *Observer* people were integrated with *Guardian* people.

As soon as the acquisition was announced, a *Guardian* team went over to the *Observer* to meet staff and explain both the process and the timetable for bringing them together. Communication began immediately, and, though the specifics of implementation could not be known until later, great care was taken to signal how things would be done, even if the details of what was to be done had yet to emerge.

When people were transferred from the *Observer* building to the *Guardian* building, the team that planned it looked at the experience from the arriving *Observer* employee's point of view. How would they feel walking up the road to the building on their first morning? Would they have to make their own way to their allotted desk, and how separate from their *Guardian* colleagues would they feel?

In the event, *Observer* people walked up to the building on the first morning to find a poster on advertising hoardings opposite the building saying: 'The *Guardian* welcomes the *Observer*.' At reception each was ushered to the staff restaurant for breakfast, where they were greeted by senior managers. Each person was given a personalized pack detailing what would be happening and what induction and training they would receive. Finally, their own managers-to-be came down to the restaurant to escort them to their desks and to make the introductions.

The aim in all this was to show respect for the title which had been acquired, to acknowledge and preserve the pride in the title and its tradition and to demonstrate a similar set of values to those which the *Observer* embodied. The integration was not simply to be structural – it was to be an integration of similar people with similar aims and similar values.

The relative smoothness of the integration meant that after a month or two the deputy managing director felt it was impossible to tell who had come from which title. This is a good result when judged against the background of many mergers and acquisitions. Issues of identity, wounded pride and different values rage for years afterwards, in some cases bringing about the failure of the acquisition.

In many companies, people still identify themselves as belonging to brands acquired long ago but kept alive in a spirit of corporate nationalism.

Years after the integration of Britoil into BP Exploration, the Britoil name still flew defiantly over the noticeboards, and in another manufacturing company overalls bearing the name of the acquired company were lovingly clung to long beyond the end of their practical life.

The failure of a large number of acquisitions and mergers in the City during the 1980s owed a good deal to the mismatch in values. In a commercial bank that took over a merchant bank, problems surfaced after only a few months following extensive merger talks. One of the issues that had never been examined was that while each side used the word 'banker', they both had quite different definitions of what being a banker meant. The merchant bank saw a banker as someone who spotted an opportunity, got in, took a couple of points on an entrepreneurial risk and made a quick profit. On the commercial banking side, a banker was someone who took a conservative view, assessed risk over a six-week cycle and looked to a longer-term return. One side saw the other as irresponsible, while the other was seen as slow and stodgy, with no individual flair.

The inability of people to work together, and the exodus of the disillusioned, testifies to the fact that acquiring a brand means not just acquiring the financial values of that brand, but also the personal values that lie behind the brand values.

First Direct is an organization that pays close attention to aligning the values of its people with the values of the organization as a whole. Like other organizations, it has articulated the values which it feels underlie the way it does business.

First Direct's managers place a good deal of importance on revisiting the values and identifying whether practices are drifting away from aspirations. The focus on making the values real is reflected in upward appraisal which asks people whether their managers put core values into practice. Every manager has been through what they call 'evolution workshops', which are designed to review how core values are expressed in day-to-day operations. Managers are asked how they relate to the values and how they can best implement them.

The importance of the part shared values play in a business is becoming clearer as organizations devolve responsibility, or try to create greater 'corporate glue', or change their structure or their ownership. Whenever change happens, the force of individuals' underlying values is felt, and the next chapter looks at reactions to change, the impact of values systems and the role of communication in managing change.

Communicating
for change

T here used to be only two certainties in life – death and taxes. Now there is a third, change, and continuous change at that. Having to manage change is not new; what is new is the pace and extent of change. Life the lid off almost any business today and there will be a host of initiatives under way – TQM, Business Process Re-engineering, customer service programmes – all demanding scarce time and attention and all of which are urgent priorities. Meanwhile staff complain of initiative overload and pray for a respite from change and a chance to consolidate.

While the pace of change in most organizations is rapidly accelerating, senior managers are becoming increasingly frustrated at the slowness of employees to respond to change. Their people nod in all the right places, make all the right noises, then go off and do something quite different.

Businesses are realizing that their cultures can provide a competitive edge that cannot easily be reproduced by competitors. The desire and will to change is there; it is the unrealized and invisible issues that tend to act as a drag on change, that heighten frustration. The pace of change can be increased if the drag factors can be identified and streamlined. For the first time, organizations are in the business of searching for cultural landmines and trying to defuse them.

In a survey published by Ingersoll Engineers in August 1993, poor communication was cited as the single substantial barrier to achieving necessary change within organizations.

> ... managers' apparent resistance to change stems from lack of understanding and the need for more or better communication rather than any underlying wish to oppose change in principle ... Only when communication and understanding of the benefits of change are achieved will commitment be given and behaviour change.

It seems that now communication does not simply have *a* role in managing change, it has *the* role.

This chapter considers typical employee reactions to change, the impact of culture on communication and different strategies for communicating change.

REACTIONS TO CHANGE

'Our people are resistant to change' is a common complaint. Research shows that chief executives are increasingly frustrated by the slowness of their people to change, when they have identified speed of responsiveness as a critical success factor.

Not all change is resisted; some is positively welcomed. Some organizations have employees who are glad finally to see change happening, and applaud management that has girded its loins to get going. However, employee reactions that managers interpret as resistance are often symptoms of concerns quite removed from a mulish refusal to change. Before redoubling their efforts to push changes through, managers are advised to put aside their keenness to 'make it happen' and to take stock of the reactions of their staff. One of the self-inflicted causes of resistance is the inbuilt assumption among managers that they are supposed to 'drive' change and make it happen.

The Japanese *ringi* system, in which there is a process of creating debate and gathering views from the bottom of the organization upwards has been contrasted with Western ways of decision making. It has been said that in a Japanese organization it takes 18 months to gather views and develop a consensus, and, once that consensus has been built up, five minutes to implement a decision. In a Western organization, a decision at the top may take five minutes to reach, then 18 months of resistance and guerrilla fighting in implementation before the decision is finally abandoned.

Almost every change in an organization creates some form of reluctance or resistance, and there is often a tendency among managers to confront or counter the resistance rather than to understand the causes of it. Managers can trap themselves into anticipating resistance and to going in with all guns blazing to overwhelm any obstacles put in their way.

People like to be in control of their environment, and any change to the status quo threatens that ability. The continual desire is to get back to a sense of stability, which puts a different light on the rallying cries that 'we must all learn to embrace change', and that 'the only constant is change'.

Welcoming change is directly commensurate with the degree of power you have to control your environment. The less power you have, and the fewer options you feel you have, the more likely you are to resist. Apparent resistance is often the expression of a desire for a greater sense of rationale, context and continuity. However, changes that may appear positive or sensible still prompt the people affected to approach them warily checking for implications, running through possible scenarios and possibilities.

There are changes happening in our organizations every day that are assimilated without much trouble or fuss. The manager's job is, by definition, one of managing changes continually. However, there are occasions when the battle lines seem to be drawn, and individuals take up their positions. Reactions can vary, from the enthusiastic welcoming of change to dogged resistance.

While there are a host of ways in which people react to changes, both good and bad, there are some common responses and underlying reasons why initiatives for change become bogged down:

- a lack of understanding of the need for change
- a lack of, or a different sense of, the context or environment
- a belief that the proposed change violates the core values of the organization

- a misunderstanding of the change and its implications
- a belief that the change is not in the best interests of the organization
- a lack of trust in those introducing change
- a lack of belief that the leadership is serious about making changes
- a lack of belief that the leadership is capable of making change happen
- a perception that the change is unfairly selective.

A lack of understanding of the need for change

In research among chief executives conducted by People in Business (1991), the most common reason given for the slow pace of change was that people simply did not see the need to change. They did not share the urgency of the need, nor did they feel the pressure on them from the environment.

This lack of understanding is the heritage of keeping employees' eyes fixed on their task, and only giving them the information required to do their job. Getting people to understand the complexities of the modern environment is all the more difficult when they have no framework for assessing the environment and have little sense of the significance of the figures in the annual report.

A chief executive of a European computer company likened it to standing on top of a mountain, looking out over the landscape of the next five years and seeing what was coming. Calling down the mountain to his subordinates, he warned them of the cold winds blowing. But they, lower down the mountain, sheltered in the warm grassy meadows, could not share his feeling of cold, or really appreciate the change that was coming. Calling down the mountain was not going to help.

A long-established brewer proposed developing an education and training programme for its blue-collar workers, with the primary objective of 'making them capitalists'. In the seven months leading up to the annual wage negotiations, these workers would learn about the mechanics of the business, how the City worked, the lower cost of labour available elsewhere in the world and the kind of profits shareholders expected. At the end of this process, these new capitalists would accept lower wage settlements, since they would now appreciate that the shareholders' expectations were paramount.

It emerged that white-collar workers, such as marketing managers, would receive significant increases, because market forces meant they would look elsewhere if pay rises were not forthcoming. Only blue-collar workers would receive lower settlements. The lesson to any new capitalist would be to use bargaining power to get a fair share of the cake, rather than meekly accept the business rationale for getting less money.

The original intention behind the education programme was sound: give people a greater understanding of the company, the pressures upon it and the options available to it. It was only the attempt to use it to sugar the pill of a lower than expected wage settlement, which was not being applied across the company, that subverted it. Yet it also showed the gap that exists between values held by people in the same company.

Although people may welcome more information about the organization, they may disagree with the conclusions being drawn from that information and with the priorities reflected in management decisions. The more information that is shared, the greater the debate is likely to be on strategy, the greater the challenging of management, and the less likely the simple acceptance of decisions.

A lack of, or a different sense of, the context or environment

A common complaint from senior managers is that the majority of their staff simply do not appreciate the complexity and the difficulty of the environment in which the organization operates. Worse, they do not seem sufficiently interested in learning about it, or share the sense of urgency an appreciation of the facts should engender. From the employees' view, the rhetoric of change can ring hollow. They may not share the imperative to make a profit, survive and thrive, and they may suspect that management is simply crying wolf. Some have observed that traditionally management start to talk about how hard life is just before the annual salary reviews.

A belief that the proposed change violates the core values of the organization

A number of changes currently under way in the public sector began under conditions of heavy suspicion that basic values were being violated. Reforms in the health service, and changes in social services and community care, were viewed by the professionals affected as a retreat from the values and commitments of the past. The redefinition of roles in the armed services, first under the Financial Management Initiative, then after the changes in Eastern Europe, stirred objections that the basic function and purpose of the services were being overthrown.

There are less dramatic examples. Craftspeople in a kitchen joinery company eye changes to apparently more cost-effective production as being corner-cutting with no respect for the true quality of the product. Salespeople resolve to give the same levels of time and service to unprofitable and long-standing customers, despite the announced strategy to 'deselect' unprofitable customers.

Those who feel their values are being betrayed are likely to stay loyal to those values and covertly continue in the old way, especially where their primary loyalty is to their profession or their craft. As the workforce becomes increasingly comprised of professional specialists and knowledge workers, with less immediate loyalty to the organization, changes that are not clearly aligned to professional values will meet greater resistance.

A misunderstanding of the change and its implications

People resist change when they have a different perception of the problem that the change is designed to solve. Their understanding of the situation may be significantly different from that of their managers or those responsible for introducing the change. They may also have a different perspective on the apparent benefits of the change, and may see that the disadvantages both to themselves and the organization outweigh the promised benefits. Some of the perceived disadvantages may involve areas which employees value differently from their managers.

In the British Navy, the possibility of a smaller team to man a helicopter was introduced, using the evidence that the Danish used a two-man rather than a six-man crew. The sceptical counter to this was that the Danish rarely flew their machines, and so it did not take many people to operate and keep it polished. There was a more unexpected reservation. A helicopter sits on the back of a frigate, and it and its crew, who are guests on the frigate, have to pull their weight in keeping their own area clean and shipshape. The reduction of one man would mean that the crew could not keep their area clean, and so would be disapproved of by their community.

People also resist change when they perceive that it might cost them more than they would gain. A factory introduced continuous working, which involved the continuous running of the production line, with no shutdown at end of shift. The maintenance of the plant was planned to allow for the achievement of volume targets. In the past, demands for increased volume had often disrupted the maintenance schedule, postponing it until the weekend, when engineers cheerfully carried it out on overtime. Changes to this practice, better planning and better scheduling meant greater responsiveness to the customer, better use of production assets, virtually wiped out the overtime which engineers had come to expect and depend on. Meetings between production and engineering staff on better ways of working would keep running aground on the engineers' vested interest in maintaining overtime payments.

A belief that the change is not in the best interests of the organization

The announcement by a food manufacturer that it was pursuing greater cost efficiencies to fund its international expansion met with mixed reactions. The explanation of the reasons for the strategy was well thought through and well presented. Resistance came from a viewpoint that the domestic operations should not be squeezed for the sake of international ambitions, and that the board was underestimating the difficulties of competing on an international stage.

A lack of trust in those introducing change

Any programme of change brings out issues of trust. Where there is not a good relationship between those introducing change, and those affected by it, there is a greater chance of disbelief and resistance.

A senior manager is at the front of a meeting room making a presentation on the changes the new strategy will entail. Board directors sit on the front row visibly attending to the presentation. In the back row, the middle managers who will have to make the changes work, occasionally nudge each other and whisper disparaging remarks, and speculate on which planet the manager has based his planning.

The game has become one of second-guessing the true intention of the senior management team. Rumours about getting out of some of the traditional businesses have been circulating, and managers are suspicious and rueful of the new plans.

In a European insurance company, a business presentation was being made to all employees in a packed lecture theatre. I was standing at the back of the room, and as the presentation proceeded employees sitting on the left side of the room would keep glancing over at their colleagues sitting on the right side of the room. Eventually, I asked a manager standing beside me what all this surreptitious glancing was about.

> Oh, don't worry about that. All the people on the left are in life insurance, which will continue to be the core of the business. On the right, people are all from the general insurance division – and we're getting out of general insurance. We made most of them redundant yesterday.

Where there is a lack of trust, people look for the 'real' agenda and the true meaning of the proposed changes. To do that they use their past experience, and put clues and signals into the context they are familiar with. Asked their opinions about the company's direction, managers smile knowingly about the last time this initiative was tried and failed. The strategic presentation they are hearing is being greeted with amused scepticism and there is little room to take on new ideas with so much existing mental baggage.

The climate of trust and relationship inside an organization has a huge impact on communication. People tend to thrive, open up, contribute and share in a supportive environment. Conversely, they tend to keep quiet and mind their 'Ps and Qs' where the environment is one of blame and fault finding.

The degree of involvement, conversation and sharing between a manager and his or her team determines the degree of their ownership and the extent to which they in their turn will share, involve and create ownership among their teams.

In an organization which is dedicated to examining data, tracking down the culprits and finding who is to blame, communication is typically low-level and unspontaneous. Uncertain about specific facts, and unwilling to make themselves vulnerable, even members of the board can sit around giving in to the cultural bias to be agreeable, and, as a group, agreeing to things that individually they might not accept.

Similarly, employees who, in response to requests for feedback and good ideas, could find themselves being grilled. In their eyes, they can have unreasonable questions asked of them, such as 'How did this happen?', 'Who is responsible?', 'How often has this been happening?' – all with the implication that they have not been doing their job properly.

Ironically, the climate of distrust and suspicion does not just prevent a free flow of communication, it also creates unnecessary information clutter. In a blame culture, people generate memos and reports both to cover their own backs and to use as evidence against others. Departments trying to justify their existence send out peremptory demands for information and publish self-promoting accounts of their own activities and value.

It is not enough simply to reduce the amount of paper being produced, or legislate for a reduction in meetings. If the climate demands that people meet together to diffuse risk and share accountability for decisions, meetings will spring up again. If the climate dictates that it is important to have your name on a distribution list for information, irrespective of whether the information is relevant or used, the distribution list will grow. Distribution lists often reflect individuals' need for visible status, rather than the need for information.

A lack of belief that the leadership is serious about making changes

There have been a number of initiatives in the past which have been earnestly launched and which have slowly slipped from memory, either because the leadership's attention was distracted by a sudden crisis, or by a more attractive activity. Where initiatives have survived beyond the flavour of the month, they have run aground on particular dilemmas, such as the director of a particularly profitable part of the business resolutely refusing to adopt the corporate initiative.

A lack of belief that the leadership is capable of making change happen

The change is being driven from the centre, which is where all the managers who are no good at actually doing their jobs are sent to keep them out of the way. The managing director is two years from retirement, and, while seduced by the management consultants in a temporary rush of enthusiasm, really wants a quiet life.

A perception that the change is unfairly selective

Other managers of similar grade in the divisions are being left untouched. Practices under threat here are perpetuated in other divisions, purely because of the political clout of their barons. Commitments to ways of working in one area are unknown in other areas, and colleagues in other departments have received no word of any change and so continue as they have done in the past.

This change is a loosely disguised way of furthering the board's fixation that local managers have too much autonomy and have to be reined in (the business divisions are being re-engineered, but the directors' chauffeurs still spend their days washing the directors' wives' cars).

One major reason why people resist organizational change is that they think they will lose something of value as a result, and they view the change as an unfair violation of their actual or implicit contract with the organization. Resistance is expressed in terms of proposals being 'divisive' or 'not respecting our culture'.

In the early 1980s, bank managers were among the first to find that the traditional career ladder they had dutifully climbed was being hacked down beneath them. The rules of advancement changed. The strategy now called for managers who would go out and market, not sit behind their desks and evaluate requests for loans. While it was all very well to suddenly prefer precisely the kind of pushy individual who used to be marked down in appraisals, what about the contract of a job that managers had bought into in return for loyalty and competent, thorough work?

Those introducing change have spent time pouring over data, reviewing scenarios and weighing up alternative proposals. They are steeped in the reasons for, and rationale of, the changes they are proposing. It is easy for them to automatically assume that those who will be affected have the same facts and information available to them and the same interpretation of the data. That is rarely the case.

Resisters can see themselves as the Resistance, or the loyal opposition, challenging the data and the interpretations, slowing the advance and defending the values of the organization. They are not resisting, they are protecting. This is all the more galling to those managers introducing change, since they can interpret questioning and challenge as resistance and react strongly to the apparent foot dragging.

While people express typical reactions in common to change, there are also some common factors that affect change programmes and act as a drag on their effectiveness.

A group of Royal Naval Officers on a barge trip pointed out a metaphor for change. The faster the barge went, the greater the bow wave it created. As the bow wave was reflected from the sides of the canal onto the barge it created a drag factor. There was a certain point at which increasing the speed of the barge created a bigger bow wave that increased the drag. The trick was to go fast enough before the bow wave itself started dragging the barge backwards.

CHOICE OF STRATEGY

Not all changes are the same, and there is no single recipe for dealing with them. However, there are some useful distinctions which can be drawn as a way of coming at a communication strategy.

Change efforts that stumble often wrongly match the degree of speed and drive to the change required, moving too quickly and involving too few people. Where cooperation is required to make the change happen, and where the people who will be affected by the change possess the information needed to implement the change correctly, the drive by other senior managers can create friction and resistance. In other cases, where there is high urgency to change, and where the speed of change is vital to survival, long consultations on issues on which strong leadership is expected can exasperate the rest of the organization at the slowness of change.

The process of communication takes time. The word 'communication' comes from the Latin *communicare* – to share. Information can be transmitted, but communication has to be shared, and sometimes that cannot be hurried. Boris Yeltsin, responding to impatience that the process of change was too slow, said, 'If you put nine pregnant women in a room together, the babies do not come in one month'.

To persuade and carry the support of your staff, you have to invest time in talking to them. The less time you spend talking, the more assertive you have to be. The more you have to assert and push, the more resistance you create.

Unfortunately, in most situations of change, time is precisely what is lacking. People are under continual pressure to get the job done, to take part in extra projects, with fewer resources, and to 'make time' to cope with everything. Under stress they tend to let slide the areas most important to helping people through change – they do not explain the rationale or the intention behind specific changes, they do not coach their people in the skills needed, and they do not have the time to counsel staff who are themselves feeling under pressure. Middle managers report that they are caught in the crunch – they are told by their bosses to communicate, but are not allowed the time to do so properly.

The dilemma that organizations often face is at what speed they should be driving change. The leaders may be arguing for a fast push that will show decisive leadership and provide a clear direction, while colleagues argue for a more softly, softly approach aimed at enlisting support and avoiding pitfalls. Faced with comments from their people that the board is either too indecisive or too autocratic and directive, directors can be tempted to adopt the style that best suits their own personality, rather than the situation they are facing.

What is the best balance of drive and involvement?

Communicating for change depends largely on the mix of reasons for the change itself, and the sources of possible resistance. The best strategy will depend upon some of the following:

- type of change
- degree of urgency to make change happen
- speed of change required
- reactions to change, and likely triggers of resistance.

Type of change

Some changes are triggered by a sudden or unexpected event: the threat of a takeover; the introduction by a competitor of a much superior product; a regulatory change; or the restructuring of the organization. These may have significant impact, but are essentially lurches. They require swift but not continual adaptation, and may be followed by periods of relative calm.

Others are driven by a larger process of change or evolution in the marketplace: the convergence of banks, building societies and insurance companies in the provision of financial services; the increasing overlap between computing and telecommunications; or the drive of consumer electronics hardware manufacturers to acquire software developers. Here, change is likely to be continual, with little respite and fresh changes coming along each day.

As a rule of thumb, it is best to involve people who will be affected by the change in the change process as much as possible. Imposing change on people can create too much bad feeling, resistance and resentment to be effective in anything but the short term. This supposes that you have the time to invest in building commitment. Whether time is on your side will depend on the strength of pressures on you to change, and the organization's ability to withstand them.

The degree of urgency to make change happen, and the speed at which the organization has to change

The two are different. Privatization of the water industry demanded changes in attitudes and practices among staff, but there was time to plan a process that helped to explain the need for change and provide the skills to make change happen. The successive deregulation of the electricity industry has allowed the evolution of a change strategy geared to each stage of deregulation. These situations could afford a much slower change process, and the involvement and education of people within the organization, taking the time to cope with reactions, and minimizing resistance.

A personal computer company faced with the collapse of the unit price in its market, and having to produce innovative products, and dramatically reduce its cost base, while its market share spirals downward, has less room for manoeuvre, and has to change fast. Such a crisis might call for rapid action, a centrally developed plan of action, and minimal involvement of others. The risk of failure in the market might override the risk of alienating and offending staff. While pushing forward on implementation, the communication might attempt to provide some degree of rationale and context for decisions, but there would be little room for consultation, venting or sharing of thinking. Resistance and resentment would be the inevitable price to pay for speed of action, and it would be vital to address those once the crisis had stabilized.

How many resistance triggers are involved?

The more the projected change is likely to trigger any of the resistance factors discussed earlier, the greater the strength of feeling there will be and the less option there will be to use power simply to drive change through.

How much cooperation is needed from employees?

The more cooperation that is needed from employees, the greater the need will be to create understanding and involvement among them.

Who has the necessary information and expertise to make the change happen?

When employees hold the information and expertise necessary to make the change happen, it is not just their cooperation that is needed. Communication in this situation needs to be much more participative, and is likely to be far more time-intensive.

What are our other options?

When the organization is under pressure to change and change quickly, the temptation is to speed up the process by imposing change. This route brings a higher risk that the change will be resisted, but there are times when the investment of time is outweighed by the risk of not changing fast enough. The less room for manoeuvre the organization has, and the fewer the options available, the more it may have to impose change in the short term, rather than trying to win people over to it.

Taking this route, when it is absolutely necessary, has a price. The less time you take to communicate, the less that you share the thinking, the more assertive you tend to be. The more assertive you are, the more resistance you create. In terms of communication you have to select a line between sharing the thinking as time-efficiently as possible and pushing your conclusions too quickly and creating resistance.

The chart in Fig. 4.1 shows two extremes of communicating change: the bottom left, where time allows for involvement; and the top right, where pressure dictates the announcement of change.

The bottom left approach will use significant amounts of time to allow for education, dialogue and the identification of what needs to be implemented. It will involve considerable questioning on all sides and allow

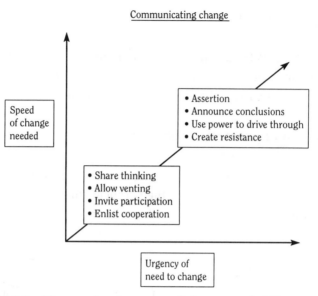

FIGURE 4.1 **The speed and urgency of change needed dictate the approach to communicating**

for clarifying and amending proposals. It is more likely to build trust and create ownership.

The top right approach is a 'lesser of two evils' choice in a situation which is inevitably going to be unsatisfactory. If the organization believes it has to go onto a war footing, and to give and obey orders simply to survive, it will not be able to afford the time for debate. However, the announcement of change will inevitably put down only shallow roots, since it provides little opportunity to create a sense of ownership and commitment, while creating a high risk of resistance.

However, the crisis situations where there is simply no time for debate, and where change must be driven through for survival's sake, are not that common. Organizations can too easily persuade themselves that they need a faster communication push than their situation warrants and then make the mistake of using the wrong channels to communicate.

Arm's length tools such as videos, newsletters and brochures are useful for distributing information, but do not provide any opportunity for ensuring the understanding, feedback and debate that is necessary for creating ownership of change. A company that is keen to get on and push change through can use informational channels quickly and efficiently to announce change and the conclusions of the board's strategy.

The belief that this is the best approach to communicating change, whatever the pressure and the pace, is a common cause of friction and resistance. The option to go for the high-speed driving through of change often has less to do with the pressure to change or the lack of other options than with a choice driven by management style, and beliefs about who should be in control.

One of the major obstacles to successfully communicating change is the attitude of the communicator, in the same way that the biggest barrier to successful selling is the product-focused seller's 'going for the jugular'. Organizations faced with making change typically set themselves to 'sell' the change to their employees, and become frustrated when employees decline to buy what they are selling. This may well be because they are practising 'foot in the door' communication, an approach to gain compliance, rather than satisfying the customer's true needs.

Senior managers can be excited by the prospect of change, can urge their staff to embrace it, but they are more likely to retain their jobs and their benefits than are their employees lower down the organization. They can thus afford to be a little more enthusiastic about the prospect of change and rising to its challenges.

An engineering company, reorganizing its product divisions, went through a process of participation and consultation. The enthusiasm of the managers was not universally shared. One grizzled engineer was deeply sceptical of the exercise, and saw the consultation as a sign of management failure: 'Working in this company's always been like working in the boiler room of a ship. When the Captain calls you up on to the bridge to ask you where you think we should be going, you can be sure you're on the Titanic.'

COMMUNICATION IN CONTEXT

People put communication into a pre-existing context

Changes make more sense in context, and without that context misunderstanding is almost inevitable. Resistance can come from arguing from different premises and interpreting within different contexts.

Day-to-day communication happens between people who more or less share assumptions. These assumptions may have been made some time back in the past and then largely forgotten, only to be remembered again if they are threatened or challenged. Successful communication relies upon a shared context, and assumes that people share common attitudes and values. When the expectations of those communicating are shared, meaning is also shared.

In a stable environment, people unquestioningly share values and assumptions, and are happier to receive information without debate. The context is taken for granted and people unquestioningly share a backdrop to their activities.

In a more turbulent environment, people need a greater understanding of the context, why things are the way they are now. The context shifts, different parts of the organization put a different backdrop behind words and actions, interpretations vary and the chance of confusion multiplies.

The greater the degree of change, the more time and effort you have to spend on setting context, sharing the thinking and fielding reactions and comments.

Since communication is effective to the degree that two speakers share the same assumptions, no shared assumptions means no communication. When it is obvious that there is a failure to communicate, the answer is not to shout louder, but to explore the mismatch in assumptions.

Context and cocooning for employees

Individuals respond to increasing complexity outside by 'cocooning' themselves at home. People at work, already stretched and with more to do, react similarly. With fewer fellow workers to help or to get support from, in a continually changing environment, people huddle closer together. They identify with their immediate team, and watch their own jobs and job security, to the exclusion of other concerns.

The individual's trust in managers two levels above tends to be low, and there is little visibility of managers above that level. Trust tends to be placed in immediate colleagues and the line supervisor, unless threat of redundancy has eroded even that. Horizons are lowered, and the focus is more on survival than self-actualization.

At the same time, organizations are trying to lift up the heads of their employees and widen their horizons, and get them to understand more about the business and the interrelationships within it. The two trends run in opposite directions, with the current running against a wider, holistic context.

The managers' inclination to communication only about task-focused issues plays into this lowering of horizons and aggravates the situation. Managers, more inclined to simply give out tasks rather than explain the reasons behind them, undermine the ability of their staff to make sense of what is going on around them. Focusing communication on too narrow an area minimizes the context and increases the chances of misunderstanding and resistance.

A question raised by managers about the level of their employees' interest is often: 'Do people really need to know what's going on outside their immediate area? Surely they are only interested in their immediate work area, in getting their job done and going home?'

While it is assumed that interest in wider issues only starts when someone makes it to manager status, one first line supervisor was clear about the need to give her staff a clear context for the apparently simplest of jobs – cleaning and preparing hotel rooms.

> My people need to be clear about the increasingly competitive environment, and what we're trying to do about it. I'm asking them to do increasingly 'odd' things, like using different materials to cut costs and different ways of working together to provide better service – they'll only be flexible if they can see it makes sense, it's not just me being difficult.

93

Once they can see where we're going, they start coming up with ideas about how we could work more efficiently. Once they are on side, and you have their goodwill, they'll move from their own area to help out others when the workload's high, knowing we want to keep the cost of temporary staff down.

We're launching new products, and differentiating the services we provide, in much the same way as the airlines offer different classes of travel. Unless people are clear about why we're doing this, they start un-differentiating the services – it takes more effort to remember that different types of customer get different packages of entitlements, as we segment more, it means more variations and complexity for them to handle. If they aren't clear on the need for ensuring we stick to different packages, they give everyone the top standard, throwing off all our cost calculations and robbing us of the differentiation we need.

One organization had been pursuing a cost-cutting programme for some time. While numerous suggestions had been given about not using the telephone until after 1 pm, turning off the lights at the end of the day, etc., little significant had come of the exercise. In one department, the manager, frustrated by the lack of progress, called his people together.

He had called them together at the outset of the initiative and explained that head office were now demanding cost cuts. While he himself had some idea about what was driving this, he had found it easier simply to point to head office as a culprit and so avoid any difficult questions that he might not be able to answer, and any unpopularity this might have brought him. Now, however, revisiting the initiative, he drew a fuller picture of why it was needed, what were the rates of return that were expected and why the return on capital employed meant that they might as well put the money in the bank and get a better return.

Once the people understood why the improvements were needed, their attitudes changed. They freely admitted that they had paid little attention to the initiative, since management were always looking for cost cuts, and the corporate centre legendarily begrudged any money spent for the benefit of the customer. They had also believed that the £1 million profit their area had made the year before was ample return for anyone but the most avaricious.

Now they saw that their view had been somewhat naive, and came up with their own ideas for improving costs. That meeting, which created their ownership and cooperation, led swiftly to the identification of £200 000 worth of savings.

Focusing on the task

Too great a task focus and too high a drive for results can tempt a manager to short-cut the process of change – cutting short the debate, in favour of getting on with the task.

Most managers will sympathize with the desire to cut things short. They might feel that they already know the answer to a particular problem, and that if they can just go in to their team and tell them to get on with the task it would save a lot of time in fruitless debate and concentrate attention on getting results. Unfortunately, we know that this is not how people are or how life works out. The less people have the opportunity to debate, discuss and gain ownership of a solution, the lower their level of commitment to it and the likelihood of their doing it well is likely to be.

Prevailing communication

The way that most communication in meetings takes place is by individuals staking out their positions early, defending their stand and attacking any countervailing position. It is the adversarial system of communication seen in Parliament and between opposing counsel in the courts. The objective is for your viewpoint to prevail over the other side's viewpoint and win the day.

Unfortunately, taking up a position *for* something creates in the other person a desire to take up a position *against*. Accusation of an individual forces him into self-justification, rarely self-examination.

WAYS OF COMMUNICATING CHANGE

What is needed?

Smoothing the path of change involves realizing that there are two aspects to the list of employees' reactions to change detailed above. One has to do with the proposal for change, its appropriateness, its validity, and its implications. The other has to do with the relationship with those proposing the change, their credibility, competence and trustworthiness. Tackling the first is a mater of *what* you should communicate; tackling the second involves *how* you do it.

The process of change has been described as a curve that demonstrates the expectations and disappointments of change. It starts with excitement and high hopes, and the liberating effect of being given free rein to slaughter sacred cows. As the sobering realization of the scale and complexity of change required sinks in, together with the slowness of visible progress, spirits drop, and people find themselves in the trough of despondency. Finally, as results start to percolate through, and greater realism takes hold, spirits climb once more, though never to the initial dizzy heights of the launch of the change.

The lesson here is that expectations are always too high, and that they need to be managed to prevent unrealistic enthusiasm and so avoid the reaction of disappointment and despondency.

However, this curve represents a change process for enthusiasts – either the group of early adopters embracing change, or an entire organization, a management buyout perhaps, unshackled and striding boldly into the future.

There are as likely to be change programmes where at the outset there is apathy, resistance and cynicism. The programme is launched to a population underwhelmed by the latest flavour of the month, fails to engage employees' participation and in a self-fulfilling prophecy achieves little, sinks into obscurity and is quietly buried and forgotten. Forgotten, that is, until its successor is launched.

The lesson to be learned is that often the way change is communicated itself creates the very resistance that was feared. One of the best ways to overcome resistance is not to create it in the first place. The pain managers feel at the hostile reactions they encounter is often self-inflicted, and caused by the way they regard the role of communication and their approach to communicating.

A manufacturer that produced for a range of international markets was trying to shift the perceptions and priorities of its employees. They traditionally saw foreign markets as 'the export afterthought' - the orders you filled on a Friday afternoon when there was little else left to do. The production manager was running a meeting with team leaders. The aim of the session was to give them an update on the reorganization within the company. In preparing for the meeting, the manager believed that the bulk of the issues and questions would be about the production problems of making short runs of a wider range of products. He was surprised therefore when questions focused on the structure of the business, and the split of responsibility between directors. Far from focusing on detail, his team leaders were interested in the whole rationale for the business, the way it would be organized to serve its markets and the relative abilities of its leaders. The manager had underestimated the depth of his team's interest and although he himself had wondered about the same issues had not discovered any of the answers.

Too specific, too late

Although people want to have the wider picture, they frequently do not ask wider questions because they believe they already have the answers. Everything they are told they put into their existing context, where it is unlikely to be interpreted as intended. People are interested in how changes affect them, but they may leap to the specifics based on a mistaken assumption about the generalities. The danger of this is all the greater when organizations delay communicating, and restrict their communication to task-related specifics.

Companies can be reluctant to begin communicating with their people too early, for fear that there will not be enough specific information available to answer the detailed questions that might be asked. This is understandable, but it also seems to be a symptom of the belief that the senior manager does the thinking and the employee does the doing. There is an assumption that employees 'close to the coal face' will only want to know the specifics of how individual changes will affect them.

97

There may never be a time when all the specifics of a change are known, and the people who know the specifics are probably the people you want to address. As individuals increasingly specialize, and become the acknowledged experts in their own jobs, it will be all the harder for someone else to anticipate the relevant questions they might have, let alone the relevant answers.

The reticence on the part of managers to begin communicating too early is a reflection of the uncertainty and discomfort playing the expected role of the manager brings. Managers, by definition, are supposed to know all the answers, aren't they? Being confronted by a question that reveals ignorance is something to be avoided.

However, pretending that you know all the answers, and getting up to tell people the details of the changes, can be a fatal error for a manager. Staff play the game, probing the specifics of the change ... Where will our new office network be located, and what will the travel arrangements be?

Managers counter by avoiding any specific details – 'A task force on branch network optimization and travel support infrastructure is working on that as we speak' – or by creating a smokescreen of management speak to conceal any lack of knowledge.

A director can find himself waxing lyrical on the strategy, only to be asked, 'How is this going to affect the stock holding policy?' Unable to answer (the only person who knows the answer is usually the person who just asked the question) he falls back on the assurance that some areas are still being looked into. The questioner settles back into her seat, having demonstrated to her assembled colleagues that the proposals are ill thought through, and that it is all rhetoric without detailed substance. The unspoken, but eloquently conveyed message is that the director should come back to them when his ideas are a little less half-baked. Question: Where is the director going to get the details to flesh out his presentation? Answer: From the people who have just attended it.

There is an even trickier question from the floor: 'Does the director realize that the vital projections the strategy depends on are based on data which are now known to be corrupt? If the data are re-analysed, the assumptions which have prompted the strategy no longer hold true. What are the director's comments, please?'

The knowledge that is needed to make the strategy work is in the heads of the audience, but the very format of the presentation prevents their cooperation. The belief that change should be communicated if not en masse, then certainly in large groups, and via a presentation, creates these unsuccessful situations.

The rules of the game are that the presenter has all the knowledge and unveils it in a masterly presentation which marshalls the facts and is compelling in its logic. The managers with the knowledge and the ability to make it work, meanwhile, sit in the audience on their best behaviour. Like any audience, they are passive for most of the time, and it is their role to evaluate the performance of the presenter, approving or disapproving. They have little to do but evaluate, and come to a 'yes' or 'no' vote in their own minds - with the likelihood that the vote will be unfavourable.

Credibility and trust

Trust is hardest to establish when you need it the most. Even where there has been trust in the past, when a change happens lack of trust can emerge as a serious obstacle.

There is often little trust within organizations. Employee research shows that, in the average organization, people have a healthy suspicion of management's motives and routinely expect a hidden agenda. Time and again, there is the automatic acceptance among employees that no matter how much they are being told, the real information is being withheld.

One new chief executive encouraged his senior managers to ask whatever questions they had that were concerning them. Managers bearded him with the rumours that he was to be transferred to run another troubled division. With admirable straightforwardness, and taking the question head on, he gave his managers his unfailing commitment to stay with them until the job they had started was finished. There was no truth in the rumour, and he would be with them for the long haul. Two days later, he was gone; sent to turn around another division in the group. He may have been the last to learn of the intentions to transfer him, and his assurance may have been candid and honest at the time, but the reactions within the company were ones of 'I told you so', and disappointment that such heartfelt assurances came to nothing.

Similarly, in one company everyone had a good time watching the corporate video in which the managing director laid out the strategy for the next five years and reinforced his commitment to it, while also asking for that of his staff. The grapevine had fed through the news that the same man had been searching for a new house to go with a new job over the period of shooting the video, and his departure was announced days after the distribution of the video.

These are extremes, and no one can deny that events can overtake the best of intentions and catch us unawares. But they do illustrate an option that companies frequently flirt with in their communication – going from being economical with the truth, to being parsimonious with the truth, to employing a truth substitute.

When times are good, organizations are happy to be as open and honest with their people as possible. Employees are relatively happy, not inclined to dig into areas beyond their immediate satisfaction, and while results are good there are probably few murky areas to alarm. It is when times are bad, and the news isn't much better, that the temptation arises to put too positive a gloss on communication. In tough times, people are scrutinizing the entrails in search of signs – do all those evening sandwich suppers being taken into personnel portend redundancies? – and the grapevine goes into overdrive. People get a feel for how bad things are, and with the additional spin of an apprehensive grapevine may well overestimate the seriousness of the situation. Either way, the uncertainty seems worse than the knowledge.

The temptation is to say nothing, or to issue holding statements. While there is often the dilemma that management do not have the whole picture, and it often seems a disservice to create uncertainty, these days there may never be a time when the picture and certainty returns. Meanwhile, your credibility is being eroded, as the grapevine busily continues its work.

The speed and pernicious influence of the grapevine depends on the climate of trust prevailing within the organization. Where there is suspicion, even the most bizarre rumour can seem plausible. Rumours spreads like wildfire when the ground is dry and flammable. An organization conducting a review of managers' core competencies and training needs found that speculation as to the 'true' nature of the exercise was rife. Managers had surmised that the true intention was to build lists of A category managers and B category managers. They then telephoned each other to discover which of the categories colleagues had fallen into. It took strenuous denials to scotch the rumour, and to lay the hours of telephone networking to rest.

Credibility is a strategic resource. It takes a long time to build, and an extraordinarily short time to lose. Ironically, thanks to the growing sensitivity to the impact a crisis can have on a business, and the examples of Tylenol, Perrier and Heinz, crisis communication has become a discipline enforced by the knowledge that a price tag attaches to the credibility brands have with consumers. Companies know that they have to be prepared to respond instantly, and that stonewalling 'no comment' will be taken as an admission of culpability, leading to a collapse of confidence in the brand. Crisis watchers will remember that Perrier's apparent reluctance to deal with the issue of benzene content in their water led to a further damaging debate about whether they were entitled to call their water 'naturally carbonated'.

Internally, managers may be more tempted to say nothing, or simply to lie, in the expectation that employees will understand later that commercial considerations made lying the logical course. While they may well understand, and it may confirm their expectations, it only erodes credibility. MORI tracks organizations undergoing change and compares ratings of communication within these with communication within more stable organizations (see Fig. 4.2). Credibility is important in times of stability, but is more under attack in times of change.

The norm for credibility of management is 66 per cent under normal, stable conditions. For organizations going through change, it drops to 49 per cent. Similarly, the norm for understanding of the organization's

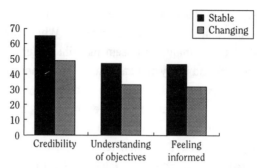

FIGURE 4.2   The impact of change on employee ratings of communication (Source: MORI)

objectives is 48 per cent normally, but in periods of change drops to 34 per cent. Whereas in stable times, the norm for feeling you are kept informed is 46 per cent, in changing companies that drops to only 33 per cent. Finally, the norm for stable companies' rating of 'I am not able to express my views' is 59 per cent, rising to a worrying 75 per cent as the company changes.

In terms of the visibility of senior management, the stable, norm preference is around 40 per cent, but again in times of change the preference for hearing direct from senior managers rises to over 60 per cent.

These scores are as likely to be reflections of employees' unease and uncertainty, as they are of managers' failure to communicate properly.

Communication needs to be continuous

On average, less than half an organization's employees knows where it is going, and less than a quarter get any feedback on progress. Left to pick up clues, they get most of their information through the grapevine, and carry on doing what they have always done in the past.

Communicating the context for change has to take place not just at an early stage, but all the time. It is difficult to start educating employees about the business environment when a change suddenly looms on the horizon.

The closer to the arrival of the change the education begins, the more people will crane their necks to see the details of the change, paying less attention to your presentation on the competitive environment and wanting to get to the meat of how this will affect them.

For those organizations whose competitiveness relies upon speed of response to their market, there has to be a clear awareness and understanding among their employees long before any change is called for – there won't be time to pull back, set things in context and educate afterwards.

Revisit past assumptions

There is, in addition to the usual human inertia, a prevailing conviction that individuals are already doing a good job which causes them to resist change. Their assessment of their performance will be based on their perception of what the job entails. Their definition of their job is probably based on their past experience, and if no one highlights those past assumptions they will continue to form the basis for self-assessment. Warehouse staff who see their job as the maintenance of stock levels, and ensuring that no eventuality arises for which there is no appropriate spare part, can be puzzled by talk of stringent inventory-level management which seems to run counter to the basic values of the job. They have prided themselves on always having what is needed, and will squirrel away spare parts that do not show up on the official records, just to be helpful.

Identify the refractive layer, and give them the chance to feed back

There is usually a 'refractive layer' of people in any organization – a layer where information coming down from above is modified or bent before being passed on, and where information from below is similarly bent to fit before being passed up. At all levels in an organization, people attempt to link the world view of those above them to the vision of reality of those below them – that is an essential part of communication. But there is usually a level in an organization where the gap between the views of those above and those below is so great that further bending is required to bring them together.

Identifying the refractive layer is important to ensuring that communication flows up and down the company. Typically, middle managers are blamed for withholding information and 'bending' the truth. This is often as much the result of wanting to protect their staff from the vagaries and inconsistencies of those above them as it is of a desire to hang on to information and power.

Where the communication habits of the organization suppress the upward flow of what is actually going on, there is bound to be a role of mediation between the two realities. Middle managers tend to feel fairly bruised that they are compelled to fulfil that valuable role and they are made victims in the process - they are not given training and it is not explained how the strategy is to be translated into actual specifics for them to enact. Under the new rules of empowerment, they are asked to put flesh on the bones of the strategy, without fully being party to the debate about how the strategy emerged.

The complaint made about the refractive layer, and about middle management in particular, is that they are resistant to change. They do not accept the torch of change handed to them, or hand it on, in turn, to their own people. Ask a middle manager and he or she will see things differently. While he or she accepts the general need for change, and may like the stirring title chosen for the quality campaign, he or she would like some more specifics about how this is all going to work.

It is not hard for them to be resistant. There is no opportunity for them to voice their reactions, and there is often no immediate, real action for them to undertake.

Acknowledge schizophrenia

The manager responsible for driving change is often seen as a prime offender, doing all the things he tells others not to do - 'a cannibal preaching vegetarianism', in the words of one senior manager. Leaders are caught between the organization of the past and their aspirations for the future – and inevitably they seem schizophrenic. Senior managers are usually the ones with the understanding to make change. However, they are senior because they have succeeded under the rules of the old culture. It is no wonder that most initiatives for change eventually take on all the characteristics of the culture they are designed to change.

They genuinely pursue change, and occasionally revert to the old-style behaviour that made them successful, whereupon their subordinates say, 'I knew it would never last.'

The most effective communication is face to face, and the most believed communication is behaviour, most visible through the management style. What makes a manager successful under one regime can be a liability under a new strategy. The management style that is rewarded is often a task-focused one, involving a high level of personal drive to get things done. The drive to make change happen creates avoidance in others; the more you push, the more dodging and resistance you create.

In any organization, its greatest strength can also be its greatest weakness. A culture that is based on directive management and compliance to procedures can find that its people are too wary to suddenly become innovators and risk takers. Employees want some structure and guidance, and if they don't get it they're more likely to stay put rather than venture out into the minefield.

It's tempting, for example, to tell employees that, with the publication of the new mission statement, they are now 'free to fail' – and that the only failure is to fail to learn from one's mistakes. Unfortunately, our human natures trail behind our aspirations. One organization said that it didn't make mistakes, it had 'learning opportunities'. However, if you created more than two learning opportunities you got fired.

Let's you and him change

Communicating your change can play straight into the cultural bias within the organization.

The force of the culture is for the status quo; culture is the means by which we bring stability to the threat of change. The mental starting position for most people is 'We don't need to change – we're already doing a good job. But if we do, it's someone else, not me that needs to change.' Individuals mentally fill in the name of their favourite scapegoat, or villainous department, and wait for the change programme to hand out the appropriate punishment.

We are equipped to rationalize our way out of changing. Organizations don't change, people do. Change happens person by person, and you can't change people, they change themselves. However, staff usually wait to see if the change leader includes him or herself among those who need to change.

Check that you are not rewarding the wrong behaviour

While the strategy calls for one kind of behaviour, the reward system is often geared to a different kind, ensuring that people pursue their pocket, not the strategy. Organizations frequently reward the wrong behaviour, with bonuses based on keeping costs down and maximizing profit – serving the customer doesn't show up as a performance measure. Measures are often short-term, while benefits to the customer may take longer to come through.

Measures of success and performance indicators are often legacies of the past, internally focused, and are often designed to reflect how efficiently the organization is fulfilling its own purposes, rather than how effectively it is serving the customer.

Recognize dilemmas

Every organization has to face dilemmas, such as how to increase value and service while reducing costs. It is the unacknowledged dilemmas that warp behaviour and derail change.

Different functions have different priorities and different objectives. These are often only pulled together, if at all, at board level, or by the manager who has to reconcile apparently conflicting objectives. It is a manager's job to balance variables, but the gap between these is often too great to bridge – leading to having to bend the truth and the figures to make it all fit.

Assess how your culture is refracting communication

People listen to communication to decipher the 'code'. What do
management really mean, where are they really going? Culture 'refracts'
communication. You may say one thing – but they hear another. If you do
not know how your employees listen, you are not in control of your
communication.

Employees 'decode' all communication they receive, listening for the
'real' message. Without an understanding of employees' *listening*,
companies, however efficient their dissemination of information, are only
in control of half the communication equation.

How people listen depends on the organization's culture. In the public
sector, for example, there is an acute sensitivity to 'business speak' – and
the suspicion that it shows a betrayal of old values.

George Santayana said 'Those who forget the past are condemned to
repeat it'. Many organizations today are repeating their past every day,
having forgotten decisions they made years before which they continue to
pursue even though it is no longer appropriate. They have become
prisoners of the past.

The culture of any organization is comprised largely of its past – not
only critical incidents that help to mythologize and define what it finds
important, but key strategic decisions which gave rise to, and sustained, its
values. While strategy is a force that drives towards the future, culture is a
force based on the past, fighting to maintain the status quo. In this way
organizations have one foot flat down on the accelerator of strategic
change, while the other foot, unknown to them, is pressed hard down on
the brake of maintaining the status quo. No wonder people within
organizations feel they are getting a bumpy ride.

The evolution of organizations is like the evolution of the human
body. There are bits of us which are no longer of any use to us, to which we
pay little daily attention but which can cause us pain – the appendix, the
coccyx and the tonsils. The corporate body has its own versions of these.

To stop being a prisoner of the past, you need to go back and unearth
it. Like archaeologists, we can look for explanations of why things are the

way they are today by digging through successive layers of yesterday. Organizations are like ancient Troy – layer after layer of new strategies and decisions from the past. Without a little excavation and digging out of those layers, you cannot lay a solid foundation for change. The signals from the past are invisible, and all the stronger for that.

Policies and practices which made sense in the past, but are no longer appropriate, are still enshrined in administration procedures, measurement and information and reward systems. They are still being enforced, and they are diverting energy and costing money.

The past is also reflected in shared and unquestioned values, accepted priorities and taboos. Any organization has unspoken rules by which people play the game, and which you pick up by nods and winks. Everyone knows what they should officially say, and what is unspoken, common knowledge but saying which constitutes a career limiting statement.

One of the most important lessons to be drawn from using communication to speed up change is that an organization's culture refracts its communication, and that without some knowledge of that culture it is impossible to create an effective change communication strategy. Fons Trompenaars points out that:

> Culture is a shared system of meanings. It dictates what we pay attention to, how we act, and what we value.

Organizations are usually a cocktail of different cultures, with different groups within the organization having their own view of the world. In some organizations, each unit is left to its own devices, and management is by financial results alone, with the way results are achieved being entirely left up to the unit. Does the word 'customer' translate as 'client' in one area and 'punter' in another? What are the different underlying opinions about what people are really like? Are people basically lazy and in need of continual control, motivated by fear and money, or are they keen to realize their potential and respond well to freedom, praise and recognition?

Communication assumes that people share common attitudes and values. When the expectations of those communicating are shared, meaning is shared. Once the assumptions are made, they are forgotten. Day-to-day communication continues between people who more or less share assumptions.

There have been numerous ways of explaining culture, and a range of typologies developed to provide managers with an insight into their organization. The working definition, that culture is 'the way we do things around here', does not provide any clues as to why we happen to have chosen to do things that way. Charles Hampden-Turner (1990) explains an organization's culture in terms of its finding ways of solving everyday problems, resolving dilemmas and providing guidelines for taking action. In other words, the situation you find inside your organization is a solution to a problem. It is impossible simply to overlay another solution, which has as its rationale a different problem. Unless there is a shared appreciation of the problem, there can be no agreement on a solution.

It is worth asking, then, when employees cling to a certain way of doing things, 'What is the problem they are trying to solve?' The role of communication in culture change is to create awareness that the problem the organization faces has changed, in the face of our human inclination to avoid harsh reality.

Changes in a culture happen when people recognize that old ways of doing things are only solutions to problems that have now passed. People will cling to their accustomed ways as long as they do not re-examine the problems they currently face. It is easier to change the organization when people share an understanding of the problems they face, the inappropriateness of old remedies and the need to find new solutions.

Internal communication can fail due to the lack of understanding about the prevailing values by which a company abides. People will resist going in any direction that they feel violates their concept of professionalism. The failure to explain how new company objectives are in harmony with the company's traditional values is a recipe for misunderstanding, resistance and conflict.

Managers are people who have succeeded by the rules of the old culture, and the skills they have may not all be appropriate. They need training – communication doesn't come naturally and learning to listen comes painfully.

Without some understanding of the cultural backgrounds, or some way of translating between different sets of values, there is little chance of real communication. You need to know what the people's concerns are, and how they get their communication. Without this information you might as well be broadcasting into outer space.

Trying to change others is a frustrating task. The more people are pushed to change, the more their current ways are attacked, the more ingeniously they are able to avoid the issue and defend themselves. Accusation breeds self-justification. People need a way of seeing their way to change that is free of blame. You need to hold a mirror up to them, so that they see the need to change, and the way of changing.

Qualitative and quantitative research helps to highlight these differences, and Chapter 6 on conducting internal research discusses options for carrying this out.

You can only sell what you own

Commitment comes from a sense of ownership, and ownership comes from participation. People need to be actively involved in discussing how the strategy can be implemented in their area. The less they are involved, the less committed they will be.

People dislike being presented with a *fait accompli*. Even where they may have agreed with the conclusion, by being excluded from the debate, and unable to contribute, they see the exclusion as a negation of their perceived worth to the organization.

Share the thinking, not the conclusions

To achieve change in an established company, people must see the rationale behind the strategy and accept it. They must also understand how the need for the change was identified, the alternatives that were considered and the basis on which conclusions were drawn. That way, they can at least see how they themselves, in the same situation, might have reached the same conclusion.

Communication should mirror the thought process that has already gone on within the organization. In a surprising number of cases, the answers to questions raised by staff have already been considered by the team who first mooted the changes. Communication of the change, however, can focus too much on announcing the conclusions of the strategy review and the actions to be implemented. What is needed is to share the thinking. People have different perceptions, and are at different stages of readiness. Sharing the thinking allows everyone to become aligned on the rationale and the strategy.

People in groups agree on generalities more easily than they agree on specifics. It is easier to get agreement in a group on the universal need for job satisfaction than it is for the same group to settle on what restaurant they will all go to together. Getting to specifics too early tends to polarize opinions and positions around individual implementation issues, before any consensus or shared agreement exists around the general approaches. A shared agreement needs to be built first; a warming-up of the relationship is needed before getting into specifics.

Senior managers tend to focus on what they believe employees need in order to fulfil their task, rather than what they need to understand and feel part of the organization. The inclination is to aim for employees' compliance with implementation, rather than their understanding.

A European bank developed its strategy and presented it to staff via managers. Managers were trained in presenting the strategy and in leading question and answer sessions to clarify and help people to understand the strategy's implications.

The structure of the sessions called for an hour's presentation, during which the manager went from the big picture to the small detail. The concluding message was that the senior managers were fully committed to the strategy. There was then a further explanation of how the strategy would be implemented in each area.

Finally, the floor was thrown open for questions. These tended to be about the minutiae (where would people's offices be, would the integration of product areas affect the car policy?)

While these were reasonable questions, the manager doing the briefing was disappointed; he had shown the employees a vision of the future and here they were nit-picking, or expressing only parochial self-interest. He had, however, brought it upon himself. The structure of the session kept involvement of staff at bay, as the focus of his presentation narrowed from the general to the specific, from vision to details of implementation, into the day-to-day specifics. Questions simply picked up at that point and continued to narrow the focus. Staff were left with a low level of understanding, little ownership and with the distinct impression that the vision was another bout of restructuring musical chairs.

Employees need to be taken through the thought process and the debate, not simply to have the conclusions of the debate announced to them. They need to know the why, as well as the what.

People look for continuity with the past. They look for reassurance that the values they abide by are being respected. Sharing the thinking, and explaining how conclusions are arrived at, is more uniting than announcing the conclusions and implicitly inviting people to take positions for or against the proposition.

Objections to specific proposals are often disguised concerns about more general issues, conflicts with values, concerns about fair treatment of people affected, etc. They are objections to rationales, which are only voiced as objections to specific issues. Managers often pursue and rectify the symptoms, rather than explore the underlying concerns. As each symptom is resolved, another pops up in its place, to the growing frustration of the manager, who begins to see this listing of objections as more foot dragging.

Communicate the context

One of the greatest dangers is that people see a series of separate initiatives which has no coherent umbrella plan that allows them to put individual initiatives into context. People will try to figure out the larger game plan from the individual moves. If the leadership does not provide a coherent rationale for the big picture, people will provide their own, and it is unlikely to be a positive one.

It is usually at times of redundancy, or shortly before wage negotiations, that companies start communicating in an attempt to educate their staff about current market conditions. One of the few occasions that people get to hear about the dynamics of the company and how it has been affected is usually as a prelude to an announcement of redundancy. While it is a rare opportunity to learn how the business actually functions, it is difficult to take this in, when what you are listening for is whether or not you have a job. It is hard when communication is an event not a process, but almost impossible when that event is redundancy. People cannot hear what you are saying to them, and each time you start talking about the dynamics of the company they take that as a signal that the axe is about to fall.

Managers do not like to make people redundant. It is usually an uncomfortable exercise and is felt by many managers to be a betrayal of the values they hold dear. The temptation therefore is usually to limit their own pain and discomfort by making it as task-focused an exercise as possible.

Figure 4.3 shows a communication funnel, which represents the process of thinking that usually precedes communication. It is depicted as a funnel because the thinking process within an organization moves from the general to the specific, from reviewing any and all factors to narrowing in on a few. At the outset, the emphasis is on open-mindedness, and the ability to think through ideas, and, as time progresses, thinking narrows and hardens into considering the specifics of a few chosen ideas. Debate at the outset moves with increasing certainty to assertion of specifics.

In any kind of decision we take as individuals, we move through a similar process. We think whether the concept of doing something fits us before moving on to the feasibility of it and how the finer details will work out. However, in organizations, different people at different levels will take successive parts of the process. The board may review their objectives, and then agree to take their respective functional slices of the whole. A director will delegate to a senior manager the job of reviewing what needs to be

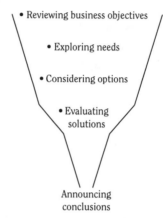

The communication funnel

• Reviewing business objectives

• Exploring needs

• Considering options

• Evaluating solutions

Announcing conclusions

FIGURE 4.3 **Announcing conclusions narrows people's understanding, and prevents them from understanding the rationale**

done to achieve an objective; a more junior manager will be assigned the task of evaluating tools which might fill the need; while the most junior person looks at the nuts and bolts required for implementation. At each successive level the focus narrows, and the whole picture is broken down into parts. While at each level the individual might be expert in a greater level of detail, there is also the likelihood that he or she lacks knowledge of the wider issues that have been debated at a higher level.

Communication is often seen as part of the process of implementation, when the focus has narrowed and the emphasis is on details of the task and the implementation plan. Managers may have mastered the issues involved, and want to get on with the job, to cut out the debate and focus time, effort and attention on getting the solution implemented. However, their staff, suspicious of management's traditional stance, and with their own value systems working differently, interpret the focus on the solution as an attempt to funnel them prematurely into doing something that may not benefit them. They may see senior management as attempting to sell them something with the apparent techniques of the timeshare salesman, and have little faith that management have their own interests at heart and are unlikely to have thought through the implications of their decisions.

The mismatch comes when those at the bottom of the organization receive only narrow communication on the specifics of implementation. The lower down the organization you are, the less context you have as background to the specifics, the less rationale you understand and the less sense the specifics make. Figure 4.4 highlights the effect of progressively narrowing the focus of communication the lower down the organization you go.

In approaching communication on such a narrow front, managers force their staff to look through the wrong end of a telescope, limiting their view to implementation issues. Since, in times of change, people scan the horizon for any sign of impending doom, this forces employees to use informal means of finding out what is going on, and hands them over to the grapevine.

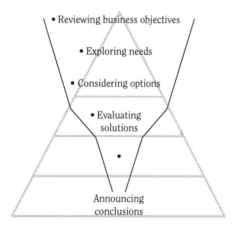

Narrowing the focus

- Reviewing business objectives
- Exploring needs
- Considering options
- Evaluating solutions
- ·
Announcing conclusions

FIGURE 4.4   Funnelling information down the hierarchical pyramid means the greatest number of people get the least context, and the lower down the organization you are the less sense information makes

At the top of Maslow's hierarchy of needs are the needs to realize our potential and to make the most of our talents. The new kind of organization with its emphasis on employee empowerment promotes precisely these needs, and promises the opportunity to meet them.

At the bottom of the pyramid are the needs for security and physical well-being. In the competitive environment, this has been the one message that people have received – there is no longer security for anyone.

Employees receive two conflicting messages: 'Let's embrace and welcome change, and realize your potential', and 'There is no job security anymore, and we cannot meet your fundamental needs.'

Given the insecurity that striking at the foundation of people's needs naturally creates, the issue of trust inevitably looms large. In times of change people want predictability: they want to know what is likely to happen and what to expect.

In the traditional organization people could expect some degree of predictability, they knew the rules of behaviour, what it took to get on and where their career path was likely to take them. In the absence of the old framework of expectations, people look to create predictability as a way of gaining some control over their lives. They look for clues, become expert trackers of the corporate world, reading and interpreting the smallest signs.

Predictability now has to consist of intentions and ground rules – what are our goals and objectives, how will we behave, what are the rules we will follow and how will we come to decisions. Managers may not be able to predict and communicate what is going to happen in the future, but they can provide regular updating and discussion of business issues, the options open to the organization and probable avenues of approach. The clearer people are on the values and ground rules, and on the processes for reaching decisions, the more they will be able to regain some degree of predictability and be able to project what might happen to them in the future.

Since day-to-day changes happen without creating strong reactions and concerted resistance, it is interesting to look at how large waves of change create quite different reactions. This may be because these initiatives are prepared and cooked by a select team, hived off and specially separated for the task. A task force is put to work by the chief executive to review the organization and come up with a new design. The task force gets to work, with enough on its plate without having to spend time on the issue of communication. They see communication as something that will need to be done a little later, when they themselves are clear on the organization's direction and when they have something concrete to say. Why worry everyone before plans are crystal clear and finalized?

However, by putting off communication with the rest of the organization, they prevent people from understanding the principles that guided them, the lessons they learned from previous experience and the choices they had to make. They unwittingly prevent the people who are expected to implement the change from sharing in their thought processes, and seeing why the conclusions make sense for the business. They also prevent any participation and involvement, and without that there will be no ownership, buy-in or commitment.

The sooner communication can begin, and the more it is part of the thinking processes, rather than the announcement and implementation process, the more valuable it is likely to be. Delaying communication may well be taken as suspicious in itself, provoking precisely the concerns and speculation that managers hope to avoid. Then the grapevine flourishes, spreading negative information that managers then find themselves having to correct.

The less time you have, the more assertive you are forced to be. You do not spend time discussing the issues that made you think, or the factors that influenced you. You do not describe the debate, you cut to its conclusions. Usually these conclusions are solutions to the problems you have identified. Without sharing the understanding of the problems, conclusions do not look like solutions – they look like disconnected ideas without any rationale to them.

The board of directors has been through the thought process and has had the chance to become comfortable with the proposals, evaluating alternatives and understanding why these make sense. The board has the most information, and, probably, the greatest level of security about its implications.

People lower down the organization also need the opportunity to go through a similar process. For people to accept and cooperate, they have to share the thinking. Announcing the conclusions gives them no chance to assimilate the thinking or understand the context – it is like trying to start a car in fourth gear.

THE COMMUNICATION COLLISION

The argument in favour of change lies in accepting a set of premises and assumptions on which the change is based – that the company, for example, has above all else to be profitable, efficient and have the funds to pursue its business strategy. Once those premises are accepted, there is a logic that shows how the proposed actions make sense. Individuals may not like what has to happen, but they can recognize the good sense of doing those actions. This constitutes the first communication task: explaining the rationale, the thinking and the logic.

This is increasingly difficult as you get closer to implementation. People naturally want answers to their own specific questions, and when the threat of redundancy looms they are unlikely to agree that international expansion is a greater priority than their continuing to draw a salary. They don't want the big picture, they want the small picture – and in detail. It is too late then to try to explain the business rationale, as people are now operating on their own personal agendas, and their individual priorities will inevitably be different from those of the company.

Communication depends upon sharing assumptions and putting information into a shared context. Without that, people will put it into their own context and their own immediate concerns. Their immediate reactions and questions come from the need for basic security, and their focus then widens progressively to the people around them and finally to the organization as a whole.

- Have I got a job?
- What is this going to mean to me?
- How is this going to affect my people?
- How much sense does this make for the business?

The later you leave it, the narrower communication is going to be. The narrower the front for communication, the greater the chance of collision and resistance will be (see Fig. 4.5).

The process of communication involves taking people through a line of logic, a process of thinking. People whose attitudes or understanding you want to change have to go through the process; they cannot just be handed the product of that process. The aim should be to share the thinking, not to announce the conclusions.

There is a need to go further back up towards the top of the funnel, upstream to where the thinking has taken place and different options have

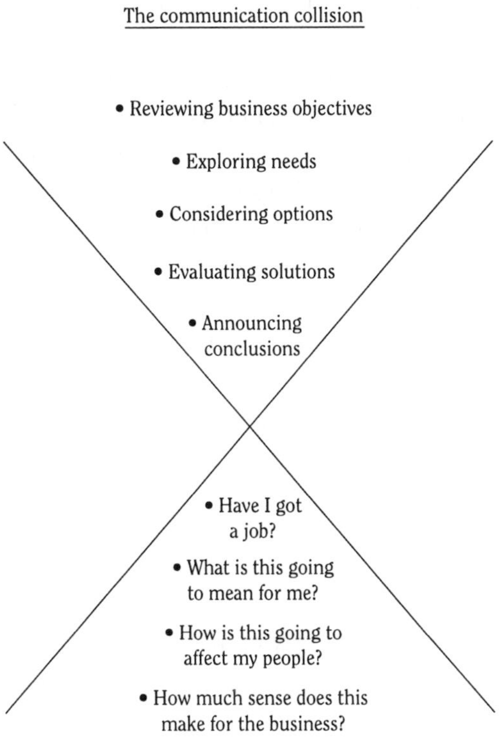

The communication collision

- Reviewing business objectives

  - Exploring needs

  - Considering options

  - Evaluating solutions

    - Announcing conclusions

    - Have I got a job?

  - What is this going to mean for me?

  - How is this going to affect my people?

- How much sense does this make for the business?

FIGURE 4.5 When communication happens on a narrow front, there is greater danger of the organization's agenda and the individual's agenda colliding

119

been considered. The greater the degree of change, the further upstream communication has to focus.

Without that context, information does not make sense or have the impact intended. Employees will decode and filter communication from their own position, anticipating that the organization is adopting an adversarial position.

The stage is set for a collision of interests, and for communication that seems to be pushing the business agenda at the expense of sensitivity to people's immediate concerns. At a time when managers are announcing the new way ahead, people's heads are filled with much more immediate and apprehensive questions about their own future, which makes it difficult to take anything else in.

The factors that make organizations successful then become a liability. The focus on getting the task done, forcing compliance, taking a position on what it is right or wrong to do, and communicating from a value system that is not shared, all add up to creating strong resistance and misunderstanding among the employees. The desire to jump to solutions, without sharing understanding of the problem and the thinking that has preceded them, aggravates resistance.

Senior management have done the thinking, they have thought through the implications, more than likely they have agonized over precisely the same issues that their staff are now raising. In their earnest desire to get the message across, they start using language which inadvertently reinforces the suspicions of their staff.

Relationships consist of shared, and conflicting, objectives. When times are turbulent, it is easy to lose sight of what is shared and connects people, and nervously focus on conflicting objectives that divide and create adversarial positions. Focusing your communication on the tasks that need to be done can trigger all the defensive adversarial resistance that you most feared.

Don't knock the past

Whether the chief executive is a fresh new arrival, or promoted internally, there is often a tendency to paint a picture of a bright tomorrow by contrasting it with the dullness and mistakes of yesterday. The implication is that the organization has been wrong in the past and now it is about to be put right.

Allow offloading

People can only take new ideas on board when they have had a chance to offload some of their mental baggage. Communicators can only be sure they have communicated when they get feedback. Managers are often shocked to discover long after the event that their words have been seriously misinterpreted.

If you do not allow people to voice the inevitable misunderstandings, acknowledge their concerns or explore their fears, you are likely to be faced not only with resistance, but resistance based on misunderstandings that you are not aware of. As people drag their feet, and you keep explaining what good sense the changes make, frustration mounts on both sides. The person introducing the change is seen to be pushing on regardless of the true issues, and the apparent resisters seem cussedly impervious to reason.

There are often supporters for change who do not speak. These are often people who have a keener sense of what is going on outside the company. The closer people are to the outside environment, the better their vantage point on change. A manager negotiating with customers picks up changes in the way they negotiate, and feels herself becoming more pressured and being played off against competitors. She detects the changing environment before her colleagues in production. People can see the signs around them – hotel rooms are not filled, taxis are emptier, there is less overtime, and less volume of product being packed and shipped.

Given the chance, and in groups small enough to put them at their ease, they are more likely to volunteer examples and anecdotes that support the need for change. By mixing people from different functions, different viewpoints help to avoid a monolithic common group view that prevents the exploration of issues. Colleagues and peers are more likely to accept corroborating evidence from each other than from a manager.

Shift from task focus

The key skills for helping employees manage change have to do with explaining, putting things in context and giving feedback. Most managers spend their time giving out instructions and checking that the tasks have been done.

The skills needed for communicating change are very different from the skills on which managers traditionally pride themselves and to which they accord priority. In an attitude survey, as a common question employees are asked how they are currently managed and then how they would like to be managed. They are also asked to detail the reasons for the contacts they have with their manager (see Fig. 4.6).

What emerges is a mismatch between the task focus of the manager – giving instructions, checking work – and the staff member's desire for context – being given background and reasons for doing things, and being provided with feedback on progress. Managers are biased towards communicating on the task, not on the context. This may merely be an

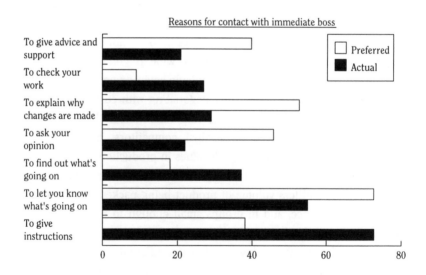

FIGURE 4.6 The traditional skills of the manager are more suited to checking tasks than to communicating change

irritant to the employee on a day-to-day basis, but in a period of change it becomes a liability.

Managers need to be trained to communicate, and given the support and the communication tools to do the job properly.

Make it safe to speak

We tend to talk about 'employees' without addressing senior management levels. Yet it is often senior managers who have to communicate, and deal with communication, without themselves having had the opportunity to test the truth of what they are hearing.

The problems that are most difficult to handle and the objections that are hardest to counter are those that the manager secretly agrees with. While it is fine for employees to ask questions, it is far less acceptable for senior management to raise issues, scepticism and doubts.

Sometimes, as part of their communication training, senior managers get to role-play, say, shop-floor workers, and this is a revelation. They get to say all the negative things they know they're not supposed to say, and you can hear years of swallowing staff members' awkward questions and their bosses' evasive answers spilling out.

People need to understand the specifics of how a strategy will work out in practice, and to do this they need to be able to ask questions and to get full answers. This process of probing and assessing is itself vital to creating comfort and ownership. Managers often complain, however, that they do not feel free to raise questions, or to continue to probe for detail. Their questions are perceived as 'negative', or as throwing doubt on the proposed changes. Persistent questioning is seen as the hallmark of the troublemaker, or may raise the suspicion that the manager is unable to handle his or her job.

One manager took his team away to address problems of under-performance. He gave them his ground rules for the day: that they could raise any issue about any obstacle, whether it had to do with him personally or the organization as a whole.

His staff responded, raising issues that they found frustrating and which he found painful to hear. However, the strongest message that came out of the day was that it was acceptable for them to raise these issues if they were obstacles. They would not be punished for doing so, nor would their contributions be dismissed out of hand. The greatest message of the day, said one manager, was that it showed that 'disagreement did not equal death', and that the old rule that to get on you had to be agreeable was changing.

Where people look for clear evidence that it is acceptable to disagree, and where the cultural bias of an organization is to stay silent when unsure, to be in fear about putting a foot wrong, and where there is a natural bias to be agreeable, management have to seek out opportunities, even staged opportunities, to show differently.

It is difficult to overcome the perception that you are not serious about making change without actually making changes. Appeals for credibility, exhortations and assurances can sound like empty sabre rattling. Some organizations choose to seed the ground with some clear actions before appealing for general support.

An electronics company simply bypassed the problem by acting first and communicating later. Small signs of change began to appear, such as altering car parking arrangements and abolishing the directors' parking spaces so that the first person in got the space closest to the office building. Intrigued staff began to ask what was happening, and the communication of the larger changes satisfied a curiosity that had already been built up.

DEVELOPING A COMMUNICATION STRATEGY

Figure 4.7 shows the communication escalator – developing a communication strategy, whether for communicating change or for sustaining it.

Typically, the formation of a strategy begins with the question of what it is that employees want from communication. This approach is based on what the organization needs from its people – the behaviour and attitudes needed from employees to achieve the business objectives. It came out of a lesson learned from researching attitudes to communication within an

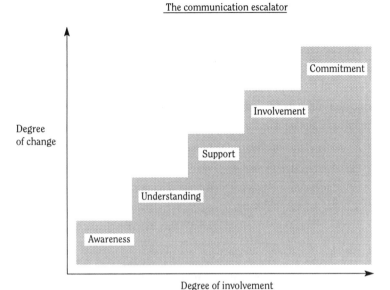

The communication escalator

Degree
of change

Commitment

Involvement

Support

Understanding

Awareness

Degree of involvement

FIGURE 4.7 **There are different steps, with different
objectives, in the communication process**

organization facing significant change in its structure, location and role.

As preparation for the creation of a new organization, those people
who would be affected by the new structure were interviewed. Interviewees
had no problem listing what it was they wanted by way of communication
(organization charts, colour brochures showing the purpose and work of
the organization, internal notices of job vacancies and maps showing the
location of the new buildings). It was realized that all of these answers
formed part of the problem that the new organization was designed in part
to address. The requests for information by employees were all based on the
assumption that life would continue as normal, whereas there was to be a
significant shift in roles and responsibilities, which would need substantial
changes in prevailing attitudes.

Basing the internal communication on what employees requested
would not have helped to achieve the aims of the reorganization, and might

have helped to perpetuate old attitudes and stoked resistance. Instead, it proved better to start with the business strategy, and begin looking at what was required from which people within the organization before looking at what communication approaches might help to achieve it.

From the point of view of achieving its business strategy, the organization asks itself: 'What is it we need from our people, right now, and in the future? Do we need all of them, tomorrow, to be aware of the change, understand its implications, support it, become involved in deciding how we might implement it and be fully committed to taking it further?' The initial reaction might be that everyone needs to go up the (communication) escalator (to commitment) as soon as possible, until the implications of the scale of the exercise and the time involved sink in.

There are usually different groups of employees from whom different objectives are required for a given time period. Some may need for the moment only to be aware, others to be wholly committed. For the best investment of scarce time and resources, the organization will need to differentiate between employees, and to prioritize from whom it needs what objective over what time period. This allows it to map out the people within the organization on a range of objectives, featured as steps on the communication escalator (see Fig. 4.8). This approach focuses on what is needed *from* employees, not what is needed *by* employees. While different groups of employees receive communication in proportion to their status in the hierarchy, prioritizing employees for time and attention needs to be based on their importance to achieving the strategy.

Different organizations will find themselves on different steps, and will aim to move up by a different number of steps. They may aim, as a priority, to be selective, and take some, rather than all, of their people up the escalator and at different rates.

Representing this process as an escalator is done for a number of reasons. It is a continual dynamic process, and the idea is to keep all members of an organization moving up it.

Different communication channels and tools achieve different communication objectives (see Fig. 4.9). The more the organization needs

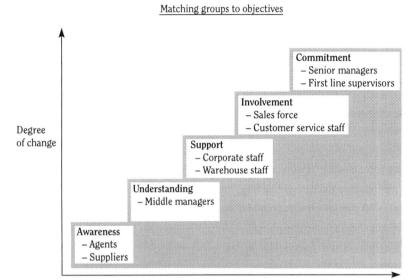

Matching groups to objectives

FIGURE 4.8   This maps what objectives are required from
which employees to achieve a strategy of greater customer
focus in a distribution company

an employee to move towards the upper end of the escalator, the more face-to-face communication is needed and the more time is involved.

At the bottom of the escalator, the focus is on the distribution of information, one-way, to a passive audience. Towards the middle, the balance shifts to greater dialogue, and face-to-face communication. At the top end of the escalator, the focus is more on management willingness to listen, and do less talking.

At the bottom of the escalator, the focus is on the task of communication, and the efficient distribution of information. As you climb towards the top, the emphasis shifts to the quality of the relationship. Managers should be alert to the vital distinction between task and relationship. Most communication managers will have had experience of a

Matching groups to objectives

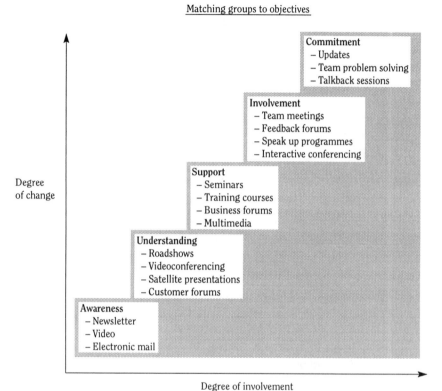

FIGURE 4.9   Different communication processes achieve different objectives

senior manager who, confident in his or her presentation skills training, is an excellent platform performer but a poor informal mixer in groups. This may not be a problem if your communication strategy stands on the lower steps of the escalator, but it may become a real vulnerability if your strategy calls for the organization to climb higher. A task-focused senior manager going through the motions of having a relationship with his or her employees is not a rewarding sight.

It may simply be too much to try to get everyone up the same step of the escalator. Organizations which lack the simple pipework of communication – sound and credible information channels, directories, pay and benefits, etc. – may need to spend time getting the basics in place before pursuing innovative technologies or radical sharing of views and opinions.

The question arises, however, as to where the majority of communication processes and activities are to be found on this escalator? Given that organizations are under pressure to elicit from employees their involvement, commitment and contribution, how is their communication matched to their ambitions?

Research into the most commonly used communication channels within organizations shows that they are concentrated at the lower end of the escalator. What the organization wants from its people tends to be at the upper end. There is a mismatch between what is wanted from people and the channels used to try to achieve it. The most commonly used communication channels include:

- newsletters
- memos
- team briefings
- departmental meetings
- noticeboards
- video
- electronic mail.

Most of these are processes that are aimed at creating *awareness*, and, on a good day, *understanding*. Employees prefer face-to-face communication, and report that their greatest source of information is the grapevine and that they prefer to hear things from their immediate line manager.

STEPS ON THE COMMUNICATION ESCALATOR

Awareness
Means of creating awareness will range from the corporate identity, press coverage, announcements on the bulletin board, internal and external

advertising campaigns, to payslip inserts, memos, continuous strip displays, direct mail and employee annual reports. They may also include video, computer disk and electronic mail.

These media will generally be distributed at arm's length, call for little interaction or response and allow for little feedback. They will be designed for consumption by a broadly defined audience, with little tailoring to individual segments. In terms of production they will require mainly executional skills, expertise in imaginative design and production quality, accessible writing and efficiency of distribution. The test for the effectiveness of this type of communication will be whether people received, or got a chance to see, the message in a form they found appropriate.

Understanding

The shift from awareness to understanding is one of feedback and additional information, tailored to the needs of a more closely defined group of people. Communication may be more face-to-face and more interactive. The aim here is not simply to present messages, but to provide rationales, get feedback and refine the communication until it gets through. It will also focus on getting feedback to check for understanding.

Such processes could include management conferences, roadshows, satellite broadcasting, videoconferencing and customer feedback forums. Meetings will tend to be presentations, with a small number of speakers presenting to audiences. The focus will be on striking a balance between professionalism of presentation, a degree of interaction and communicating to large enough groups to make an efficient use of time. There will be a disciplined format in which the presenters retain the initiative to communicate, and interaction is through question and answer sessions at the end of presentations.

Support

Pursuing the more ambitious objective of support means a significant shift in interaction. It is not enough here to get people to understand what is happening, and what its implications will be. The aim is to elicit acceptance, if not of the change itself, then of the need for, and the rationale behind, the change. Employees may not like what is happening, but they can accept why it is happening, and support the logic with colleagues, family and customers.

The focus will be more on education than presentation, with input from outside the organization, a review of parallel trends in other industries and a review of the changing dynamics of the business. Such sessions could include business forums, training events and customer seminars. A guest speaker from another organization may share relevant experience, or a management guru may be asked to chair discussion and challenge thinking.

Numbers will be limited, and the room will be arranged to foster interaction. Presentations will be less formal, with continual discussion rather than set question and answer periods.

Involvement

The aim here is as much to get employees to share their pre-existing reactions, concerns and objections as it is to provide them with management thinking. These processes will be far more of a dialogue, with the avowed aim of sharing thinking, assessing implications, exploring alternatives and reviewing the best means of implementation. There will be a greater recognition that communication is a dialogue between partners, with the aim being less of getting the message across than of listening to reactions and pooling experience and expertise across hierarchical boundaries.

Communication will not be limited to conversations between managers and staff, and colleagues within specialties and across functions will gather to talk independently and exchange ideas and information either face-to-face or at arm's length.

Team meetings will be used not only to disseminate management thinking, but to identify and solve issues that prevent the team working effectively, improve processes and reduce costs.

Cross-functional project teams will work to solve issues identified by the team meeting process.

Feedback forums will be called in which employees feed back to their managers the issues that are proving to be obstacles, and request they resolve the issues with their own colleagues.

Speak-up programmes will be used to encourage the raising of issues or concerns that stand in the way of the organization.

Interactive conferencing will use IT systems to continue the debate, to share information and to set agendas prior to meetings.

Commitment

Commitment comes from a sense of ownership – and ownership comes from having participated in the development of strategy and solution. Gaining commitment will entail a high degree of talking through the pressure affecting the business, reviewing possible competitive scenarios and strategic options open to the business. High levels of interaction and participation, flexibility for expansion of particular points and ensuring that everyone is clear and has the opportunity to contribute, means this is a process that takes a good deal of time.

The parameters for contribution will be clearly set – a divisional management tier may work on the application of group strategy to their division; customer engineers may focus on matching the need to reduce inventory costs with the need to support a wider range of customers.

There will be time spent in syndicates and 'breakout' sessions for colleagues to share thinking and check each other's perceptions. Feedback will be in 'shirtsleeves' sessions, airing concerns and challenging management thinking. The format will be relatively informal, with a loose agenda and room for employees to set the pace and the issues for discussion. There will be a facilitator rather than a presenter, and the focus will be on ensuring that people feel comfortable about raising issues, and that the debate is aimed at a constructive resolution of perceived problems.

Communication will be lateral as much as vertical. Update sessions will be held across functions to raise cross-boundary issues and to update senior management on developments. Team meetings will be used as much to keep seniors up-to-date as to disseminate management information.

What will drive communication is the quality of the relationship and the degree of trust. The style of meetings will focus on openness, and feeling comfortable about raising issues. Talkback sessions in which the chief executive meets with people from all levels of the organization, informally at lunch, or more formally through invitation to team meetings, will demonstrate a willingness to accept feedback without retribution and in a spirit of constructive enquiry.

Communication by itself cannot change people, but it can certainly help remove the barriers to change:

> You cannot change an organisation without courage, and you cannot induce courage from above, not even by example. What you can do, though, is make goals and methods transparent enough that your employees will be willing to take some calculated risks. You want hundreds of people making informed choices and taking timely action. You do not want them all second guessing each other or wondering if the boss really means what he or she says. (F Martin, 1994)

The next chapter looks at creating specific changes, to create greater focus on the customer, higher levels of quality and using communication to sustain a competitive advantage.

Customer and quality communication

O ne of the major challenges to organizations is to acquire customers, retain them, build relationships with them and identify ways of being more valuable to them – before the competition does.

One of the constant cries of chief executives is 'How do I get my people to be more customer-focused, and to deal with them in a way that communicates professionalism? How do we get people to cooperate across departments to present a single consistent face to the customer, and how do we share knowledge internally to make us smarter and more responsive in the customer's eyes?'

This chapter looks at the move towards greater customer focus and businesses' quest for an offering to customers that differentiates them from the competition. It looks at what an organization needs to do well to achieve differentiation, what gets in the way and the role of communication in helping to achieve it.

For present day firms, understanding and meeting customers' expectations and those of employees is inextricably bound up. The simple fact is: in services, the offering and the employee are inseparable. This has always been the case, but now with reliance on know-how, it is no marginal issue. Increasingly, the behavioural dimension – or how people interact – impacts on the potential of long-term customer relationships. And, needless to say, the state of a relationship affects a customer's perception of service quality (Vandermerwe, 1993).

Now that companies are trying to break down the walls between departments, to improve internal cooperation and service, they will also start bringing the traditional outsiders inside. Closer working with customers and suppliers will identify ways of working together more valuably for mutual benefit.

By being close to the customer you can provide greater value in service, and the closer you get, the better. Over the past few years, for example, the relationship between the supermarket food retailers and the food manufacturers has shifted significantly. Food manufacturers, identify the retailer as the customer, seeing the final customer, the consumer as further down the chain. They have adapted the product, how it is delivered, packaged, designed and labelled, payment systems, invoicing procedures – in fact, every facet of how they interface with the supplier. All this, while giving the customer greater margins and more responsive service. This is not done out of altruism, it is a reflection of the power that retailers have in their ownership of the customer.

Links between manufacturers and retailers get closer day-by-day, as the supply chain between them is shortened and unnecessary costs are identified and reduced. Now, as with other industries, it is common to find managers from the supplier side actually living with the customer, able to identify and respond to needs before they become apparent to anyone else. This trend will continue from being close to the customer to being within the customer to more intimate collaboration, where the supplier helps the customer explore and defines for the customer what will be of value, anticipating needs that the customer may not yet have thought of.

This symbiotic approach to business will bring a number of challenges. Organizations will have to maintain a continual dialogue with their customers, seeking not just comments and reactions, but digging into the reasons behind them. They also have to create a strong sense of belonging among their own people, while at the same time having them put the customer's needs before their own. In a world where the old distinctions between 'us and them' are breaking down, there is all the more need to hang on to a sense of 'us'.

The desire to be responsive to customers may have started as a recognition that power was migrating to the customer, who was spoilt for choice and free to go to the competition. Now, the drive to please and retain customers is based on a sound economic calculation. Competitive pressure is forcing companies to shift away from simply acquiring and transacting with a customer, to retaining and developing a longer-term relationship with a customer.

The Chartered Institute of Marketing/Henley Centre concluded in 1993 that 'The more competitive environment will focus greater attention on the potential of existing customers', and this will mean:
- assessing the lifetime value and therefore the value of promoting loyalty;
- increasing the contribution of a given customer through cross-selling/ upgrading programmes.

This is due in part to the realization of how expensive it is to acquire a customer in the first place, and the appreciation of how much revenue a customer could potentially provide over his or her lifetime if he or she could be retained. The cost of acquiring a new customer is calculated as being five times higher than the cost of retaining existing customers. Upfront marketing costs are not the only expense associated with winning a customer. Many companies pay intermediaries and agents commissions for introducing customers initially, and then have set-up costs. In the cellular telephone market, the average cost of acquiring a customer is £200, and where 25 per cent of customers lapse in the first year there is a significant price to be paid in the pursuit of new customers.

Rover Cars' dramatic resurgence owed something to the calculations it made on customer loyalty and customer lifetime value. The typical customer replaces his car every three years and spends £10 000 on it. He buys his first car at the age of 30, and his last at the age of 60 – a total of £100 000. In terms of after-sales servicing, the typical customer spends a total of £3000 servicing over his car-owning lifetime. So if a new, typical, customer is lost after the purchase of the first car, the opportunity cost is £90 000 in sales revenue and £2700 in servicing revenue, a grand total of £93 700 per lost customer.

For Rover, in the UK alone, where current new car sales loyalty levels are running at around 56 per cent, the revenue lost with customers who do not stay is a grand total of around £9000 million. Thus an increase in loyalty of just 1 per cent would yield an incremental £200 million revenue to Rover and to Rover dealers.

The service and repairs parts market is estimated to have a total value of £220 million per annum. An increase of just 1 per cent in actual retention of the after-sales parts market would yield an incremental £2.2 million revenue per year to the dealer network (an average of £3500 per dealer).

This appeals to suppliers who can offset the cost of acquisition of a customer against the revenue derived from a customer over a period of years. Having the best of all worlds means retaining existing customers, getting the loyal customer to spend more, converting occasional customers to being regulars, creating new customers and winning the competitors' customers. This allows the supplier to build up familiarity with customers' individual needs and preferences, and provides information on which to base new product development. From a purely defensive viewpoint, it minimizes the chance of competitors worming their way into customers' affections, and lessens the chance of customers shopping around for an alternative supplier.

Too many companies concentrate too much effort on attracting new customers, not because they do not recognize the logic of retention, but because hunting, not farming, is in the blood. If conquering and winning customers has been the drive in the past, then the cultural heroes will be the new business getters and the firm closers. The salesman conquering a customer, and, once the thrill of the chase is over, disappearing to look for fresh conquests, is not uncommon in sales-driven organizations. Caring for the existing customer seems in comparison a less exciting prospect. When a new sale is closed, the champagne is opened; when the existing customer stays, nothing noticeable is celebrated.

The drive among suppliers, then, is to build increased levels of relationship with, and loyalty among, their customers. As part of that relationship building, the aim is to increase the number and range of contacts with the customer, and to make each contact pleasant and valuable.

This conviction on the seller's side of the importance of relationships is matched by the customer's desire for a relationship with a trusted supplier, who provides not only a product or a service but also information on which decisions can be taken. Who they choose depends upon how distinctive and valuable they perceive a potential supplier to be.

WHAT IS IT THAT CUSTOMERS VALUE?

Customers expect some basic things as a matter of course, and the supplier has to provide them, simply to be a credible option for customers. These include the ability to provide the basic service or product in a timely and professional manner, with prompt follow-up and servicing and efficient back-up. These are things that the customer expects, and only really notices if they are not there. They are not seen as remarkable, nor do they earn the supplier any brownie points with the customer.

There are, though, those 'X' factors that customers may not at first think of or expect, but which are more valuable to them and more appreciated. These include such things as advice, creative ideas and problem solving. These do provide competitive differentiation and can justify higher pricing to reflect extra value.

Companies find themselves attempting to identify value characteristics when they are in a competitive market, and when they need to combat price sensitivity and customers' perceptions of them as undifferentiated suppliers of a commodity. The quest is for an offer which the customer will value, and which will set the supplier apart from the competition and create such satisfaction as to foster lifetime loyalty.

WHAT ARE YOU OFFERING TO CUSTOMERS THAT DIFFERENTIATES YOU FROM THE COMPETITION?

Customers will expect the supplier they choose to meet high standards of product quality and speed and responsiveness of service. Only by providing them with unexpected additional value, in advice, helpfulness and support, will a company create a differentiation.

Product leadership

One way of differentiating is to offer customized leading-edge products and services that make rival goods obsolete.

The fact that telephone companies now provide access to what is in effect a single network has driven them to develop different new products and services to create a competitive distinction. The videophone is one attempt, as is the aim to provide a single telephone number which will allow a call to be forwarded to wherever the owner might be.

Lyons Tetley has pursued a strong drive for product leadership. Drinking tea seems a simple enough occupation, but tea-drinking habits vary across the world. In the USA, tea is drunk iced, in Europe hot and black with lemon. It is drunk quickly in the morning, in order to get to work, more leisurely on Sunday afternoons, and out of vending machines at the office. Lyons Tetley have focused on creating innovative and attractive ways of tea drinking to meet varying needs, such as the round tea bag and instant tea. While the basic commodity is simple enough, the value added is in the variety of packaging and convenience.

McDonald's established itself as a place where you could go for fast food of a consistent, reliable quality. It prided itself on being able to reproduce the experience wherever you went, and focused its people on complying with procedures that had been proven effective. In terms of what it offered to customers, McDonald's distinctive offer was operational efficiency.

Operational efficiency

Operational efficiency means providing customers with reliable products or services at competitive prices and delivered with minimum difficulty or inconvenience.

The Automobile Association is an example of this kind of organization. In the most familiar part of the organization, emergency rescue and recovery, speed and efficiency in getting to stranded motorists and solving their problems is what the customer wants.

Direct Line provides customers with time-saving ways of accessing financial services, insurance and mortgages, and is organized for speed and responsiveness. First Direct, banking unencumbered by a branch network, has organized itself to be available whenever the customer might need it, rather than during working hours when customers are themselves at work and unable to get to a bank. It has also organized itself so that the customer can get service via the telephone rather than having to go to a branch.

First Direct operates 24 hours a day, 365 days a year, with a service conducted entirely over the telephone and employs 1500 staff. Its objective is to be the best by providing a high-quality service quickly and conveniently, offering competitive interest rates and simple, easy-to-understand products around the clock. Its mission is 'To be the best in the world at personal banking', in terms of being market leader, most used and most recommended.

First Direct is growing at a rate of 10 000 new accounts a month, and 30 per cent of customer acquisition is by word of mouth.

First Direct claims that it is recommended every 30 seconds, and that one in four of new account openings are via personal recommendations from existing customers. It is based on the promise of operational efficiency and friendliness, and is now moving into greater customer closeness, identifying customer profiles and more specific needs.

First Direct was developed by the Midland Bank as a step change in personal banking. Midland saw the opportunity to increase market share among upscale customers by responding to customers' increasing frustrations with the traditional bank networks. According to research, one in five customers had not visited their branch in the last month, and said that they would rather visit it as little as possible.

Research showed that customer demand for better service was higher among banks than any other retail sector. Friendly and knowledgeable staff were considered most important, alongside convenient opening hours and quick and easy transactions.

In an attempt to beat McDonald's, Burger King has set out to respond to a greater desire among customers for individuality and tailoring, with their claim to provide you with a hamburger as you like it, rather than how they want to prepare it. McDonald's, on the other hand, has built its strength on offering a consistent, identically delivered product wherever you choose to go. When it was first established this was a viable proposition, but one which has now been matched and eroded in its strength by competitors. Now it needs to shift to respond to food trends and a greater desire among customers to be treated as individuals. It is now pursuing new food ideas, with greater flexibility in how it deals with its customers and the products it offers them.

In any service organization, success in the past may well have been based on ensuring that staff complied with procedures to deliver consistency. Getting staff to act as individuals, and to be infinitely flexible and variable at the sharp end, runs counter to proceduralism, and a culture based on enforcing compliance militates against creating flexibility to deliver customer value.

In a refinement of its strategy for the future, and a shift from operational efficiency to greater closeness to the customer, McDonald's is likely to feel, in the short term, the drag of the culture it has built up in the past.

In the same way that businesses have to shift from a production focus in communication, they will also have to learn the rules of having everyone focused on a customer. To change in the future, they will have to review their past.

Whatever the end-product being offered and however companies choose to position themselves, customers will buy information, know-how and ideas.

The ability of suppliers to make a valuable contribution, and the willingness of customers to open up and share their real problems, where help is needed and would be valued, will come down to the ability of people on each side to relate to each other. Inevitably, organizations are moving into the relationship business, pursuing greater closeness to the customer, where it is the chemistry and the quality of the communication that counts.

Faith Popcorn, described by *Fortune* Magazine as 'The Nostradamus of Marketing', says:

> What will make us buy one product over another in this decade is a feeling of partnership with the seller, and a feeling that we are buying for the future. Anonymous, impersonal selling is over ... we want to buy from a person ... a person whom we trust. Trust will be implicit in every purchase (Popcorn, 1991).

Closeness to the customer

Closeness to the customer means segmenting and targeting markets precisely and then tailoring offerings to match exactly the demands of those niches. Knowledge of the customer and flexibility in their operations allows organizations to meet specific requests, or to tailor individual products.

In terms of pursuing a strategy of becoming increasingly closer to the client, and identifying ways of adding value to the client's business, Price Waterhouse, one of the world's Big 6, has invested time, energy and resources in orchestrating its knowledge and expertise inside to the client's benefit.

In Denmark, the Sterling chain of DIY stores identified that a significant group of customers lacked the confidence to undertake jobs around the house, let alone buy the products they might need for those jobs. They now operate local clubs where they teach the necessary skills, build customer confidence and reap the sales of the related products as a reward.

Spotting the opportunity to make a proposition to customers that differentiates is not enough. A company has to match the offer it makes to customers with its own capabilities and culture. There may well be a gap between the route the organization chooses to take and the capabilities and attitudes that prevail internally.

This is not just something that affects consumers in the retail marketplace. In relationships between businesses, the drive is the same. On the professional services side, banks, advertising agencies and accountancy firms are all trying to reorganize themselves to provide a single point of contact with clients to make sense of the complexity of products and services for them.

QUALITY AND COMMUNICATION

Providing a quality service or product to the customer, and good communication, are inextricably linked. Listening to your customer, whether internal or external, is a founding principle of quality, as is changing the way managers and staff deal with each other. Research among customers showed that 60 per cent of those who reported reasons for leaving a particular supplier attributed this to encountering indifference among that supplier's staff.

Are we Marks and Spencer or are we Kwik Save?

Employees who have been told to serve the customer, or serve someone who does, reasonably ask the question how much and how well should they serve? Achieving the correct degree of customer orientation first requires agreement of who the customer is and what he or she is buying in terms of service and value.

What is offered to customers is not just physical products, but the full relationship between supplier and customer, including the supplier's reputation, brands and service levels. What behaviour and attitudes are needed from employees, and how communication should be organized, will depend upon the offer being made to customers, and how a company chooses to deal with it.

The organization needs to have struck the correct balance and decided what its quality positioning is going to be. Is it providing a prompt, value-for-money service, or is it offering a unique, premium-priced product?

Figure 5.1 shows a number of possible positions a company might take in striking a balance between the price and the quality of what it offers to the customer.

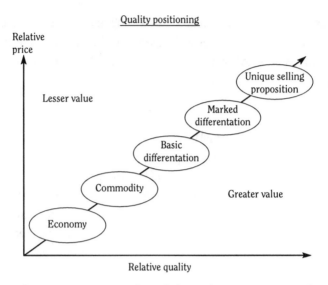

Quality positioning

FIGURE 5.1 Businesses strike a balance between price and quality in what they offer the customer

The creation of separate businesses from the monolithic British Rail in 1982 produced entities with very different ways of serving the customer.

Network SouthEast was in the business of moving thousands of people between 7 and 9 am each day, and then getting them back home again at night. As a commuter business, with some leisure and some corporate travel, it was an operation of extreme peaks of demand and activity.

It was also a business which had to deliver a service of transport between two points in safety and on time. Network SouthEast was interested in high-density seating – getting everyone sitting down – and meeting timetables.

While Network SouthEast's interest was in operational efficiency, InterCity's focus has been on closeness to the customer, providing high-quality service, with time and attention devoted to providing service face-to-face with customers.

InterCity decided that it would offer business customers a quality of service dependent on high-quality interaction between staff and passengers, and comfort and care while they travel – far more in the manner of the business class of airline travel.

Network SouthEast, on the other hand, adopted a quality positioning focused on functionality – that trains run on time, that tickets are easy to obtain and that carriages are clean and serviceable. Their quality positioning does not depend on face-to-face contact with staff.

Without having decided what your positioning is, having a strong customer focus among your employees could actually be a recipe for disaster, with people offering an expensive service for which the customer does not fully pay, which he or she does not appreciate or value and which appears purely as cost to the business. Everyone within the organization needs to know where they are positioned, or energies are likely to be misdirected. Different parts of the organization are likely to have different customer focuses, and communication emanating from different areas will provide mixed messages that will divert energy and increase cynicism.

The chosen positioning also needs to be valuable to the customer. In the pursuit of quality, organizations which are achieving customer satisfaction scores in the high 90 per cent, can end up chasing incremental improvements at increasing costs in areas that their customers do not actually value. If they are not valued, such improvements are purely cost without benefit, pursued under the banner of continuous improvement.

You can only pursue continuous improvement if you know what it is that needs to be improved – and that means listening to the customer, whether internal or external.

Research shows that while employees may agree that quality should be got right first time, their feeling is often that senior management will sacrifice quality to expediency, that getting the job done and out is more important than getting it right. This points to the different definitions people have of what quality actually is. Employees believe that if managers were serious about quality they would be investing more heavily in equipment, tools and training. In companies where there is no agreed shared definition of what quality is, people tend to supply their own definitions and judge management harshly by those criteria.

Employees can see a contradiction between published management ideals for customer service and quality, and the traditional values of service that they have pursued. This is a particular issue in the public sector where differences are perceived between the values of public service and those of customer service.

Quality programmes fail when employees buy into the culture change they provide, but then find management more interested in the costs and production performance, 'bottom-line' benefits. Where there is little attention paid to the organization's bedrock attitudes and values, there is little chance of getting employees' and management's objectives aligned.

Communicating in boxes

Rather than pursuing new initiatives to create customer commitment, organizations should first weed out all the things they currently do that actively stop their people from focusing on the customer.

Some of the issues that derail quality – empowerment, re-engineering and renewal initiatives – are caused by communication emerging from one prevailing mentality and being interpreted by a different mentality.

Culture refracts communication, and part of an organization's culture is reflected in the decisions it makes and how it balances competing priorities.

Each part of an organization suffers from some degree of schizophrenia. Each function will itself have decided what its quality positioning is going to be, the service it will provide, how it will be measured and what the rewards will be. Each may decide this in isolation from other functions. This results in differing degrees of customer orientation, towards different sets of customers, some internal, some external, some overt, some covert. The internal collisions of competing priorities and misinterpretation then result in confusion, diversions and cost that add value to no one.

All of us serve somebody, if only to survive to continue to draw a salary. The hierarchical organizations of the past had a career ladder, which represented a flight from the customer and enabled you to start serving the person who was your real customer – the person who had your next job in his or her gift.

Once the organization has established what it is offering customers, and how it chooses to serve them, it has to recognize that there is already an existing customer orientation within the organization – it is just that the definition of who the customer is differs. People serve a customer, and are rewarded for doing so, but there are many internal customers competing for attention and resources (the boss, other departments, etc.) who are given priority.

Different individuals and different functions within the organization have a different unconscious interpretation of who their real customer is and what it is that they are providing.

Figure 5.2 demonstrates the axes of the balance which organizations typically have to strike: how best to balance the efficient running of the operation with being responsive to individual customer requirements; how best to balance the management of cost and resources for the organization's profit and success with the need to provide value to the customer. They have to decide the balance and the trade-offs involved in

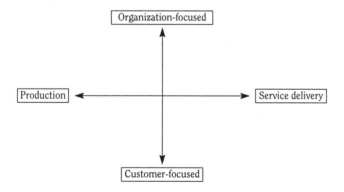

FIGURE 5.2 Organizations strike a balance between competing priorities

how much they will bend towards the customer's needs and convenience without 'giving away the shop', and to what degree they are focused on operational efficiency, rather than closeness to the customer – whether it is more important for the customer to be fitted into the existing system or to tailor individual solutions to his or her problems.

These dilemmas, tensions and balances are reflected within the individual. We are able to hold in our heads mutually inconsistent beliefs and values, and, like the organization as a whole, we tend to become schizophrenic and engage in double-think to resolve some of the apparent contradictions. Anyone who has seen credit control personnel on a customer service course can see these contradictions happily at work. Individuals try to buffer themselves from these, and taboos inside the organization protect people from facing overly difficult value clashes or dilemmas (see Fig. 5.3).

Every business strikes a balance. The problem comes when different parts of the business strike different balances unbeknownst to each other.

Typically, people with frequent contact with the customer would place themselves in the bottom right-hand box, and would describe helping

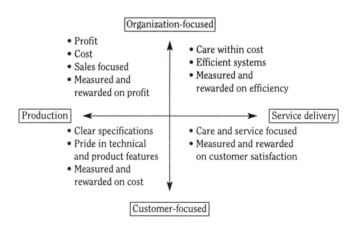

FIGURE 5.3   Different and conflicting balances exist simultaneously

customers as a main source of job satisfaction. Others would see themselves in the top left-hand box, maximizing the return for the company. Moreover, it is not impossible to have individuals in each box happily working on a different focus, with different objectives, with different reward schemes based on different measures.

Protecting the customer from the management

Customer-facing managers buy into the strategy of establishing long-term relationships and of offering the best advice, and recognize that sales will flow as a result. It suits their inclination to help people and to solve their problems. Then they get tired of having short-term campaigns and product pushes which fly in the face of the avowed strategy. Their enthusiasm for the strategy is checked by the pressure to shift products.

Typically, employees will intellectually agree that the pursuit of quality makes sense, but privately and unspokenly that agreement is qualified by each individual's personal values and his or her sense of priorities. Each may agree, for example, that professionalism is important – but what constitutes professionalism in specific situations, for example trading off between serving the customer and ensuring the best use of resources? They may temper the agreed approach to providing quality, within cost, with a personal decision not to 'skimp' on the job.

People's values will be expressed in how they see their role, who they think their real customer is, what gains rewards, what is measured and what they see as the real business purpose of the organization. The organization signals its values by its measurement, reward and management information systems, by its allocation of resources and by what it celebrates.

In times of change, people are forced to *prioritize* values, to decide which are pre-eminent and which are needed to guide decisions in a new environment. Everyone faces these questions of balance, and comes up with their own way of striking a balance that relieves the pressure on them while maintaining their sense of values. In most organizations, people do this in isolation from each other, sometimes unconsciously, and the mismatch of their balances causes unrealized friction and misdirected energies.

149

Inevitably, there will be differences in perceived values inside the organization. A finance manager at head office will strike a different balance of priorities than will a front-line customer service person. People strike their own balance of competing priorities, guided by their own values. Since this balancing act is largely unacknowledged, different, sometimes conflicting, balances operate simultaneously within organizations.

Communication between the boxes will be based on different priorities and different views of what the core business is supposed to be. Customer service people receive the glad tidings that one of their branches has been closed, couched in terms of optimism and cited as an example of rebalancing of the property portfolio. Customer service people believe the business is about serving the customer, and cannot see how closing branches helps that, while the property management function at the centre is delighted at the improved rate of return on assets.

If different parts of the organization have different customer focus, and are rewarded and measured differently, there are bound to be conflicting signals and mixed messages. Anyone caught in the minefield of trying to keep all customers happy, whether internal or external, is likely to freeze, since that is the safest thing to do.

Companies espousing greater closeness to the customer and high levels of customer service have to ensure that their people understand the whole business equation or risk seeing staff give the store away to customers. Understanding how the company makes its money, how it sets out to make a 'win-win' situation with customers, is vital.

Those who like people and like serving them can also be squeamish about charging them for the service. If customer service staff do not understand, for example, the rationale for charges made to customers, their own values may dictate that they waive them, in the belief that these are yet another example of rapacious management wanting to squeeze more money out of customers. They see themselves faithfully protecting the customer from the management.

To have an organization which truly delivers value throughout, people do need to see themselves as part of a chain of interlinked activities.

Working in functional boxes prevents people from seeing the interconnections, and the different and competing objectives of those boxes work against a sense of being connected.

Finance departments, for example, are in the unenviable position of having a whole range of customers, some of whom have conflicting objectives. Trying to serve all these different customers is bound to lead to a level of schizophrenia.

A first step towards creating better communication is to identify existing orientations and to become clear about who people are already serving. Simply overlaying and exhortation to serve a customer, whether internally or externally, will not work, because the exhortations are drowned out by the unspoken priorities implicit in the organization.

Whose convenience?

Any organization strikes a balance between serving the customer and serving its own objectives.

The Industrial Revolution put machines in factories, and insisted that workers come out of their cottages and congregate around the machines. From that moment, the most efficient running of the machine for most efficient production become the priority, and people were fitted around that priority. The pursuit of economies of scale, and the focus on reducing cost per unit, placed a high priority on operating efficiencies, as engineers used their ingenuity to squeeze incremental efficiency from the machinery.

Traditionally, organizations are set up to serve their own convenience first and then, only under pressure from the marketplace, the convenience of the customer. Customers have not known what they wanted because they have not known what they could have; they have simply taken the choices on offer.

Responding to customers means hassle, variability, complexity and greater unpredictability. The Newtonian Law applies that organizations keep on heading in the same direction until a force is applied on them. That force is customer choice, backed up by negotiating power.

Malcolm MacDonald (1993), Professor of Marketing at Cranfield School of Management, said:

> The truth is that marketing is an attitude of mind manifested in a management process that uses all the resources of an organisation to satisfy the needs of customers in order to achieve the objectives of both parties.

In the relatively easy 1960s and 1970s, characterized by growth and the easy marketability of products and services, production orientation was possible, largely because demand seemed limitless. The focus was on producing volume, not value.

Traditionally, a factory would turn out products that were stored in the warehouse. The responsibility for shifting these was given to the sales force. The products were moved and the warehouse space was emptied, allowing the process to begin all over again. The product went to the customer, and it was up to the customer to make it fit the individual needs or circumstances.

The undermining of quality service comes from applying a manufacturing mentality to what is essentially a relationship. Manufacturing went into mass production to attain economies of scale, to achieve greater efficiency and to reduce unit costs. Customer service has pursued the same approach for the same reasons, treating and serving its customers as an undifferentiated mass, organizing them to fit the demands of the system using mass communication.

Most organizations are structured for their own convenience, not for that of the customer. They were designed around a production focus, so employees wanting to serve the customer have to first escape the restrictions of the structure.

Organizations frequently reward the wrong behaviour, with bonuses based on keeping costs down, and maximizing profit. Serving the customer does not show up as a performance measure. Measures are often short-term, while benefits to the customer may take longer to come through.

Measures of success and performance indicators are legacies of the past, internally focused, and are designed to reflect how *efficiently* the organization is fulfilling its own purposes, rather than how effectively it is serving the customer.

It is often quoted in customer service programmes that for every complaint you hear, someone goes away disgruntled and tells two of their friends about a negative experience. However, in those customer service organizations where compliance with internal procedures is paramount, staff might be forgiven for thinking that a disgruntled customer going off silently is preferable to having a very vocal manager descend on you for breaching procedures.

Even in traditional manufacturing, there is a drive to shake off the production focus that prevents greater responsiveness to individual customers' requirements.

Volvo Cars is getting away from central stocking and fields full of cars tying up money and slowly rusting. The aim now is only to manufacture after a customer has ordered a specific car. Currently manufacture time is four weeks, but the aim is get that down to two weeks by 1995.

Volvo is turning the factory production focus on its head. It will be possible to go into a showroom, use an interactive system to select your car on screen, see how different wheels would look, try the metallic paint and see how it would look under different lights, and then push a button to send the order to the factory.

Volvo's new factory is more advanced than any other factory except for Toyota's in Japan. The factory is geared to be as flexible as possible, with customer demand dictating work flows. It will be able to run a variety of different models on the same assembly line, allowing capacity to be used flexibly, rather than allowing capacity and output to dictate what cars need to be sold to customers. Typically, Volvo will contract for 2000 hours of work from an employee, which will be called on flexibly, depending on levels of demand from customers.

While customer-facing staff may feel that the rest of the organization pulls against them, staff in areas supporting or producing for the customer can feel similarly aggrieved by what is done to them.

Highly motivated customer-focused salespeople are often viewed by their colleagues internally as importers of problems and cost into the business. In the interests of apparently serving the customer, they promise what is difficult to deliver without thinking through the implications internally. Without the knowledge of such implications, they may indeed be bringing in business which is costing more than it is earning.

THE IMPACT OF COMPLEXITY

'Product clutter' is the term used to describe the proliferation of different types of the same basic product. Instead of one packet of cereal in your kitchen, you may now have four or five; instead of one type of toothpaste for the family, three or four different types for different teeth and different ages. One store, for example, has 110 types of personal stereo on display. The current Nike catalogue describes 347 separate varieties of trainer. As markets become increasingly competitive, manufacturers feel they have to meet the customer's needs ever more specifically.

While the creation of new products gives customers ever more choice and ever more tailored products, it confronts them with a bewildering series of decisions that they have to make and an escalating amount of information that they have to digest. It also has a similar impact on employees, who now have to master a greater number of procedures, change over lines to produce shorter runs of different products, produce more brochures and commit different prices and discounts to memory. As the variables proliferate, the chance of confusion and miscommunication escalates.

What does it take?

Building relationships rather than stimulating product transactions lies at the heart of customer retention. The relationship cannot be based on exploitation, or seeing the customer as a target to fill with whatever products the factory has produced.

Microsoft, an organization that has succeeded on its leading products, is now having to shift to become closer to its customers. Bill Gates, the head of Microsoft, has called for the restructuring of the entire company, warning that the days of stratospheric sales may be coming to a close. In an attempt to meet increasing competition and to avoid the threat of complacency, Microsoft has been examining how it has to change.

In the future, as sales no longer increase at historic rates, the company will have to tailor more closely to customers. Staff, he tells them, 'will live, eat and breathe with their customers, understand everything about them, sell to them and be their advocates'.

Seeing customers as a lifetime stream of revenue may be attractive, but succeeding in hanging on to that stream demands attention to people, inside as well as outside the business.

To create a customer- and quality-focused culture requires strong and clear leadership. Senior management need to be committed, because lack of commitment is transparent and readily detected. Demonstrating that commitment goes beyond agreeing and repeating messages, or going out on the road to meet people. For the board director and the chief executive it means that how they behave, and what they signal, are now crucial parts of the communication strategy.

Companies that are well on the way down this path (e.g. Xerox, IBM) have had a rude shock and have had to fight their way back to competitiveness. Their commitment came out of having few other options.

The late Dr W. Edwards Deming, authoritative leader of thinking on customers and quality, was asked by managers how they could convince their own bosses to take focusing on the customer more seriously, and replied 'Pray for it to get worse.'

The company's leadership will favour listening, coaching and teaching rather than supervising and controlling. They will demonstrate their personal values rather than just communicating the business's corporate stance and policies. Leaders will centre the corporate culture around service to both customers and colleagues. They will spend a great deal of time with customers and employees, experience their company's service processes and listen to employees for suggestions for improvement.

The face which the company presents to the customer – accessibility, respect, friendliness, helpfulness – has to be reflected in how staff are treated, or the gap between the claim and reality will be clear to all. Unless the culture and the proposition to the customer are completely in step, it will not be differentiating or confer any competitive advantage.

Customers want to be treated as individuals, and customer contact people need to be able to respond as individuals. In asking employees not just for their muscles but also for their hearts and minds, companies are redefining the relationship between themselves and their employees. Carers need care themselves if they are to generate the level of concern and commitment needed. They need high levels of information to be able to take action and prioritize demands, and they need to understand why things are happening, for their own peace of mind and to answer the questions of customers.

Greater customer loyalty promises greater profit, but also depends on greater employee loyalty and satisfaction. Value is created by satisfied, loyal and skilled employees. Their satisfaction comes from having the support services and policies that enable them to deliver results to customers. It is also affected by the feelings that employees have towards their jobs, their colleagues and their companies. Employee research shows that what people want, unsurprisingly, is openness from their leaders, to be treated fairly and with respect.

Research shows that service workers most value having the ability and the authority to solve problems and provide value to customers. AA patrols like to get people fixed and on their way, nurses like to tend patients back to health and production teams like to solve challenges set by customers' specifications. Satisfaction is also affected by the attitudes that people have towards one another, and the way people deal with each other inside the organization.

ICL Service Systems provides field engineering support both to its own customers and to those of third party computing suppliers. In an environment where every contact from the customer seemed to be a complaint, it set out to make a step change in the level of service it provided. In the course of that it learned a number of lessons.

ICL observed a strong link between employee satisfaction and customer satisfaction. It believes that satisfied staff provide excellent service which then satisfies customers. So as well as asking customers what they wanted, it asked engineers what frustrated them about the company. The slow processing of their expenses, leaving engineers with a cash flow problem, came up as an area that could be improved. ICL now tracks the speed of processing expenses as a way of monitoring the level of the company's service to its own people.

Engineers also said they would prefer not to wear the suits and collar and tie that they had been accustomed to wear when with customers. ICL responded to their request for smart practical uniforms which gave a greater sense of professionalism.

ICL decided to measure employee and customer satisfaction to complement the wealth of statistics that its management information systems provided. The Commander system displays statistics on the activities of field engineers, including such measures as:

- call-outs
- call to fix (the time elapsed from the customer's call to the problem being fixed)
- parts used.

The system tracked measures of operational efficiency, the best deployment of engineers and the stocking and turnover of parts. What did not show up on the system was feedback from the customer. Measuring operational efficiency runs the danger of squeezing the softer side of the service provided, the time to talk with the customer and advise on how to avoid problems in the future and so minimize call-outs later.

'Call to fix' is a good example of one of those measures which is based on what the supplier thinks is important, and focuses on the supplier's desire to use the assets most efficiently and cost-effectively. It is tempting to measure it because it is easy to track, though it might not be relevant to customer satisfaction.

Now, instead of fitting both engineers and customers to the system's drive for efficiency, ICL agrees individual service level agreements with each customer. Some customers may not want immediate service, but bookable service at a specified time. The service provided is then measured against the service level agreement, rather than according to measures that suit the organization's system.

Customers look for value, and staff look to be valued. Customers want flexibility, and want engineers to call at whatever hour suits the customer. Getting engineers to turn out at almost any time calls for flexibility from the engineer, and from his or her employer.

Engineers now feed back on what gets in the way of meeting service level agreements, identifying the things that need to be changed to allow them to provide a better service.

ICL measures the 'feel good' factors for both customers and staff. Now ICL runs an annual employee satisfaction survey, as a way of reflecting how well customers are likely to be satisfied. The lesson learned is that one way to provide greater satisfaction to customers is via greater satisfaction of staff.

One of the main attractions for customers of First Direct is its ease of access and approachability. A key finding among customers is that 'staff sound happy'. First Direct believes that staff only sound happy if they are happy.

It also believes that the quality of service to customers is only as good as the people who deliver it. It believes it has an operation based on people, and its success or failure is down to how well it manages people. New recruits are not allowed to speak to customers until they have undergone an intensive seven-week training course. This is reflected across the entire culture of the organization, with open-plan environment, flat structure and open and accessible communication.

First Direct started off with a blank sheet of paper; it has not had to change an established culture and it has the advantage of a young workforce. It tries to be open both in terms of physical space and psychological atmosphere, with spacious, bright open-plan offices and informality between teams.

First Direct receives up to 18 000 calls a day, more than half of which are outside traditional banking hours. Flexibility is at the heart of its offer to customers, and this is reflected in the flexibility it offers its own staff (e.g.

crèche facilities). Employees report that one of the major attractions of First Direct was its flexibility, in that they can negotiate a 'partnership agreement' in which they agree the hours that suit the rest of their lifestyle.

Central to First Direct's offer is the rapport that the banking representatives establish on the phone, and the personal service that customers can expect. First Direct's aim is to make personal service the hallmark of anyone that the customer comes in contact with, rather than just the individual they might speak to on any one occasion.

The company selects outgoing individuals, with creativity and initiative, and then develops them. When trained, they are able to deal with 85 per cent of calls without referring to anyone else. The one skill everyone shares is communicating. The ability to create rapport on the phone, and to relate to colleagues, is essential.

While everyone seems to enjoy the rapport and open atmosphere, high standards are set for team members, team leaders and managers. Staff answer telephone calls working shift patterns, 24 hours a day, 7 days a week. These staff typically do not have a banking background, but are skilled in customer service.

First Direct has gone to great lengths to work at communication, and see it as central to the service it offers. The philosophy is not to behave as employer/employee but to act as a team, with a common sense of direction and aligned goals. To do that they feel that people have to know what it is they are supposed to be doing and why they are doing it.

Communication is everywhere: walls and partitions are plastered with notices, jokily designed, which alert people to business information, procedures and social events. On the banking representatives floor – where the people who answer the phone are based – there is a buzz of excitement reflected in the charts that the teams have created for themselves. Each team has its own name – The Gladiators, The Flexible Friends – and each team creates its own chart showing its service performance. A flipchart full of colourful kites, each representing an individual, shows their service level scores. There are photo galleries showing pictures of who's who and who does what, with team leaders' photos stuck on top of circus performers' bodies, or on the heads of tombstones in a cemetery. Invitations to fun runs are put up beside flowcharts showing account service processes. Partition walls are covered with displays of information marked 'Need to know' and 'Nice to know', and 'Did you know?' files are laid out for people to look through.

On the walls there are display boards showing service level, calls waiting to be answered and how well staff are doing. Noticeboards are filled with letters of commendation and thanks from customers. These do not just appear pinned to an ordinary noticeboard, they form the centrepiece of graphic displays which also include the exasperated letters of dissatisfied customers to avoid staff becoming complacent.

There is little divide between official communication on the wall and the normal office graffiti. Anyone can put signs up, as long as they are responsible for taking them down when they are out of date. Communication is not solely the responsibility of the internal communication department; it is the responsibility of everyone.

Avis, the car rental company, maintains that the quality of service to the internal customer directly impacts on the quality of service to the external customer. It also runs an annual company-wide employee satisfaction survey, in the belief that caring for customers, requires it first to care for its own employees.

Management consultants, Bain and Company has investigated the value of customer retention and the impact of retention on profitability. Its research shows a link between high levels of customer satisfaction and lower staff turnover. Higher retention of staff means not just reduced hiring and induction costs, but, more importantly, the retention of skills, experience and knowledge of the customer within the business.

Where value to the customer is the competitive differentiator, knowledge of the customer, familiarity with the company's capabilities and the ability to match them is the key factor. Knowledge and skills are the company's real assets, and they reside within individuals. 'Our people are our greatest asset' is often a platitude included in the annual report as a sop towards employee involvement. Aiming for customer retention brings home the hard truth behind the statement.

Reward systems have to be tailored to whether or not the customer is satisfied, and recognizing value in what is being done. Reward systems should not be tied to the efficient fulfilment of procedures. Rank Xerox and IBM have introduced customer satisfaction indices as a basis for performance-related pay. The Automobile Association has introduced a team-based reward system to ensure that individuals' self-interest does not get in the way of satisfying the customer.

Although typically customer service people already possess 80 per cent of the skills they need to do the job, they can under-perform simply because they know it is better to frustrate a customer, who may never complain, than to violate internal management strictures. Making mistakes is usually seen as an internal management taboo, and staff may prefer to do the wrong thing rather than to be spotlighted for failing.

Burston Marsteller, one of the world's largest corporate communications companies, ran weekly breakfast sessions for its account people to enable them to learn what was being done in areas other than their own. To counterbalance any tendency of people to blow their own trumpets, presentations were divided into highlights – things that had succeeded – and lowlights – failures that carried a useful lesson. Acknowledging failures as lessons gave people greater latitude to experiment.

Quality – the communication mismatch

We all know of some of the crazy things that organizations do. People at the bottom of those companies see them too, but don't feel that they can say anything or that they will be heard.

In one aircraft manufacturing company, the dispatch department decided to save money on the sending out of spare parts which had been repaired. It waited until it had gathered together 20 gearboxes before getting a truck to deliver them. This saved thousands of dollars in better use of trucks. Meanwhile, all over the world, there were aircraft stranded on the tarmac, waiting for parts, losing hundreds of thousands of dollars in revenue. The dispatch department was fulfilling what it saw as its own role, possibly after brainstorming ways of saving costs, but in the absence of a wider picture it was undermining the overall effectiveness of the company.

To avoid this, what is needed is knowledge of how different parts of the organization link together to deliver value to a customer. The aim of Total Quality is to continually improve the business process, and the drive for continuous improvement is fed, again, by information and knowledge.

A quality organization needs strong upward communication of ideas and problem-spotting skills. It also needs strong lateral communication to follow the lateral processes that deliver value to the customer.

Most organizations are structured vertically, in separate functions, so there are immediate barriers to lateral communication. The majority of channels are designed for downward communication, with little opportunity for upward feedback. Where opportunities for upward feedback exist, people may be reluctant to speak up, and managers reluctant to listen and act.

Quality is about 'connectedness', where people have a sense of the whole relationships with their internal and external customers, and an understanding of how the process of which they are a part fits together to produce the desired result. Employees want more information about parts of their organization beyond their immediate work area. They want to know exactly what other parts of the organization do, and to receive feedback on their performance. Pursuing cost improvement programmes without educating about neighbours in other boxes inevitably leads to blame. Without understanding the objectives of another area, it is inevitable that employees will say, 'Why should I slog to save a few pence when that lot over there are throwing money away?'

The division of the organization into functional boxes, and communication only about employees' strictly local work area, works against the sense of connectedness. Instead of having separate departments pursuing separate departmental objectives, a customer focus aims to link the different elements of the company together in a single chain, across the organization. It also aims to create among managers and employees a sense of how the whole business fits together to provide service to the customer.

To achieve this, what is needed again is knowledge – knowledge of how different parts of the business link together to deliver value to a customer. Research among employees has highlighted an interesting twist to relations between different departments – a syndrome called 'the unknown incompetent'. People in one area may not actually know what another area does, but in the absence of any knowledge about it they nevertheless feel it is pretty bad at whatever it does.

It comes as no surprise that people fill the vacuum of information – usually for the worse. Employee attitude surveys consistently show that, on average, less than half the employees know the objectives of the organization. The lower down the organization you go – that is, closer to the customer – the less clear the objectives become.

Where people do know the objectives, they do not get feedback on progress. It's a relatively simple thing to do – telling people where we are all going, and giving them regular feedback on progress – but it tends to get lost in the shuffle of just getting the job done day to day.

Being focused so much on serving the customer, and on reporting on anything that gets in the way of their own satisfaction, it is important to keep people aware of the balance of business issues so that they focus on serving the customer as a way of also making the business successful.

At First Direct, the chief executive runs sessions with between 30 and 35 employees to give them an overall picture of the organization, and one member of staff commented that she, for once, felt that she 'understood the entire picture, not just her department's part of it'.

THE ROLE OF COMMUNICATION

The role of communication in helping deliver the offer to the customer falls into two parts: getting started and keeping going.

For strategies to succeed, people need to understand what the strategy is, and what is the proposition that the company is making to its customers. They need to understand the context to the strategy and the rationale behind the proposition. They also need to know their own role and how it fits into the whole, and they need to be involved in turning the strategy into specific actions.

Educating people, creating understanding and involving them in the discussion of how to make it work, all comes under the heading of getting started. Keeping going means using communication continually to refine the organization's ability to deliver on the offer it makes to the customer. It involves:

- providing feedback on how individuals, their team and the organization as a whole is doing;
- looking for ways of improving continually, based on feedback from internal and external customers;
- developing an understanding of how the organization works;
- refining the interpretation of the information the organization receives about its activities;
- sharing best practice and learning;
- networking knowledge and expertise;
- creating links and interconnections between individuals.

Communicating to compete

As suppliers get closer to their customers, communication will have to be designed to serve the supplier's chosen positioning. Communication needs to be based on what it is that the organization is offering to its customers and what it has chosen to emphasize as its competitive edge.

Operational efficiency and communication

Companies competing on operational efficiency aim to deliver products or services to customers with the least inconvenience, and to beat competitors on price. They try to refine the service or production process, reduce costs and increase the effectiveness of business processes across functional and departmental boundaries.

To support this competitive strategy, communication should focus on creating greater understanding of roles and priorities across functional and structural boundaries. Team meetings discuss ways of eliminating snags in the process, and are updated on measure of efficiency, progress on costs and the implementation of the team's ideas. Meetings are run by the team leader, assisted by a facilitator from elsewhere within the company, and representatives of departments that share a process attend to alert the team to upcoming changes, to hear about problems that have arisen from their areas and to feed back remedial actions.

Closeness to the customer and communication

While companies pursuing operational efficiency concentrate on making their operations lean and efficient, those pursuing closeness to the customer tailor products and services to fit an individualized profile of the customer.

Employees try to make sure that each customer gets what he or she really wants. Salespeople will spend time with a customer to become familiar with his or her needs and objectives, and to figure out which product or service will solve a problem, or add value.

For this strategy, communication has to stress flexibility and responsiveness, and communication systems are tailored to meet the varying needs of different departments and functions, rather than there being a single regimented model for all.

Selection, induction and training programmes stress the creative decision-making skills needed to respond to individual customer needs. Internal information in directories or on screen, quickly shows who can provide expert advice in which area to speed up problem solving.

Communication focuses on feeding the views and attitudes of the customer into the organization. Team meetings focus on customer feedback, complaints and commendations. Customers are brought in regularly to provide feedback directly. Employees from the supplier visit, or are seconded to customers; employees from traditionally backroom departments man the stands at trade shows. Upward feedback sessions are run, at which front-line staff update senior management on customer reactions, needs and requests. Employees are given the authority to make decisions to solve problems, and are empowered to spend the necessary money to do this. Communication focuses on stories of employees' ingenuity in solving problems, and of those who put themselves out to help customers.

The Burton Group's internal magazine shows its desire to be close to the customer, with a story celebrating the shop assistant who solved a customer's quest for a hat for a wedding by lending her her own hat. There was no sale, but the customer was happy and a relationship was created that may pay off in the future. In the same magazine were articles on fashion trends and issues, providing front-line and backroom staff with coverage of issues that customers would be interested in discussing.

In industry after industry, as products and services are commoditized by competition, clients are saying it is the knowledge of their industry, and the ability to relate specialized know-how to their problems, that will win their business. Organizations want business partners who will have a long-term relationship with them, and who will become more valuable as they become more familiar with the client's industry.

Clients are faced with a growing number of interconnected problems and a clamour of professional advisors, lawyers, accountants, management consultants and merchant bankers, all jockeying for a place at the boardroom table.

Within the professional advisor's own business, there is a proliferation of services and products, as new ideas are systemized and transferred across industry sectors, and their range of offerings becomes more complex.

At the interface between the client's increasingly complex business and the advisor's proliferating services is usually some kind of relationship manager whose job is to present a single face to the client and orchestrate the contacts between his or her organization and that of the client. The key competitive differentiator for such a firm will be how close it can get to the customer, and how well it manages its relationship with clients. The ability to provide valuable advice, know-how and innovative ideas depends on the advisor's ability to get to know the problems which most affect the client, and the ability to network knowledge and expertise within his or her own organization.

For all of these firms, working with a wide variety of clients, across a range of industry and market sectors, there is a pressing need to have a wider and greater understanding of market dynamics, the factors affecting clients and greater knowledge and understanding of the expertise and capabilities within their own organizations.

These advisory businesses, where ideas are the currency, are comprised of knowledge workers. Increases in efficiency among knowledge workers will involve making best use of people with expertise wherever they may be located in the company, either in terms of the organization's structure, or geographically.

The need to match internal knowledge to increasingly diverse client needs, while concentrating resources in the best location and keeping headcount down, will make networking knowledge and expertise the prime challenge for these businesses.

Making the link

Creating a level of service that customers will recommend to others depends upon listening for feedback, learning from it and being able to respond. Communication needs to provide the means for maintaining the flow of learning around the organization. The customer is often the missing link in internal communication.

Getting customers in to visit, taking back-office and support staff to visit the customer, etc. are ways of creating contact that gets people out of their boxes. People who do not know who the customer is, and do not have contact with him or her, are unlikely to take a keen interest. Unfamiliarity breeds contempt.

Figure 5.4 shows that a circular process of feedback and improvement is more useful than cascades of information.

Barriers to hearing the voice of the customer, or of employees who serve him or her, are twofold – the lack of channels and the cultural bias against listening.

The problem often is that the channels do not exist for feedback from customers, nor is there any place to capture and store reactions. The

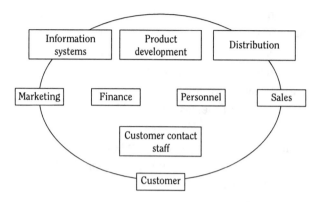

FIGURE 5.4   A loop of communication and feedback needs to link both the external customer and the internal customer together

customer relations department has traditionally been the place that customers are referred to, on the assumption that whatever customers have to say will be a complaint. The role of customer relations has been to handle the customer and keep the sound of any raised voices away from the rest of the business. This means that the communication line from the customer leads into a siding of the organization and feedback is shunted off to the side. There will be little systematic connection from the points of customer contact to the management of the business, and feedback will end up dead-ended in a communication cul-de-sac.

What are the feedback points for collecting reactions from customers, such as reports from field sales and service personnel? Solo field engineers who have close contact with the customer often have little day-to-day contact with their own employer. When meetings are called, the emphasis is more often on handing out operational guidelines than on pooling experience of customer issues.

In an environment where the drive is to package products and services and push them out down the distribution channels, getting comments from the customer, or from front-line staff, can seem like swimming against the current. Where the communication model is to craft messages and push them out, getting feedback into the organization can be like trying to get toothpaste back into the tube.

Managers need to be trained to listen rather than to tell, and they need to be trained in exploring underlying barriers to good service and unrealized customer needs.

Product leadership and communication

Companies that pursue product leadership aim to produce a continuous stream of state-of-the-art products and services. That takes creativity of ideas, applicability of those ideas and speed in getting them into the market. Creativity means recognizing and embracing ideas that originate outside the company, so communication focuses on feeding in ideas from elsewhere and keeping track of competitors' activity. Team meetings include feedback on customer experiences and problems, competitors' advances and brainstorming exercises on improving products and processes.

Internal seminars on technical developments are complemented by overviews of social trends and the circulation of reports by futurologists. Outsiders are regularly brought in and supplier forums are held to identify areas for improvement, together with advisory panels and customer user forums.

To increase the speed of getting innovative ideas into the market, internal departments spend time familiarizing themselves with each other's roles and identifying ways of accelerating the development process. Marketing and research and development hold team meetings together, and communication is organized along project team lines with the project leader coordinating lines of communication.

The link between internal communication and product innovation was particularly important to Lyons Tetley. As a supplier of hot beverages, it manufactures and sells household name brands such as Tetley Tea. Tetley Tea is the number one tea bag brand in the UK and number two worldwide.

Building on the phenomenal success of its innovative round tea bag, Lyons Tetley's mission was 'growing our share of the UK hot beverages market through innovation'.

In 1992–93, the UK saw a very tough trading climate. Tea drinking in the UK is a habit which is declining slowly over time, as coffee drinking becomes more popular and more widespread. Ironically, across most of Europe, where traditionally coffee drinking has been strong, there is an increasing habit for drinking tea.

In the UK, the company faced intense competition not only from its traditional competitors, but also from the growing strength of 'own label' products. Facing a diminishing market, there was intense pressure on price and on margins. Meanwhile, worldwide the increasing international scope of the business meant that the Lyons Tetley brands were having an increasing impact outside the UK.

Building on its success in terms of quality and innovation, the company reviewed its markets and its internal operations to see how it could give itself increased market strength, growth and continued profitability.

Lyons Tetley aimed to be a quality organization. As with most organizations undergoing change, it was looking for more commitment and contribution from its people. It knew that communication was central to this and it knew it needed to be good at it. It reviewed its communications and found that some of the levels of communication needed were not intact.

Figure 5.5 shows the levels of communication which an employee needs, if a company is to deliver its promise to the customer.

People need to know what their job is, and how they are doing in it. They need to know their immediate team's role, objectives and priorities, and how they are doing against them. They need to know of other teams, functions and departments: the aims and objectives. They need to have a sense of belonging to the organization, and a clear sense of the direction and aspirations of the business. All levels need to be served and intact.

It was discovered that people had a high level of understanding of their own role and that of their team, but less for their department, and a

Levels of communication

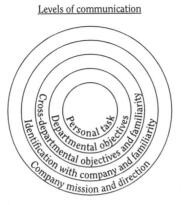

FIGURE 5.5 People need communication at a number of levels, and all levels need to be addressed

---

much lower understanding of other departments and of the company's overall objectives.

As a traditional British company, Lyons Tetley had focused on downward communication. It now embarked on a quality strategy which needed strong upward communication, a high degree of knowledge among all departments of each other's activity, and strong lateral communication. Lateral communication was virtually non-existent, and, where it did take place, relied upon informal contact among senior managers. Culturally, managers found it hard to raise contentious issues between departments. For the strategy to succeed, these cross-functional issues were precisely what needed to be raised, to identify root problems and make improvements. Other businesses have discovered that the majority of cost and quality improvements are to be found at the interface between functional departments.

Lyons Tetley is part of J Lyons, which produces an internal magazine called *Lyons Mail* that is extremely popular and well read. As an important part of the division, Lyons Tetley frequently finds itself featured in the magazine, together with its sister companies in the division.

It was discovered from the communications survey that *Lyons Mail* was being used by individual parts of the business to glean a better view of the overall business objectives of Lyons Tetley. Managers were looking outside for information on what was going on inside.

A business newsletter was created with specific attention to middle management, who were discovered to be missing out on business-related information. One of the main aims of the newsletter was to educate individual parts of the business about each other, as a means of creating greater understanding and cooperation across component parts of the company.

Communication skills training aimed to change the communication style. The training of senior managers in communication skills was focused on facilitating, developing a more open style of communication, and specifically at raising contentious issues and handling conflict. Once senior managers began acquiring the skills, the training was extended from senior management down to first-line team leaders.

Team meetings were introduced to allow teams to discuss issues at a number of levels – company, cross-departmental and their own area. Meetings also allowed discussion on improving problems which the team saw as getting in the way of doing the job properly.

Better lateral communication began with the senior management group. While team meetings created better lateral communication at senior levels, business breakfasts were introduced to link senior and middle managers. They also allowed more informal and open conversation about issues affecting the business. These breakfast sessions are held every two to three months and are aimed at 20 or so senior and middle managers at a time, allowing a two-hour breakfast session with board directors. These have no pre-set agendas and the aim is to allow open, frank discussion of any issues which the senior and middle managers choose to raise. The sessions also serve to provide a greater context to some of the information coming down from the board into the team meetings, and to allow for more challenging debate about areas of commercial sensitivity and confidentiality.

At these business breakfasts, managers are encouraged to speak out openly and frankly, with the aim of giving them direct access to the board and feeding back issues as they hear them from their own staff. They also serve to build better cross-functional links between managers as they come into contact with each other and hear common issues arising from their individual areas.

The common factor in all these channels of communication is feedback, with a focus on providing service to both internal and external customers. It is clear that without feedback an organization is likely to keep on doing what it, rather than its customer, believes is important. Listening to the voice of the customer, and, since employee satisfaction breeds customer satisfaction, to the voice of the employee, is vital.

First Direct points out that as employee satisfaction improves, customer satisfaction increases. They track both regularly, via internal and external research, and publish the parallels between the two.

First Direct regularly polls its customers, in a number of ways:

- 'First response': a sample survey into new customers and how they found the account-opening process. It also looks at how they felt in terms of being valued/not valued and the smoothness of the account transfer process.
- A quarterly questionnaire of 1000 people, with operational questions, for instance on the length of time taken to answer the phone, fleshed out by research with focus groups.
- Quarterly NOP survey looking at both its own customer base and that of its competitors in other banks.

First Direct also carries out an annual staff survey and benchmarks the results against the norms for other financial institutions. The staff satisfaction rating is part of a 'business barometer', which is updated monthly and is displayed prominently on large triangular black obelisks at strategic points across the floors. This also displays information on:

- level of customer service
- financial success
- customer satisfaction
- employee satisfaction.

Listening to the voice of both the customer and the employee, and using research to feed back into the business, is an important part of creating a greater customer focus and a competitive differentiation. The next chapter looks at the use of internal research to help create change within the organization.

Using internal research to create change

T he use of research as an instrument on the corporate dashboard is helping to speed up the changing of behaviour within organizations. What gets measured may get done, but changes in attitudes and behaviour are rarely measured with any frequency. Companies do not usually measure their market share only at the end of each year and they try to get feedback from customers fairly regularly, but internal tracking tends to be done at best annually, and, in terms of the traditional attitude survey, every two to three years.

Research is one name for feedback, and organisms that evolve successfully have swift feedback mechanisms from their environment that allow them to detect and respond to change. Increasingly, organizations are asking their customers what they want, through a variety of mechanisms, whether by means of regular questionnaires, focus groups, use of market research, inviting customers in or going out to speak to them. A similar drive is taking place internally, as organizations ask their own employees what they think, what they believe needs to change and what they need to make change happen.

In the past the employee research survey has been seen primarily as a means of letting employees 'have their say'. Now there is a move towards using internal research as a means of both identifying drag factors to change and helping to remove the drag. This chapter argues that using internal research is a potent tool for change. It looks at using research not just as a measuring stick but also as a means of fostering and sustaining behaviour change.

Ideally, in the search for a competitive differentiator, a company conducts research among existing and potential customers. It looks not just at the basic characteristics that customers expect as a matter of course, but digs further to find the X factors – those things that customers would not normally expect but which they would value. Having spotted a competitive opportunity, the company has to take advantage of it.

The next stage is to conduct research internally to evaluate how suited employees are to delivering what the organization has chosen to adopt as its competitive strategy. Ideally, the research should be used to highlight the gaps between the current situation and the desired one, and the communication strategy should then focus on closing these gaps.

Research is one of the most useful tools for improving communication and creating change. It gives an insight into the state of the organization, and prompts the re-examination of issues that normally go unexamined. There are very few occasions in organizational life where you get a chance to do this. Even where organizations suspect they already know what research will show, the process of conducting it is invaluable – if only because it is one of the few upward communication vehicles available.

However, there can be confusion about the aims of research, and internal research particularly can fall victim to mixed ambitions and objectives. Research can be undertaken regularly to provide a benchmark for progress, or intermittently to resolve suspicions about the state of play inside the organization.

There may be a general unease about communication, a desire to assess progress since the last review, or a desire to become more professional and improve practices. Research is conducted – and itself becomes a source of confusion, muddying, rather than clarifying, the waters. What should be a great opportunity for helping change to happen becomes the focus of frustration and dissatisfaction.

Why do some of these mismatches of expectation and outcome occur?

RESEARCH TAKES PLACE IN A CONTEXT

There is a real danger in testing whether people are satisfied or happy with the communication they receive. Scores which say that people receive enough communication beg the question, 'For what?' Even questions which ask, 'Do you get enough information to do your job?' pose the further question as to whether the employee actually understands what his or her job involves. With most organizations undergoing change, and looking for more commitment and contribution from their staff, the role of the employee is likely to have shifted, and the definition of what the job entails is likely to have changed. Therefore the danger is that responses may be based on an outdated definition of the job to be done.

In one IT organization, comparing findings from different questions showed a very interesting picture. Asked if they understood where the organization was going in terms of strategy and direction, the vast majority of employees said they did not know. However, asked whether they themselves were helping the company to achieve its objectives and go in the right direction, they all resoundingly said yes. They did not know where they were going, but they were unquestionably helping the company to get there.

Organizations that conduct surveys and compare themselves with British norms can be deluded into being satisfied that they are above the norm. The communication needed for an insurance company is very different from that which is required for a fast, responsive engineering servicing organization. The scores for one survey can be identical to the scores for another, yet the implications can be totally different.

Traditional research into communication channels, commissioned every two years as a way of keeping a finger on the pulse, may be a useful health check for an organization in a stable market. For any organization in a changing market, however, the role of communication is likely to be more complex. It will not be sufficient to check communication only every two years, the equivalent of doing an MOT on the communication vehicles. Research has to be used more frequently to help reduce the drag on change, and help the company to achieve its strategy successfully.

Researching communication in the absence of the business strategy can be misleading. Communication does not exist by itself, so it is a wasted opportunity to attempt to measure it in isolation. Research is less useful when it is based on assumptions that do not match the organization's stage of development or its business strategy.

A pharmaceutical company registered almost maximum scores among employees in its survey. The survey showed that employees were extremely contented, received precisely the right amount of communication and were entirely happy with the benefits package they received. And rightly so. They were looked after superbly and were happy in what they were doing.

Unfortunately, times were changing. Where the past strategy had required long-run production where people had to comply with stringent quality procedures, a greater responsiveness to customers was going to mean shorter runs and more frequent change-overs of the lines. This meant that engineers who were responsible for the change-overs were going to play a much more important role in relationships on the shop floor. This had implications for the workforce's understanding of what their job actually entailed. They needed to be flexible, responsive and to be able to adapt to quick changes on different products, in contrast to the old culture of steady rhythms, long shifts and relatively undisturbed work routines.

Factories concentrating on long-run production have different communication needs from those factories that make short runs to order, where employees need to be able to switch between lines as demand requires and to have the knowledge and skills to be able to operate different machines.

At first glance, the research into the pharmaceutical company showed a happy, satisfied and productive workforce – good news if the company was dependent on the degree of happiness of its staff. Contrasting these results with what the company needed from its people in order to achieve the business strategy showed a different picture. The survey results revealed the kind of organization which was currently unsuited to the new strategy. Faster and better communication between the sales function and the production function was required; production staff needed to understand better why it was that they were having to run up different kinds of products for different kinds of customers, in far greater varieties of packaging and form. Flexibility of working practices, the need for continuous running, the shift to multiskilling and the need to match production standards of their other production sites across Europe were issues that were soon to disturb the even tenor of the ways of working to which employees had become accustomed.

CONDUCTING RESEARCH

When looking at whether to conduct internal research, it is easy to focus on the technical issues involved and to forget that internal communication is merely a means to an end. Conducting internal research itself is a process that should help to make change happen. Organizations are full of research reports which are technically excellent and whose analysis is incisive, and which have simply ended up being shelved.

Conducting internal research opens up the whole debate about what might be going on inside an organization, and allows people to advance theories, hypotheses, reactions and opinions in a protected way. Employees are engaged with their manager in trying to identify the unconscious rules by which the organization is run and which are holding it back. They are freed from the day-to-day focus on the task, and have temporary protection from retribution.

Typically, any organization which begins to look at internal research is interested in discovering the flow of communication, the usefulness of communication channels and the appropriateness of content. A typical set of objectives would be to:
- assess how well people understand the organization's goals and strategy;
- establish where communications are getting through and which channels work best;
- evaluate how well team briefing or a consultation process is working;
- gauge the effectiveness of in-house journals;
- assess the impact of customer service, quality or training programmes;

- determine the view of the company on such areas as terms and conditions and morale;
- establish the effectiveness of current internal communications at all levels within the organization;
- identify communication best practices where they currently exist.

Usually the brief is very focused and the emphasis is on being able to identify remedial actions which can be taken to improve communication. However, during internal debate about the objectives the more important agenda lying behind the brief usually emerges. Internal research is often encouraged by managers within companies who recognize the need for improvement and change. There has usually been an internal debate as to whether or not suspicions about internal communication are well-founded and argument between different factions as to what course of action, if any, is necessary. Managers have debated anecdotal evidence, and are seeking some more authoritative quantitative view to achieve a more objective picture.

The outcome of the internal debate is usually a fairly low-risk decision to conduct some research, sometimes by independent outsiders, to settle the issue one way or another. Senior management may want actual proof that there is some kind of problem, while others in the organization may see internal research as a means of educating and convincing senior management that there is an issue, and that there is a way of actually beginning to take some action.

The rationale for conducting research, and the expectations of what it will produce, differ between managers at different levels within a company's hierarchy. Senior management may give the research the go-ahead as a way of developing a score card on the business, while their juniors may hope that the process will allow fundamental issues within the organization to be drawn out.

Since what holds communication back within organizations is less likely to be issues of media and execution, and more those of culture, values and the 'prison' of the past, research allows for the identification and removal of some of the prison bars.

Measuring communication

Internal research is often used to answer queries about the communications budget and what precisely the internal newspaper is delivering. Assessing the effectiveness of communication tools is impossible without knowing the job they are supposed to be doing.

Organizations tend to want to know whether their communications are being effective. Again, without looking at the wider issues, communication departments can only look at whether their communications are efficient. Communicators are limited to looking at how much it costs to produce items, how well the newspaper is distributed, whether employees have the opportunity to view a video, or whether they attended and liked the management conference.

This is like measuring the efficiency of an engine, without ever discovering whether the engine is taking the vehicle any distance in the right direction. It is quite possible to get high scores in all of these measures and yet see no major shift towards meeting the attitudes and behaviours needed to make the strategy work.

It is almost impossible to answer the question, 'What is the company gaining from its communication budget?', without pulling back and looking at the wider issues that will have an impact on communication. Asked about the usefulness of the internal newspaper, for example, but not about wider issues, respondents may express their dissatisfaction with communication as a whole by marking the newspaper down. Then, on design and relaunch of the internal newspaper at a later stage, the company's communication objectives may be no closer to being met.

One editor of a divisional newspaper conducted research into the readership of his newspaper. The results were extremely enthusiastic and positive, and it emerged that the newspaper was widely read and was valued at all levels of the organization for its usefulness. A lesser man might have circulated the report and bathed in the glow of its warm sentiments. This editor, however, pointed out that the strength of positive feeling pointed to the real problem – the newspaper was never intended to fulfil the purpose on which it was now being congratulated. Its popularity reflected a lack of communication and a lack of appropriate additional channels. In the absence of communication about the organization's overall direction, and any feedback on its progress, the internal newspaper had become the pre-eminent vehicle for communication because it was virtually the only vehicle.

The review by one organization's corporate headquarters of its communication practices concluded that its media needed to be more professional in their execution if they were to get their message across. Time, effort and money was invested in producing videos with high production values, and revamping internal magazines to make them glossier. Ironically, this made things worse. It was discovered that the misperception of the corporate centre's role was exacerbated by the perceived extravagance of its self-promotional literature. Anything landing on anyone's desk which bore the chairman's photograph went immediately into the bin. Making the magazine glossier only meant that it skimmed across the desk that much faster.

Even where the aim is to quantify the return on the communication budget, the focus tends to be on the costs of production. Employees have a limited amount of time to read information, and there are often higher costs in terms of audiences' time in 'consuming' communication.

In a decentralized organization, there may be a number of different units who have set out to communicate with their own people and with colleagues in other units. Freed by their autonomy they produce information, and items of communication proliferate as communication is effectively deregulated. While the assessment of the effectiveness of communication may focus on the activities of the communication department, the real problem besetting the organization may be the clutter caused by everyone getting in on the communication game, with no coordination.

Internal research allows you to set benchmarks to measure performance and return on investment, and to target your communication more effectively. Before it can begin to communicate to its best advantage, a company has to become aware of the particular ways in which its people already communicate. Once it has identified the formal and informal channels that people use most and which are most effective, it can match what it wants to say to the best way of saying it.

Issues of communication tend to revolve too much around media and execution, or around morale and employee happiness. Research is one of the best ways to start the debate with senior management about communication and the attitudes and behaviour needed from employees.

Matching research to the organization's stage of development

What should be assessed depends on the stage of development of the organization and its business strategy (see Fig. 6.1).

An organization which is at the systemization stage may want to test the effectiveness of the communication channels and procedures that have been put in place. Research will test for the effective operation of channels,

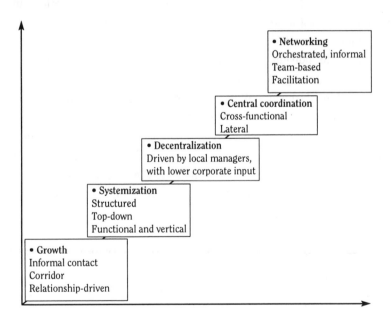

FIGURE 6.1 The stage of development will highlight what aspects of communication need to be reviewed

those most preferred versus those most used, whether key messages are getting through and whether the distribution process is working efficiently.

Questions would typically focus on such areas as:

1 Channels of communication – current usage versus preferred usage
2 How well informed people feel they are
3 Credibility of management information
4 Opportunity to comment on matters affecting work
5 Management listening and taking account of views.

An organization at the decentralizing stage may be more interested in testing for whether people understand the direction of the company, individuals' knowledge of areas of the business outside their immediate area, how management style is perceived and how ideally people would like to be involved and managed.

Prime areas for questioning at this stage would be:

1 Understanding of, and feedback on, goals, objectives and performance
2 Understanding of information received about the team's results
3 Communication style
    • how the individual's immediate boss communicates day-to-day
    • reasons for contact with boss
4 Level of involvement – attitude towards current level of involvement and desire for more or less involvement.

An organization which is trying to shift towards central coordination may want to assess the employees' knowledge of, and identification with, the group as a whole, and may be interested in assessing people's understanding of career development and training within the wider group of businesses.

Issues of concern at this stage would be:

1 Understanding of goals, objectives and performance for the business as a whole and the individual division
2 Understanding of goals, objectives and performance for the local team and for the individual
3 Current knowledge of other departments
    • rating of effectiveness of other departments

- importance of receiving information from other departments
- importance of providing information to other departments.

Networking

An organization that has reached the networking stage recognizes that the formal structure has become too cumbersome to cope with the complexity of its relationships and reporting lines. When that happens, the role of research is to look at orchestrating the informal network to better effect.

Managers have tried for years to control the grapevine, or to drop selective nuggets of information into the ear of someone whose tendency to feed it into the grapevine is assured. Managers have their own sources of information, and those in the know who provide them with information.

As companies continue to delayer and flatten their hierarchies, and there is an increasing reliance on teams with shifting membership, the ability to understand and form informal networks becomes more important. This begins with finding out how it works and who are the key players within it:

1 Who speaks to whom
2 Who has credibility and provides support
3 Who is sought out by colleagues for their expertise and knowledge
4 What information people accept, and what importance they assign to the departments originating it.

This can help identify gaps in information flow, and the mismatch between areas' rating of each other's credibility and their importance to the business.

Organizations who use a network of key communicators can use the mapping of informal communication networks to identify who already has standing as credible communicators, as a basis for selecting people to take on a formal communication role.

Isolation and insularity

Communication maps often show departments that have few links to other groups. In these situations, employees in a department spend all their time talking among themselves and neglect to cultivate relationships with the rest of their colleagues. Frequently in such cases only the most senior employees have ties with people outside their areas, and they may hoard these contacts by failing to introduce these people to junior colleagues.

Gaps in the network

Mapping of flows of information and communication within Oil Co. demonstrated that areas, especially support areas, which needed to have close contact with their internal customers were not part of a two-way communication flow.

Oil Co. is a highly developed and professionally managed multinational oil company which has moved from a monolithic and centralized past to a decentralized approach to managing its business. It has a wealth of communication processes, the majority of which rate well among its employees. However, with its habit of keeping its eye on the ball, it wanted to review whether that concentration on the ball was leading to ignoring the other players on the pitch.

Oil Co. is a well established company, with a range of internal communication channels and a fully formed and effective team meeting system. In comparison with other organizations, it would have rated highly as a well structured and professional company in its communication. However, Oil Co.'s business needs highlighted issues which were quite different, and reflected a company at a different stage of development.

Oil Co.'s business strategy focuses on maximizing profitability while achieving the highest standards of quality and safety and working within environmental standards. Oil Co. is highly decentralized, and there is a strong focus on business lines and profit centres.

Within Oil Co. the natural work units of most businesses are the departments or divisions within them. However, the increase in workload, without a vast increase in resources, meant that there had been compartmentalization into smaller units. Fragmentation has made it more difficult for employees to understand and relate to the wider business unit.

Many of the departments within the company did not have extensive communication with one another. However, there were many business processes which ran laterally, connecting and involving a number of different departments.

In a company-wide review of communication which included interviews with staff at all levels followed by a questionnaire survey, five levels of communication were examined:

1 *Team-level communication*: communication between members of a work team.

2 *Cross-team communication*: communication between individuals who work within teams in the same department.

3 *Departmental-level communication*: communication more general or about wider issues in the department.

4 *Cross-departmental communication*: communication between different departments.

5 *Company-wide communication*: communication on company-wide issues.

The survey showed that team-level communication was very effective, with the team meeting system being highly regarded by most people.

Ironically, the emphasis on devolving authority to the point closest to the customer had successfully strengthened communication at a local team level, at the expense of communication between teams and between departments.

Local teams provided a sound channel for feeding back team issues and team performance. Oil Co.'s internal publications provided a good conduit for news of national operations. What was being lost was the communication between departments.

To further a quality strategy, lateral communication was increasingly important in creating an understanding of the different objectives of, and constraints affecting, other departments. Part of the research entailed tracing the information linkages between departments. People in each area were asked to assess how important information from other areas was to doing their job properly. Each area was also asked to assess how much information they currently received from each of the other areas.

From this information it was possible to map out which areas needed to exchange information with each other. It also tracked the relative importance each department placed on both giving to, and receiving information from, the others. This highlighted the actual amount of information which was flowing in each direction, and any mismatches between what was needed and what was provided.

This information provided a blueprint for closing the gaps in information flows. It identified whether the flows of information were aligned with the business processes, or whether there were departments vital to a process which were being starved, or starving others, of information.

RESEARCH BY COMPETITIVE POSITION

Whatever the specific focus of the research, there will be a foundation of assessing the basic effectiveness of communication channels. Simply mapping out the channels that people use, and contrasting them with how their users rate them, can bring some useful savings. Organizations that have flattened their structures and reduced the number of employees can find that they are still happily producing in-house magazines aimed at management audiences that ceased to exist some years before.

There are some basic questions that will need exploring, for example, what are the channels most used for communication, what are the channels most preferred? However, if the research is to provide some competitive insight, it will also need to include questions that test for areas of strength or weakness around the chosen competitive positioning.

Operational efficiency

If operational efficiency is central to the business, there are some key factors which need to be in place and which need to be measured.

Degree of involvement

How involved do people feel? Is there a desire to be able to contribute more, or are people unwilling to put themselves out for the sake of the business?

Clarity of role
How clear are people on what they are supposed to be doing, and on how their job contributes to the whole?

Knowledge of objectives
While people tend to be clearer on the objectives of their own jobs, they are apt to be increasingly hazy on the overall objectives of the business the lower down the organization they are.

The feedback they receive on progress against objectives tends to focus on their own job, but feedback is, on average, low for all levels of objectives (see Fig. 6.2). If people do not know what they are supposed to be doing, are unsure how or whether their job fits into the overall scheme of things and receive little news of progress, they are unlikely to feel deeply involved in the business as a whole.

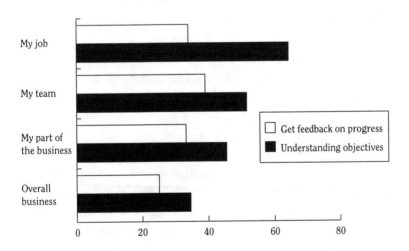

FIGURE 6.2 Average ratings of understanding of, and getting feedback on, objectives

Are individuals' ideas listened to?

Employees are likely to have ideas on how the job they do can be improved, if there is someone to listen and take notice. Operational efficiency relies on the organization listening for, and constantly encouraging, a flow of good ideas.

Understanding of the process you form part of

Operational efficiency requires people to understand the process they form part of, and to have a clear understanding of the priorities and objectives of colleagues on the same process.

Use of team meetings

The use of the team to identify snags in the process, and to brainstorm solutions and improvements, is the hallmark of the company focusing on operational efficiency. Team members should feel that they are able to raise issues and use the time to come up with ideas for improvement.

Where research shows that team meetings are in fact used to broadcast corporate news from the top that is perceived as time-wasting and irrelevant, there is a clear mismatch between strategy and practice.

Closeness to the customer

If closeness to the customer is the basis for competing, the following areas should be included in the research:

Perceptions of customer objectives

While it is important for all employees to know the objectives at all levels of their organization, for a company focused on the customer it is vital that employees also know the objectives and priorities of the customer.

This is particularly an issue in organizations which have shifted their focus to new groups of customers. The traditional picture of the former customer can live on within a company long after the strategy has started to focus on a quite different sector of the market.

Contact with customers

As well as knowing who the customer is, it is important for people to get feedback and acknowledgement for a job well done from the customer. This is all the more important for those who work in back-office rather than front-line functions. Do those who have contact feed in to colleagues' team meetings, for example, or do customers attend meetings?

Feedback on customer visits

When customers visit the company, do employees receive feedback on their reactions, comments and suggestions? Having been on their best behaviour for visitors, do employees get to hear what the outcome of the visit was?

Knowledge of internal customers

How well do people know their internal customers' objectives and constraints, and the expectations they have for the service they receive?

Communication with other departments

What are the processes for communication with other departments? What is the frequency and who are the named contacts there?

Effectiveness of upward feedback

What channels exist for feeding up comments and suggestions, and observations of customer problems, and how are responses passed back?

Research among customers should be run in parallel with internal research, so that the two perspectives can be compared and contrasted (see Fig. 6.3).

What is it that customers value as their top priority? In a financial services company employees confidently ranked speed and accuracy of transactions as paramount. Customers said they wanted good quality advice on investment options.

Employees were putting all their time and effort into speeding up transactions, largely unnoticed and unvalued by their customers. While the business strategy was to focus on getting close to the customer, the majority of staff were pursuing greater operational efficiency.

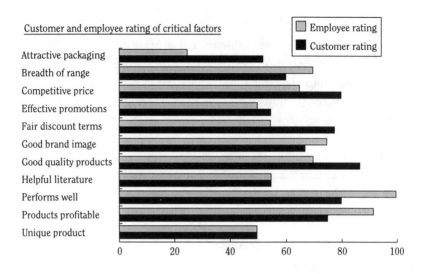

FIGURE 6.3   Contrasting views between what employees and customers rate as important

Contrasting customer and employee views brought the message home clearly to staff.

Through questionnaires and one-to-one discussions with patients, BUPA Health Services uses its 'heart to heart' programme to receive continuous feedback on how well it is meeting its patients' needs and the needs of its other customers – insurance companies and the consultants who use the hospital facilities. These are fed back regularly each quarter to employees, and used as a basis for discussing how to improve service.

As a means of exploring further what their customers might want and value from them, individuals at different levels in the organization have been trained as facilitators to run customer focus sessions. The same individuals will run cross-departmental communication sessions to look at resolving issues that run across departmental boundaries.

Product leadership

Where product leadership is the chosen competitive positioning, research should include:

Understanding of customer needs

How well do employees know and understand customer needs and objectives, how much feedback do they get from customers on products and services, and how well do employees understand their priorities?

Relationship between R&D marketing, sales, production and distribution

How well do departments involved in developing new products understand and cooperate with each other? What channels exist for fostering and capturing new ideas from all employees?

Perceptions of customer service

What do employees believe customers have a right to expect? Which, if any, customers are more important than others?

Perceptions of quality

What are the criteria by which employees judge quality and how do these compare with customers' criteria?

Rating of how customers see us

How well do employees know how their company is perceived by customers, and how their products and services are rated?

Rating of how we differ from the competition

How do employees regard the company's strengths compared to what the customer is seeking, and how do we compare with the competition on those aspects?

When BT was gearing itself up for the major change necessary to take it into the 1990s, to become more responsive to customers and to focus on

Total Quality, it conducted one of the largest employee surveys undertaken in the UK. The Communication and Attitude Research for Employees (CARE) survey aimed not only at reviewing the effectiveness of communications programmes, but also to identify areas for improvement in business operations. One of its key findings was that there was an uptapped desire for greater involvement, with 40 per cent of BT staff wanting to feel more involved in the business.

The Automobile Association also discovered from its internal research that a sizeable proportion of its staff wanted more involvement in the business. They wanted some way of contributing ideas and solving some of the day-to-day problems that got in the way of providing a good service to members. At a time when the organization was looking for people at the sharp end to take ownership for the quality of service to their customers, this demonstration of an untapped desire to get more involved in doing a better job fitted both the staff's desires and the company's needs.

AA Roadside Services is by far the largest part of the Automobile Association, with over 6000 staff, supplying a personal service to nearly 8 million members. The 5500 employees of the Roadside Services Division include 3600 patrol staff, 1400 emergency operators and 350 mechanics repairing AA vehicles. The rest are support staff. The majority of these staff, the patrol force, are not based at any particular location and are given breakdown jobs from one of eight regional telephone answering and deployment centres. In 1993 Information and Breakdown Emergency Centres answered over 8 million telephone calls. AA patrols went to the help of stranded members on more than 4.5 million occasions.

In a service organization that relies both on operational efficiency and the ability to handle people in trouble sensitively, front-line staff have over 12 million opportunities to make a lasting impression on customers, either at the roadside or at the end of a telephone. As the quality of service is central to the promise it makes to its members, the AA believes it is crucial to inform and motivate its employees to deliver a memorable service.

At the level where strategy is translated into action, managers and team leaders, who frequently have the lowest involvement in creating the strategy for change, and limited access to the thinking behind it, bear the most responsibility for implementing that change. In their business, they have to communicate the key message that they are totally dependent on the market for survival. Today, they are less inward-looking and far more customer-focused.

The senior management of Roadside Services decided to close the gap between what they needed to be to deliver service, and what their past traditions had made them.

Traditionally, the AA has been run on somewhat militaristic lines, within regions, and with long chains of command and the prevailing management style being one of command and control. Those at the sharp end were expected to comply with precisely laid-down procedures, with little room for deviation. The need to have patrols at the roadside owning the quality of service meant giving them more latitude to take the decisions necessary to ensure that members were well served.

Often key staff, the patrols who actually go out to answer members' calls for assistance at the roadside, were thought of as 'loners', working on their own, mending vehicles. They spent the majority of their time out in their vehicles, with only the radio link giving them any sense of connection to the rest of the organization. Often they were individuals who wanted to escape being over-managed in a garage workshop, were quite capable of motivating themselves and liked being out on the road meeting and helping people.

Towards the end of 1989 the company was reorganized, and this inevitably brought change. From feedback, it was obvious that staff were becoming isolated from management and that they were not fully aware of the company's strategic direction. There was the particular problem of communicating with a remote and geographically spread workforce, and staff were not buying into the objectives and vision presented by senior management.

With a clear strategy for differentiating itself through the efficiency, speed and quality of its service, the organization wanted to identify any gaps between where it wanted to be and where the majority of the organization currently felt itself to be. It decided to conduct internal research to identify the situation inside the company and the priorities for action to align their employees with the business strategy. Following interviews and group discussions with staff, a wide-ranging opinion survey called 'Talkback' was undertaken, to find out what staff thought, both of the changes the company had been through and of their impact on communication.

Any call to the AA is answered by a telephonist, who would send the details by computer to the radio room for transmission by data to a patrol out on the road. The survey showed that staff wanted more contact and cooperation between telephone operators, deployment operators and patrols. This led to the creation of radio channel teams, with radio operators organizing shifts to ensure overlap with 'their' patrols' shifts. This allowed them to get used to each other, to build some familiar contact. It worked better for the patrols, ensuring they got to the site of a breakdown quickly, and gave better service to the member.

The AA regularly organizes a phone-in that encourages staff to speak directly to senior management in work time. They can give their comments, question policy or voice a complaint. They also have an answerphone where staff are invited to leave comments and questions, with a guarantee of an answer within 24 hours. In addition to a corporate newspaper, regular monthly mailshots to patrols, a monthly magazine and a quarterly audio tape specifically for field staff are produced.

Although these provide direct lines of communication from senior management, the research showed that the preferred medium of communication for staff was with their own team leader. It also showed that there was a desire for the team leader to spend time not only giving them information, but also listening to their ideas and working on the team's day-to-day problems.

It was obvious from the opinion survey that in order to improve communication they had to begin not only with the communication framework, but at the heart of the team/team leader relationship. Therefore a first step was to establish an effective team briefing system and to ensure that managers were seen in the field.

How the AA built upon its team briefing system in response to the research, is covered in the following chapter.

Lyons Tetley conducted customer research that identified the crucial factors that customers wanted. To complement this external research into customer views, an internal communications review was carried out. Individual and group interviews with employees were conducted among a cross-section of the company, issues were identified and then tested by a questionnaire which was issued to all staff.

The communications review came up with a range of findings which reflected the history and tradition of the company. Each individual part of the company had grown strong in terms of its communication within itself, but as a whole it resembled an industrial estate of separate businesses rather than a single united company. The review also showed that while there was greater understanding about local objectives and feedback on progress, there was a low level of clarity about the direction and objectives of the company as a whole.

A lack of contact below the most senior levels between different parts of the company had led to a decline in understanding and familiarity with what each part of the operation did. This encouraged a parochial focus on individual departments' objectives, and increased 'boxitis'.

In addition, the survey results showed that there was a wide range of differences between different parts of the company concerning clarity of the business's direction, and their sense of closeness to, or separation from, that direction. A closer analysis of which departments were most separated and least clear about the company's direction became the foundation of the targeted communication strategy.

One of the specific aims of the research was to test for the effectiveness of lateral communication. The questionnaire asked individuals to assess their knowledge of other departments, and later to rate each department on their perceived effectiveness. A number of lessons emerged from this particular strand of the research. Almost every department felt like a Cinderella – that other areas did not understand the pressure that they faced, or appreciate the job they were doing.

It also emerged that there was a correlation between an individual's degree of familiarity with a department, and how effective at its job he believed that department to be. If someone knew a department well, he tended to rate it more highly, but if he did not, he tended to rate its effectiveness as being much lower. It was interesting that even where people had little actual knowledge of a department, they still had strong opinions about its effectiveness. However the less that was known, the less was the perceived effectiveness.

This was a key issue for the company. Cooperation between departments was a key factor in their quality strategy. Since a lack of knowledge meant a poor rating of effectiveness, the trust needed between departments to get their part of the job right was being undermined by a lack of information about each other's activities.

The flip side of this was that, if greater familiarity created a perception of greater effectiveness, more trust between departments could be created by more contact with, and information about, each other. Part of communicating for quality therefore meant educating each part of the company about the others.

The main findings were that:

1 Employees' understanding of the overall objectives of Lyons Tetley and how well the company was doing against them was low.
2 People had a slightly better understanding of the objectives of their own part of Lyons Tetley and of their individual jobs.
3 Too little information was provided on the business context for the company as a whole.
4 There was little linkage between departments.

Overall, the organization was seen as compartmentalized, with cellular, closely-knit departments.

Although the results overall were slightly higher than the averages to be found in other British companies, they did not fit well with the company's own aspirations. The clear aim from the board became to create a common direction and shared sense of purpose, and to unite different parts of the business in a united company.

The communications strategy was based on creating a communications system that linked different parts of the company together and cleared communication blockages to deliver news and information that was clear, visible and honest.

Lyons Tetley showed all the characteristics of a decentralized organization, where local communication was relatively good but linkages between the departmental and functional areas were poor. It would have been impossible simply to role out a centralized communications strategy on to such a culture, particularly at a time when the overall quality strategy was to listen and respond to the needs of local customers. The communication strategy itself had to demonstrate precisely the principles it was advocating: of listening, responding and tailoring solutions to local customers.

Clear objectives were set for the communications strategy:

1 In terms of downward communication, there needed to be a greater understanding of company objectives, and regular feedback of progress against them.

2 In terms of upward communication, the aim was to encourage greater listening and responding to issues, and more opportunities for feedback to directors.

3 In terms of lateral communication, there needed to be a greater knowledge of other departments, and more frequent contact between departments that needed to cooperate more closely together.

The first steps to implementing the communications strategy entailed creating a shared understanding of what the communication issues actually were. It was clear from the communication review and from the survey that people have very different views of the role that communication should fulfil. Before rushing ahead into implementation, it was imperative that a shared context for the role and the aims of communication should be established, particularly among senior management who would have to make the strategy work.

A first step was to feed back the communication review and survey results to staff. Since a key finding had been that staff wanted more visibility of board directors, that they wanted to feel they could speak openly and see some response to the survey, the first wave of feedback actually came from board directors.

The board had included in the survey the question, 'Do you think the board will actually implement any of the issues from the survey?' Interestingly, the response to this was overwhelming positive, as people did have faith in the board to take action.

Board directors prepared in pairs to run informal feedback sessions and to lead discussion of the implications and suggested actions to be taken. This entailed gaining a working knowledge not only of the details of the survey results but also of their significance and what the results taken together pointed towards.

One of the findings was that individual areas had good communication, but there was no-one at an overall company level providing a picture of where the business was going as a whole. This was the role that the board directors had to take, and in the feedback of the survey results they were the ones who presented the overall company results and the overall company viewpoint.

Traditionally, employees would have been told to go to such sessions, but, in an interesting reversal of cultural expectations, employees were actually invited, without coercion, to attend.

The feedback sessions were run fairly informally using overhead projectors, in groups of around 30 people to allow for a reasonable amount of conversation and feedback. The aim was to provide honest communication using new methods, to share the understanding of what the survey was telling them, to seek ideas of how to improve things, overcome fears among employees that it was not safe to speak, and begin to show greater visibility of the board.

Few people attended the first couple of feedback sessions. The temptation must have been, given the time and effort that directors had put into preparation, to have managers deliver bodies, willingly or not, to fill the rows of seats in the sessions. However, they kept their nerve and kept the invitation open, and word rapidly spread that these sessions were useful.

The remaining sessions were filled with people keen not only to hear the survey results but also to volunteer their own views.

The second wave of feedback was done at local level by senior managers themselves. The research had shown that senior managers, though the first vital link in the chain of communication, often did not have the time to debate issues affecting communication and did not always receive the tools or the skills to do the job that was expected of them. The feedback process had to address some of the issues that had been highlighted by the survey. The senior managers were seen as key to communication, and had the responsibility to make communication happen in their areas.

In order to prepare them for the job of doing the feedback, each area received an individual report which reflected the different findings in its own area with as much detail as was consistent with respondents' anonymity. Senior managers were then brought together for two-day training courses, both in facilitating feedback sessions, and in presenting data and being able to interpret and understand what that data meant. They then ran sessions in their individual areas which consisted of feeding back information, encouraging discussion of its implications among their teams and identifying immediate local actions that could be taken to improve communication. Given that day-to-day work normally focused on the task in hand, it was unusual to be able to pull back and look at other issues, and the feedback process itself was seen as a first step to concrete improvement in communication.

While the feedback process was continuing, the time that that process was taking was being used to further the communications strategy. The board developed a communications charter as a clearly articulated statement of intent about communication, both to advertise what they would offer and to clarify expectations that were realistic.

Internal research does not have to be in the form of questionnaire surveys. It can simply take the form of bringing groups of employees together and listening to them. It is possible to learn as much about the state of communication from the jokes that people make, and the graffiti in the loos, as from anything else. A piece of graffiti on a hand-dryer at one organization read: 'For a 30-second message from the chairman, please press.'

Sometimes it is necessary to conduct only qualitative research – talking to people, either individually or in groups – and in many cases organizations recognized the findings clearly enough to begin taking action.

Having decided that research is something which should be conducted, it is too easy to be trapped into discussing response rates, questionnaire design or the relative merits of census or sample surveys. Even though it is absolutely vital to get technical issues correct, so as to defend the statistical purity of the results, researchers have to maintain an equal realization that almost all the issues they are about to highlight will have their roots in the senior management of the company. If you are about to open a can of worms, it is inadvisable to limit your attention to the shape and design of your can opener.

The real issue facing an internal researcher is how to get on with perfecting the research tool while at the same time trying to find some way to get back upstream to address the real issues. One way of approaching this problem is to view internal research both as a means of providing hard information and as a way of seeding the ground for changes which any report will inevitably recommend.

Surveys of communication often produce information which is seen as bad news. They can be a dispiriting experience for the chief executive, who may secretly fear that this is a reflection of his or her leadership ability, rather than a syndrome which affects almost every organization that has people in it.

Internal research can be an albatross around senior managers' necks. They began the survey in earnest, hoping that it would help settle some of the debates among senior colleagues by providing something more than anecdotal evidence. When the results come out, however, there may be concern about the findings, scrutiny of the methodology and apprehensiveness that information will leak out either to colleagues in other companies or to competitors.

Most of the issues that internal research will highlight will have to do with senior management and leadership style within the organization. If you take on responsibility for conducting internal research, and go off and do it on your own, using your own resources or an outside consultancy, you are unlikely to make many friends. If senior management's first real involvement in the project is listening to the presentation of the final findings, their responses are less likely to be constructive.

Findings can be resisted, and management's defence mechanisms triggered. It is remarkable how, in a presentation of the findings, senior managers suddenly become experts in research methodology, asking questions about statistical validity, phrasing of questions in the questionnaire, individuals selected for interview, five-point scales and false positives. Resistance to uncomfortable findings is expressed in questions about the way the research has been conducted. The findings are then talked out of court without any real discussion or acceptance of their validity, and any hope of commitment to action disappears.

The prime objective of anyone conducting internal research should be to create a sense of ownership among those who are involved in the survey. Research is a means to an end, and recommendations will only be acted upon if some commitment to change has already been created. Commitment only comes out of a sense of ownership, and that ownership can only be created if the target groups have a chance to participate and to guide the process.

When conducting internal research, then, it is useful to divide a project into two strands:

1 The content of internal research, for technical issues such as whether to use qualitative or quantitative techniques, interviews and/or discussions or a questionnaire survey, census versus sample and the selection of a representative group of interviewees.

2 The process, including such issues as who should be involved in managing the project, how the commitment of senior management can be gained, and how resistance to findings can be anticipated and reduced.

In conducting an internal research project, it is important to separate out these strands. It is far better to have a series of presentations to discuss methodology at the first stage, and to flag up emerging issues and suspicions at the second, as a way of warming up and preparing the management group before the final presentation.

How an internal research project is conducted is itself a major communication. For this reason it is often a good idea to pay close attention to what you call internal research. 'Staff attitude surveys' as a term too often gives the impression that it is management scrutinizing employees, rather than that the whole organization is under review. Using the term 'employee survey' gives a similar impression, and reinforces senior management's tendency to see all problems as being at the lower end of the organization. Similarly, 'communication audit' reinforces the notion of communication as a functional task, with researchers and interviewers being viewed in much the same way as accounts departments view the annual visit of the auditing team. British Telecom calls its rolling survey 'Care', and the Automobile Association calls its questionnaire survey 'Talkback'.

One of the positive messages that can be conveyed if the survey is conducted properly is that this is a major demonstration of management's willingness to listen. People are willing to give their views honestly if they believe that some good is going to come of it. Without commitment to feedback and to change, people can feel manipulated, resulting in suspicion and lack of cooperation.

Creating ownership of the project among those who will need to carry it forward to implementation, calls for senior managers to be involved in the project from the beginning, through a project steering group. This group usually comprises representatives from operational and support areas chaired by a senior manager who acts as project champion and as a link with the board.

The role of the steering group is to:
● manage the day-to-day running of the project;
● determine the detailed project plan;

- provide advice and guidance on internal points;
- agree the selection of interviewees;
- input to, and agree, the design of the questionnaire for the quantitative research;
- act as a sounding board for the conclusions and recommendations.

When carrying out a staff survey, good communication is essential. The maximum number of people can be encouraged to participate by informing them in advance of the survey, its aims and what is expected of them. This can be reinforced by including a letter from the managing director explaining the importance of the survey and asking for their participation.

Managers need to be well briefed, since staff will probably turn to them if they have queries. Briefing managers can also help to overcome suspicion or potential apathy.

The key communication to staff about a survey is the questionnaire itself. It needs to be carefully prepared, designed and tested to ensure that it sends out the right message to employees. Clear instructions, and careful design and layout of the questionnaire, help to ease completion for the respondent and increase the numbers returned.

To ensure the correct interpretation of the questionnaire data, and to allow for the investigation of any apparent anomalies, it is sometimes useful to conduct group discussions to probe identified areas. This may take place in cross-functional groups of 10–12 people, to gauge the strength of feeling behind particular issues, reasons for attitudes held and the likely feasibility of recommendations.

Feeding back

The act of asking questions also creates expectations. Research of this kind is a contract: you ask people to tell you what they think; they have a legitimate expectation that you will take note of and act on what they tell you. A commitment to survey work entails a parallel commitment to good communication, not just of the results but also of the action to be taken in response to those results.

Feedback is a great way of starting a debate, of inviting explanation and understanding of apparently contradictory findings. It is even better when line managers start posing some of these questions to their own staff – What does this mean for our team? How does it show up for us? What can we do to solve the problem? This is one of the most useful ways of allowing the team and the manager to pull back from their day-to-day relationship, redefine it, set some new rules and start again.

In one organization the single finding that most struck the board was that 70 per cent of people did not feel they could say what they thought without some fear of retribution. It was that finding alone that caused the company to invest time and effort in running feedback sessions.

In running a feedback session, the danger is that managers may go through the data, bar chart by bar chart without discussing the significance or implications of them. They tend to rate themselves against other departments as not having done too badly. However, successful sessions focus on having the team first look at what some of the issues are in their communication. Feeding back results and then immediately asking for suggestions on how to improve communication is an invitation for a list of at best, bright ideas which might not be implementable.

In some organizations, teams suddenly asked to contribute their ideas start to throw out suggestions which they have not thought through but which are suddenly found on the flipchart as a list of actions to be implemented. Getting groups to talk about what they see as some of the issues and to discuss their opinions before exploring solutions is a wiser way of running the sessions. It also requires managers who have been trained to facilitate sessions, especially where the survey has shown that managers do not listen to the feedback they get from their staff.

In a task-focused organization, once realization that communication has to be improved takes hold, there is a temptation to begin developing new initiatives. A survey has now been completed for three months, people are impatient for results and want to see what senior management's reaction will be. Senior management are not in a position to react well, since they have some inkling of what the problems might be but probably have more questions about what the data is actually saying.

The feedback sessions do two things: they fill the gap quickly in that they start to provide feedback; and they start to identify actions and create ownership of them, without which senior management can do little. These sessions are not just to fulfil an implicit commitment to tell people what the survey shows; they are themselves signals of a new way of communicating. Organizations have used the sessions as the inauguration of team sessions to look at issues and problem solving within the team itself. While the first session may be about communication, the next may be about problems that are affecting the team.

The temptation is to run off and start doing new things. In one organization, at the end of a mission statement process the chief executive declared: 'We want honest and open communication in the organization.' His colleagues suggested that, rather than launch some new initiative, they should ask themselves the question, 'What do we already do that suppresses open communication?' The board had no trouble identifying what had prevented open communication from happening – not giving people the opportunity to talk, labelling information unnecessarily as confidential, verbally punishing people for voicing their opinions, etc. The new effort then went into removing what had suppressed openness, rather than into new, and misdirected, initiatives.

'What does it mean?' not 'How did we do?'

While asking people internally about their experience of communication is obviously important, care needs to be taken in interpreting what they say.

A board of directors were receiving feedback on an attitude survey and becoming increasingly dispirited by the results, although the scores they had achieved would have delighted other organizations. The reason for the disappointment was fairly simple: they had embarked on a quality strategy which needed strong upward communication, a high degree of knowledge among all departments of each other's activities and strong lateral communication. What they had, not untypically, was an organization where communication was mostly downward. Lateral communication was virtually non-existent, and, where it did take place, relied upon informal contact among senior managers. Comparing themselves to the norms told them that they had reasonably good communication; comparison with their business strategy revealed that they did not have the communication processes in place to succeed.

Comparing the scores that one organization may have achieved with those of other organizations in the same country, or even in the same industry, can be misleading. Again, the question should not be, 'How did we score compared with other organizations?', but rather, 'How do we measure up to our own aspirations and objectives?'

A pitfall of the employee attitude survey is viewing it as a scorecard. In an American oil company, the worldwide employee attitude survey is coordinated out of the USA, with each country participating and responding to questionnaires tailored to their local differences. The results flashed up to senior management show the UK lagging behind, say, Italy. The UK chief executive's major problem, as he sees it, is to increase his scores before the next European executive committee meeting.

Use research as a mirror

The importance of internal research is that it holds a mirror up to the organization. There is no Richter Scale of communication, and the issue is not how well the organization scored but whether it has the kind of communication that helps it to pursue its strategy. The value of conducting internal research is that it brings people to an awareness without triggering their defences – it gives you a chance for education, not accusation.

Right now, you could predict 60 per cent of what research in your organization would show. In any organization where people live and work together, the following findings will typically emerge. These seem not to be a function of any particular organization structure or culture, but more a reflection of human nature.

Typical findings
- The grapevine is most used but least preferred
- Most people prefer communication through their immediate boss

- People are more interested in information about their own immediate work unit
- Managers want more information while at the same time complain of being deluged with paper
- There is a reluctance to speak openly within the organization
- Employees want more involvement
- There is a preference for being asked rather than being told
- Management style is a major contributor to poor communication.

The best use of research is to open the debate by asking, 'What does all this mean?' What does it mean, for example, when people say that they want communication from their line manager, but also feel that receiving communication direct from the chief executive is more important and glamorous? In periods of change, people want to hear from more senior managers – perhaps because their own managers are not sufficiently in the know.

What does it mean when employees report that their favourite form of communication is face-to-face meetings but that they also like to receive communication on paper? Surveys usually show that there is a dislike of a cascade or deluge of paper. What this meant in one organization was that although meetings were conducted face-to-face, they were used to diffuse risk among colleagues, and memos were gathered and filed as protective evidence for when the inevitable rocket came from above.

What does it mean when the survey results say, 'I see the corporate video quite enough' – when on closer inspection it turns out 'enough' means 'never, thank you very much'?

One review of communication showed that employee ratings of team briefing were high. It was only during the feedback sessions with teams that it was discovered that the team's definition of team briefing was very different from that of management. The team believed that the briefing was there to give them management propaganda, while they had a cup of tea and a break. They valued the sessions not for the information, but for the chance to catch up with their colleagues and take a break from work. Those briefings which were conducted at the beginning of a shift rated particularly highly, and conversation and involvement were high, as workers filibustered to delay going back to work. Similarly, briefings held at the end of the shift tended to be rated as 'giving just enough information' – enough to get away quickly to get the bus home.

A recent acquisition that had been integrated into the organization reported that its most used channel for communication was the in-house journal, and that it received very little information from the grapevine. This bucked the trend from the rest of the organization, which showed that most information was gathered from the grapevine. Why was it that this part of the organization had an apparently positive score – it did not rely on the grapevine as much as did other areas – and did this mean it was free from the negative spin that the grapevine tends to put on communication?

On closer inspection, and after further discussion with people in the organization, the acquisition seemed to have been integrated in name alone. While this part of the business had shared the same site for many years, there was so little contact between it and the rest of the business that there was no informal network to feed communication. On closer inspection, the high ratings attributed to the internal newspaper were signs of people avidly scanning information trying to glean some sign of their fate.

Holding the mirror up to managers

One of the most interesting sections of a survey is where managers rate themselves on their management skills and are also rated by their employees. Both of these ratings are compared in turn with what managers and staff see as the ideal management style for the organization (see Fig. 6.4).

In feedback sessions managers laugh ruefully over the fact that all their colleagues rate themselves so unrealistically highly, before the truth sinks in that they too have rated themselves too highly. Managers almost universally see themselves as open and available, while their staff have quite a different view. 'My door is always open' is a typical comment from such a manager – employees report, however, that they never go through the open door.

210

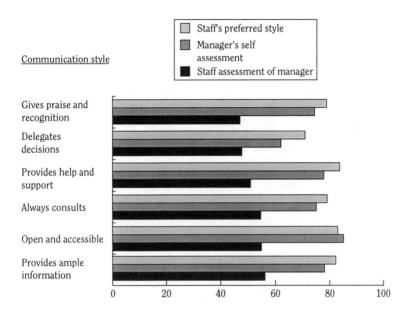

FIGURE 6.4   Contrasting perceptions of managers' communication style

Why is it, for example, that managers rate themselves modestly as two points behind the ideal of management style, while their staff rate them in the mid-50 per cent range? When this question arises in a group, it is easy for managers to admit that yes, on Monday mornings they can be consultative, but as pressure builds they tend to become more and more directive. This is a useful way of holding up the mirror as opposed to playing on the fear of managers that their scores will show their departments in a poor light.

What is interesting is that managers usually rate themselves highly on task-focused skills – giving instructions, checking progress, keeping on target, and control. They tend to give themselves a lower rating on the whole issue of explaining, setting the context and giving feedback. This fits in with the manager's perception of his or her job as telling people what to do and ensuring that they do it.

An organization that is pursuing quality needs managers who facilitate and explain, who create understanding of different parts of the system and how it fits together, give clear directional objectives and provide regular feedback on how the team is going to achieve them. Skills are based far more around relationships – of creating involvement and discussion among team members and facilitating their creativity and ideas – rather than around giving instructions. Figure 6.5 shows that the typical reasons for contact between manager and staff member are focused on giving instructions and checking tasks. When the survey comes out, even where managers are highly rated for task-focused skills, these may be the wrong skills for the new role of the manager.

Lurking behind the question of 'How do you rate your manager?' is the unasked question, 'What is the role of the manager?' It is quite possible for a manager and a staff member to rate the manager with exactly the same scores – the manager seeing that as someone who gives instruction and ensures they are carried out that he or she is a good manager, the

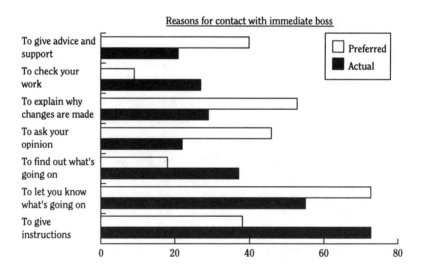

FIGURE 6.5 What staff want from their manager, and what they feel they get

employee, having a different perception of the role of a manager, sees that he or she is a bad manager. There is no common ground for debate, since they have different criteria to begin with.

One of the questions that is always asked is about the role of middle managers. Middle managers brought up in the traditional way in the old school may have skills and attitudes which are no longer thought appropriate to the new style of organization. The impulse from the top is to go round them, get rid of them, or try to train them to get it right. One way of using research is to hold up a mirror to the senior or middle managers so that they begin to explore why some of the anomalies arise in people's perceptions of them.

The fallacy of employee attitude research is that employees know what they want. When asked what information they want to receive, people tend to say they want to know everything about everything. They also say that they are tired of being deluged with irrelevant paper. They may ask that only relevant information is passed on, but jib at anyone else presuming to decide what it is they 'need to know'.

EXTERNAL AND INTERNAL RESEARCH

Increasingly, organizations are seeing research as a means of integrating an outward-looking attention to the market with the internal focus of the organization. Rather than separating external market research and internal employee research, the two can run in parallel and reinforce each other.

Tracking studies are used externally to continually feed in the reactions and assessments of the market, and there has been a move to increase the frequency of internal research and the rate of feedback from employees.

Typically, questionnaire research takes place every two years within an organization, with the exercise being used to benchmark, and then track, progress. Companies now want more frequent and less cumbersome ways of keeping up-to-date with issues and attitudes, and the increase in frequency has meant finding more flexible ways of assessment than the questionnaire survey.

Research is being seen not as the biennial inspection of the dipstick, but as an instrument for the corporate dashboard, providing continual feedback that allows greater responsiveness. The term 'communications audit' conjures up the visitation of independent outsiders running checks on policies and procedures, and while an outside view may help remove some of the internal cultural blinkers, continuous assessment needs to be pursued internally.

Research is a continual process within BT. As well as the annual CARE survey, it researches specific initiatives via eight-weekly interviews with around 800 BT people. The Leeds Building Society has a quarterly programme of questionnaire research which allows managers to get employee reactions to a range of initiatives. First Direct feeds back regular results from customer research and employee research to its staff.

While companies are tracking both employee attitudes and customer attitudes, the information is only useful if it is shared throughout the organization. Peter Chadwick, a continuous improvement consultancy, studied 300 companies in Britain, France and Germany. Eighty per cent of companies reviewed monitored customer satisfaction, but only 20 per cent made the information available below middle management.

While customer service departments and sales departments may have access to regular customer feedback, it is not unusual to find that other departments do not receive that feedback. Organizations that are focused on the customer, spread the information around and include it as a regular feature of team meetings. BUPA Health Services, for example, feeds its quarterly feedback from its customers to its staff, who then use their team meetings to discuss areas for improvement and ways of raising satisfaction.

To make the best use of both internal and external research, as the raw material for teams making improvements, requires better under-standing of how teams communicate and how to get the most out of team meetings. The next chapter looks at communication in teams.

CHAPTER

7

Communicating in teams

I n *The Wisdom of Teams*, Jon Katzenbach and Douglas Smith (1993) make the case for teams forcibly:

> Managers cannot master the opportunities and challenges now confronting them without emphasising the team more than ever before. The performance challenges that face large companies in every industry – for example, customer service, technological change, competitive threats and environmental constraints – demand the kind of responsiveness, speed, on-line customisation, and quality that is beyond the reach of individual performance.

A team represents something greater than the sum of its parts, and by playing to each member's strengths more can be achieved, more ideas can be inspired and more fun can be had than by individuals working alone.

The last few years have seen attempts to combine individuals in teams, create closer bonds of cooperation and greater job satisfaction to solve problems and improve processes. The team provides a safe setting to come up with the ideas, and the support of the team is more likely to allow greater creativity.

The amount of knowledge and information that needs to be mastered and transferred is rapidly outstripping the ability of any one individual. The team provides a useful means of allowing individual strengths and expertise to be pooled, and specialized information to be shared for the benefit of the team as a whole.

Equally, the range of qualities and skills required of the modern manager grows longer every day. While it may be impossible to find any one individual who embodies them all, a team goes a long way towards combining the best balance of necessary attributes and qualities.

A team can build up a collective store of information, experience and expertise which can be preserved and handed on as members depart and new members arrive. It is a force for institutionalizing knowledge and for continuity, and represents one of the best means of creating and sustaining change within an organization.

The composition of the team, the chemistry between the individuals, how they interact and how their roles and approaches complement each other are all important to getting the best results. When setting up in the UK, Nissan paid great attention to the composition of the teams working on production, and to the role and attributes of the team leader. Having the technical ability to do the task was not enough; team leaders also had to have the skills to make the most of their teams and use the team to get the best out of individual members.

Usually on the production floor, the team's composition may be an accident of history, rather than the result of careful selection processes. People who work together on an assembly line, for example, may have joined the job at different times, and their selection will have boiled down to their ability to perform the assigned tasks which the job involves. The team that gets together for a meeting may simply have been the first eight people at the head of the queue for jobs one day.

People have at least two roles in a meeting, as Dr Meredith Belbin observed: their functional one as production manager, or service engineer; and their team role as the one who comes up with bright ideas, or structures lines of enquiry, or appeals for common sense.

The focus of team meetings has been on the first of these roles, the bringing together of individuals who share functional responsibilities, to focus on a task. Except for off-site team-building activities, or specific training courses, the second role of the team member – what he or she brings in terms of outlook, and how he or she interacts with others – tends to be ignored. Anyone who has been in a meeting, however, will recognize that a great proportion of its success is affected by the chemistry, the interaction and the relationship between individuals.

In the same way as organizations are having to go into the relationship business to deal with customers, so they will also have to learn to understand and manage the relationships within their teams, in order to use the teams as a tool for competitive success.

Team meetings are the forum in which individuals come together, the place that helps or hinders their interaction and determines how the team's energies are channelled. They offer a variety of ways to arrange teams, a range of formats in which people can come together, and a gamut of techniques to provide information, stimulate thinking and unlock the creativity of the team's members.

The attraction of communicating in teams tends to vary with a company's underlying feeling for the value of teams, and why people are brought together in teams in the first place. Is it a convenient and time-efficient way of repeating the same message to the maximum number of people at one time? Is it a way of creating greater team spirit and identification between individuals, a way of giving individuals companions to talk to, a means of creating logical and discrete process owners, or a way of generating more innovative ideas?

There are often confused and very different perceptions within an organization about the purpose of team meetings. At board level, for example, the aim behind team meetings might be to create a flow of creative ideas for improvements within the company. At middle manager level, the focus might be on simply passing on information, and avoiding the use of meetings to raise old and familiar complaints. At first-line supervisor level, the desire might be more to identify and solve day-to-day problems that keep cropping up. The difficulty arises when the board looks forward to a feeding up of ideas that never seems to materialize, the middle manager complains that the information passed down is not interesting or entertaining enough to hold the team's attention, and the first-line supervisor bemoans the fact that she never receives feedback from above on her team's recommendations.

Meanwhile, employees are confused by the mixed signals they receive about the purpose of, and the rules for, team meetings. They are invited to raise matters of concern to the team, yet when they want to discuss pay, grading or safety issues they are cut off and told that discussion of these subjects is inappropriate, even though the team feels they are burning issues.

Where there are failures, problems or breakdowns, these are not always due to the team briefing system, or whatever variant of it has been implemented. Team briefing as a system is fairly straightforward, and there are a great number of organizations who have continued to use it in its classic form, or have adapted it slightly to their needs. Where organizations have reported failure of team briefing, the failures are often reflections of their own organizations' cultures, and over-optimism in hoping that the system would solve all of their problems. As a system or framework it cannot alone address or overcome basic cultural issues inside the organization or fundamental attitudes to communication with employees.

The culture of any organization refracts communication and bends any formal communication process. This is why you find as many passionate advocates of cascade briefing as you do those who have been disappointed and frustrated by their experience of it. A couple of examples of different cultures and their reaction to briefing illustrate the point.

A large diversified organization, with many management tiers and geographical locations, decided to adopt team briefing as a means of addressing its communications problems. A long-established company, it was attempting to become more marketing-led, and it was widely felt that its overly bureaucratic systems were slowing down its responsiveness. Team briefing was seen as a means of quickly communicating down the management chain, and of bypassing bureaucratic paper-based systems. Ironically, their experience was that, after an initial honeymoon period, the system assumed all the characteristics of the bureaucracy it had set out to avoid.

Managers, uncomfortable about their roles as communicators, and used instead to dictating or supervising tasks, were uneasy about risking a loss of status by failing as team briefing leaders. Rather than speeding up the communication process, a Catch 22 situation emerged whereby managers hoarded information to ensure that they could fill the full one hour set aside for their team briefing without lapsing into embarrassing silences.

Similarly, employees, unused to being consulted, and brought up not to question their managers, were reluctant to engage in real issues within the briefing, or to ask more than the politest of questions. This was exacerbated by a cultural issue of the organization that asking questions or raising real concerns would be viewed as a 'career limiting statement'.

A young high-tech company with an informal culture felt that its fast growth required a more formal means of ensuring consistent communication. Its adoption of a cascade briefing system took place against a history of 'corridor communication', informal meetings and a fairly flat hierarchy. Although in a period of vast change the grapevine had begun to take on more power in the organization, the introduction of formal briefing sessions tended to make people more self-conscious, and the more structured meetings tended to reduce interaction and make employees more of a passive audience.

Many organizations introduce team briefing or cascade briefing without taking account of the rules that govern attitudes and behaviour within their own organization. If this is not done, any briefing system introduced will take on all the characteristics of the communication problem it was designed to solve.

Having a common, clear understanding of the aims behind team meetings, and of what they are expected to achieve, is an important first step to making teams work to the advantage of the company. A second step is understanding how the different elements of the meeting need to be balanced to achieve the desired aim.

The manager who starts a meeting with a blistering attack on the poor performance of the team, demands to know who is to blame for escalating absenteeism and then appeals for creative ideas to help solve a problem dear to the manager's heart, is unlikely to unleash the creative potential of his or her team. Similarly, bringing a team together to discuss and understand business issues is likely to be undermined by reading out long lists of instructions, 'while I've got you all together'.

Figure 7.1 shows how different formats of team meetings can be used to achieve different objectives.

The team meeting role

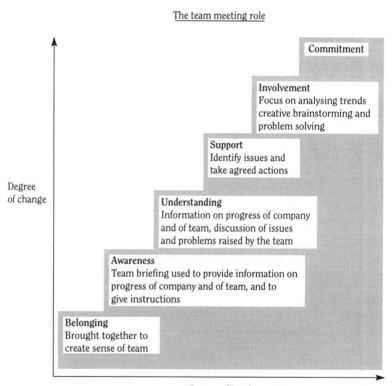

FIGURE 7.1 Team meetings can be used for different objectives, and their formats developed to encourage greater participation and involvement

Team meetings can be used for any, and all, of the following:
- giving instructions, reminding people of procedures and regulations, and alerting them to problems, issues and complaints
- providing information about developments, work-related issues, background, news and developments
- seeking reactions, opinions and responses to particular issues that the organization is considering
- stimulating discussion and greater understanding of issues affecting the organization, and creating greater support for the business strategy and actions being taken to implement it
- involving team members in problem identification and solution.

At their most basic, team meetings involve getting together for between half an hour and an hour on a regular basis, usually monthly. The leaders at each level talk to their teams and give them an update on how the company and their own area is doing, so that all employees are kept informed by their immediate supervisor on what is relevant to them.

In communication surveys, employees rate their line manager as the most important channel of communication. People also say they prefer face-to-face communication, and they like to receive information in groups so that everyone hears the same messages and gets to hear each other's comments and questions. Team meetings can be used to strengthen the role of the team leader, and the relationship between the leader and the team.

In terms of managing change, the most important skill for the manager in communicating is the ability to put things in context and explain the reasons behind changes and the intended benefits.

One of the rules of thumb of team briefing is that 70–80 per cent of the information should be 'local' items, with the remaining 20–30 per cent being information passed down from above. This emphasizes the importance of allowing time at each level to discuss and understand information, and time for preparation for each line manager, as a significant part of the local information will be developed by him or her.

However, many organizations are finding that team briefing has had limited success in getting information down the management chain.

Making briefers into victims

One of the problems of team briefing is that it relies upon the passing down through the line management chain of the baton of information, with little opportunity to investigate, flesh out or challenge the messages being passed. This passing of the baton continues down the chain until it meets the point of impoliteness. White-collar areas tend to be much more circumspect and careful about probing a piece of information, whereas blue-collar areas tend to be more direct, not to say brutal, about testing information.

The message is cascaded to the point where it is challenged. The person who is challenged has not had the benefit of probing and discussing the information with his or her boss, so he or she is unlikely to be able to answer any questions or elaborate too much on the bare bones of the brief. Without the ability to explain and elaborate, and to make it relevant to the team, the team leader can add no value, and is reduced to denying any responsibility for the communication, staying in with the team by denouncing the information more vehemently than they have done.

One manager was responsible for running a team briefing for lorry drivers. He felt that they were loners by nature, and at their best alone in the comfort of their cabs out on the road. They disliked being brought together to listen to a manager, and they had to be brought in at the weekend, on overtime, to attend the briefings. However, the company had identified communication as a key issue, and was willing to invest the time and money to make it work.

When the manager began to read from the prepared brief, he was quickly halted by questioners asking for clarification and explanation of some of the points. It became clear that the manager could add nothing to what was written on the page, and the drivers demanded to know why they couldn't just take a copy of the brief and read it for themselves.

The manager felt that he had been placed in a difficult position, and was left feeling bruised and aggrieved by the process. Similarly, with so much reliance on the extent and the style of the core brief, it was a bad day when, with his team assembled expectantly around him, he opened the briefing pack to see the immortal words 'There is no core brief this month', with 45 minutes to fill stretching before him. It is not surprising, then, to find managers adversely affected by the process, but still keen to get something out of it.

What are some of the other pitfalls that can reduce the effectiveness of team meetings?

1 *Lack of clarity at the top*: the 'management speak' used to formulate the messages in the core brief can be misunderstood by those putting it together. If these people lack clarity about the messages, by the time they reach the end of the management chain messages have become impenetrable.

2 *Lack of translation*: the failure of local managers to set overall messages in a local context often results in the core brief being seen as both remote and irrelevant to the local job.

3 *Management style*: various forms of heavy-handed 'management style' can inhibit the team and prevent it from getting involved in the team briefing process. Responses like 'Yes, well, anybody got any sensible suggestions?' are guaranteed to limit the extent to which people want to get involved.

4 *Disowning the brief*: managers can be guilty of distancing themselves from the core brief. The 'don't blame me, this is what they have told me to tell you' approach immediately undermines the credibility of the core messages and usually means that the manager will not bother to set the core brief in a local context or add any local information.

5 *Information is power*: many managers still consider that employees should come to work to do as they are told. The increasing emphasis on cost control, customer service and quality all point to much greater empowerment of employees. However, managers may believe that what employees need is a kick in the pants instead of dressing things up in a 'caring and sharing way'. Many managers feel uncomfortable with what they interpret as a dilution of their traditional, hierarchical power.

Those on the shop floor are automatically thought of as the customers for any team briefing process, but it is often middle managers who seem to get the least information. They find themselves wrong-footed by those below them who are well informed via other routes, such as their union shop steward or the grapevine.

6 *Chinese whispers*: the classic distortion of messages as they are passed from layer to layer, with little opportunity for discussion and amplification.

7 *Limited feedback*: senior managers can often be disappointed with the lack of response they get from those further down the management chain. You can often hear the cry: 'But I am telling these people all this information and nobody is passing anything back to me!'

Information both down and up the management chain is perceived to disappear into a black hole. No one is clear how far the message got before it disappeared, or where feedback is supposed to go, who is supposed to deal with it, how and within what time-frame.

8 *Lack of review*: quite often team briefing is introduced and then left, and initial enthusiasm soon wears off. Few organizations take the time to review their team briefing process to see how much success or otherwise it is having.

9 *Timing*: where team briefing takes place at an inappropriate time such as over lunch or late in the afternoon, participation will be limited. People soon get 'hurry up' signals from colleagues and learn that it pays not to say too much. The opposite of this applies where briefing is held at the beginning of a shift, for example, where the team may stall in an attempt to put off the evil hour of returning to work.

Even where managers at local level fail to translate core messages, at least they are delivered intact to most parts of the organization. However, in the absence of any translation and setting of context, those messages when they do reach the bottom often have little meaning or relevance. This inevitably reduces people's ability to make any useful contribution to the team meeting, resulting in a lack of feedback upwards.

Most practitioners of cascade briefing systems know that, while the system is not perfect, it is preferable to the alternative of making no real provision for communication. However mechanistic the process becomes, it at least provides employees with more information than they had in the past, and acknowledges, to whatever extent, their importance to the organization.

Why is there such a gulf between the realization that communication is important within teams, and the ability to establish satisfying forums for communication?

Part of the answer is in the number of different agendas team meetings have to accommodate. The board wants a means of keeping everyone up-to-date on company issues, educating their people about changes in the market, and putting actions in the context of a changing market. Local managers want their staff to understand how their individual area is progressing, and how they can improve things. The team itself wants to spend the time addressing its own local problems and getting some actions implemented. An individual team member may want to use the forum as an alternative to staff consultative channels for raising a specific issue.

All of these agendas jockey for time and attention and need to be balanced. Frustrations can arise when a top-down approach to communication collides with a customer-focused, bottom-up approach, where the employee is the customer for communication. The top-down approach is based on the belief that everyone is entitled to receive information on the company's direction and progress, and that they should receive a single consistent message. Team meetings may provide information which may not be of interest to the team but in which senior management believe it *should* be interested.

The struggle is for consistency within an organization that has different people and different needs. The pursuit of core briefing is based on a production line approach to communication. The desire for uniform standards means that a single core brief has to be read out, with some local tailoring and additions. This tends to reduce the team leader to an automaton, and managers complain of being used as messengers, in a way that undermines their relationship and credibility with their team. Worse, the production-focused approach to communication assumes that uniform delivery of a message is possible, let alone desirable.

Inconsistency is almost inevitable. The aim should not be to eradicate it, but to accept that it is inevitable and to encourage feedback in the session to check perceptions and to fine-tune the communication in response to feedback.

The starting point for organizing team meetings has to be the needs of the customer at the lowest level of the organization – the team itself. The starting point for communication should not always be simply what people want, but what the organization needs from them in terms of attitudes and behaviour to make the strategy work. In team meetings, however, there does have to be a greater focus on what the team wants. Without responding to how the team wants to run its meeting there is no meeting. Involvement is not mandatory and cannot be forced.

The limiter on team meetings is the level of energy and involvement among the team. When that is absent, when proceedings are turgid and the brief makes little sense, everyone is disappointed; no one, including the team leader, wants to be there and few want to return next time. To raise and maintain energy levels, team meetings have to be seen to be valuable *to the team*. The team's immediate interest is in finding ways of being more effective and reducing the day-to-day hassles of its job, and if these are not addressed the team tends to question the value of the meeting.

Most team meeting structures rely on team leaders at each level to exercise judgement on what information will be relevant to his or her team, and what issues should be raised for discussion in the meeting. The ability of the team leader to make those judgements, to relate to, and work with, the team, are central to successful team meetings. Yet there is a continual debate within organizations about the amount of filtering and information blocking of which managers are guilty.

The fear at almost every level is that messages are being blocked, filtered and omitted. Team leaders, however, will claim that they are not filtering information: they are tailoring it to the interests of their team and leaving out what is not relevant. However, without a clear understanding of the context and implications of the message that is supposed to be passed on, how can a team leader make a judgement about its relevance and importance, beyond the groans he suspects such an issue will prompt within his team? Handing on the message may be seen as a time-efficient way of distributing information, but without discussion and understanding even this basic approach is fraught with problems.

Conflicts in the system may be resolved on the hoof, with the team leader having to mediate between two different customers and two different views of the role and value of team meetings.

At some point in the hierarchy, a team leader will be caught between two 'customers': senior managers who see the team meeting as a means of delivering messages from above; and the team itself, who wants to use the time profitably for its own issues. Team leaders, left to themselves, solve the problem by suppressing the brief or the team discussion, or calling two separate meetings – one for the brief and one for the team's issues.

One way of resolving the problem is for everyone in the chain to understand that the process as a whole is designed to satisfy the needs, both short-term and long-term, of customers throughout the organization.

What information?

The aim of the process is not simply to produce as efficiently as possible a series of messages tailored to different levels and audiences. There are easier ways to distribute information, via more neutral media. The aim is to use team meetings to strengthen the links between the team leader and his or her team. The translation of information helps to make links between the levels, and forces leaders to think through what the messages mean, but the relationship between the team leader and the team is paramount.

People enjoy meetings when they get something out of them, either by solving a problem that annoys them from day to day, or by having their views aired and listened to. The task-related information rarely excites them – it is usually the team leader's ability to maintain energy levels, and to involve people, and the cross-conversations between team members, that makes the session worthwhile.

Raising people's horizons is necessary, but it is not always something that they ask for. They will tolerate a small amount of non-local messages if the rest of the meeting is useful in addressing their local problems. Interest in wider issues depends on creating discussion and interest in their immediate issues. The core brief rides on the back of local issues – too heavy a core brief and the horse dies beneath the jockey.

In the same way that the best way to delight the customer is to give him or her the product for free, the best way to capture the interest of a team is to talk only about *its* problems – that is what bothers them on a day-to-day basis. Even if there are no solutions to be found, the discussion may be therapeutic in the short term, and may put problems in perspective.

However, the temptation for the local team leader is often to jettison anything but local issues and concentrate on the problem solving that teams find valuable. The danger is that this will reinforce parochial short-term views and the habit of teams looking at the priorities of their local box, rather than taking the longer view across the company and across the lateral business process of which they form part.

When people ask for information only on immediately relevant issues it is based on the assumption that the bedrock of the company is sound – the business is moving along and their jobs are secure. If team leaders base the balance of local to wider issues on the same assumption, however, they will find themselves in a corner. If you have shrunk the focus of the team meetings to a task-focused, local point, the communication process will be inadequate to cope with any fresh demands on it.

Difficulties will inevitably arise when the environment becomes turbulent, the volume of orders drops and the rumours of redundancies start. That is when the interest of the team will suddenly expand, and when they will look for information and clues to the significance of what is going on. They will start scanning the newsletters for references to the company's financial soundness, and will turn to the grapevine to answer the bigger questions about how the business is doing.

Similarly, when the company starts to focus on lateral business processes, and greater cooperation between departments, the lack of awareness of other areas and their priorities will make it all the harder to create cooperation. Team leaders may find themselves fielding complaints from teams that arise from the very lack of mutual understanding that the leaders have helped to create.

People want to know how they are doing personally, how the team is doing and how the local unit is doing. They want to know the direction that is being taken at local and at organizational levels, and they want feedback on progress against objectives.

For the local team leader, there has to be an understanding that it is in the interests of the team to have a perspective that includes local and business-wide issues. For the board, it means that only by creating interesting, local problem-solving meetings can they generate interest in wider issues. They cannot afford to overload them with non-local information.

Communicating in teams

Managers running team briefing sessions can simply hand over dilemmas to their staff. The manager in a distribution warehouse was running a team briefing for his people. He had a number of issues on the agenda he wanted to discuss.

1 Racking damage – there had been a significant investment in new racking, and the forklift truck drivers were colliding with it and not reporting the incidents.

2 Unsafe driving – the manager was a forklift truck driving instructor and took standards of safety in driving very seriously. He was worried that slipshod practices were starting to creep in.

3 Volume – to meet the pressure of customer orders, drivers needed to be faster and more efficient at shifting pallets.

As he finished dealing with each of these items, his message was clear: 'Pull your socks up and improve your performance'. In discussion after the meeting, it became clear that all three issues were facets of the same problem: (a) to meet the pressure of customer orders, drivers were going faster in order to hit their volume targets; (b) they were taking short cuts on the safety of their driving practices; and (c) inevitably there were collisions with the racking. Simply telling staff to improve their performance and to treat each of the issues as a separate item denied the basic problem, which was how to strike the best balance between safety, meeting volume targets and protecting the investment made in the racking. At the next meeting, the conversation revolved around a shared agenda of how they could best balance the demands of safety while meeting customer demand and providing good service.

Organizations have different perceptions of the role of teams, varying ideas about the role they want them to fulfil, and therefore different formats and structures for communicating with them. These tend to be a reflection of the current stage of development of the organization is in, and the degree of compliance and contribution it therefore needs from its people. Taking each of the stages of development a company goes through, it is possible to see what types of team meeting are typical of each stage.

Figure 7.2 shows the characteristics of communication at each stage.

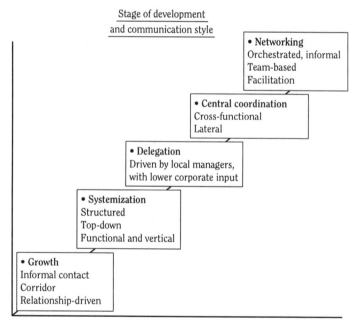

Stage of development
and communication style

• Networking
Orchestrated, informal
Team-based
Facilitation

• Central coordination
Cross-functional
Lateral

• Delegation
Driven by local managers,
with lower corporate input

• Systemization
Structured
Top-down
Functional and vertical

• Growth
Informal contact
Corridor
Relationship-driven

FIGURE 7.2   Team meetings will be used differently according to the stage of development

A first step to getting the most out of team meetings is to agree what is the problem they are designed to solve. Different formats of team meetings are appropriate to different stages of development, and to different degrees of involving team members.

The following section looks at how team meetings are used at different stages of development, highlights the problems that arise and possible ways of adjusting team meetings to solve those problems.

Growth

At the outset of an organization's development, people will communicate relatively informally. While the company is small there are likely to be only a few small teams, with members passing from team to team, with little formal separation, and everyone getting involved in teams designed to update or progress particular products or manage individual clients.

Team meetings may be relatively informal, and with less distinction between work time and social time meetings will take place both inside the organization and outside in social settings, over a drink or a pizza, called to meet a need rather than at a set time.

Characteristics
- Team members represent all functions
- Each member updates the others on his or her activities
- Immediate feedback and reactions
- Focus on customer feedback and product developments or problems.

Systemization

As the organization grows, and the number of people outstrips informality, informal systems are not enough to guarantee the flow of information the organization needs. There is mounting frustration at the lack of consistent messages, and the dominance of the grapevine as the main means of finding out what's going on. Information seems to be limited to the favoured few, and the selective feeding of the grapevine and the intrigue of who is a rising star and who is falling creates a clamour for systemizing communication.

The introduction of management disciplines may include the introduction of team briefing as a consistent way of transmitting information face-to-face. It may not in any way compensate for the loss of warmth, spontaneity and speculation that the informal system offered before the organization got too big, but it does offer, as a minimum, a mechanism for the monthly dissemination of consistent information to everyone.

The purpose of team briefings is to ensure that everyone in the company is regularly informed about the company's and their own unit's performance, and that they receive regular information about the company and about the changes within it. They ensure regular face-to-face updates, and also ensure that the manager who will be responsible for implementing any new policy or procedure will be the one explaining it. They provide one of the few opportunities for the entire organization to pull back and take a wider view of what is going on in the individual's own area and in the organization as a whole.

Team briefing is primarily about downward communication. Its aim is to create local understanding and awareness of both corporate and local issues. It does not aim to involve teams in discussing or resolving team issues. Its focus is on presenting information to the team, and discussing it. Traditionally its focus has not been on upward communication.

The role of the team leader focuses on presenting the core and the local briefs in an articulate way, and being able to translate information into the language of the team to make it immediate and relevant. He or she may also need to be able to lead discussion and to field questions.

The term 'team briefing' tends to be interpreted as a team's passive acceptance of the information that is delivered by management, and tends to be viewed by the team as a vehicle for management propaganda. While it will represent a means of distributing information in a structured way to an organization which has been starved of information, it will also bring with it a disadvantage. The company will now be structured vertically, with briefing organized within functions; and based on passing information down the company. This will serve to reinforce the separation between functions, the role of management at the top as the thinkers and those at the bottom as the doers, and the threat of conflicting functional objectives and 'boxitis' of the organization.

Characteristics
- Structure created to distribute consistent core information
- Uniform meetings structure
- Employees attend to hear information and key messages
- Focus is on presenting, not involving
- Mandatory standards of presentation and timing
- İnformation is communicated vertically, within functions
- Core messages decided at the top
- Primary aim is to provide information.

Decentralization

Once some form of regular team briefing is in place there is a foundation that can be built upon. The drive towards greater decentralization, however, changes the nature and focus of team briefings. In a decentralized organization, the way the meetings are organized, and who attends, become almost more important than the content. The structure is used to engineer a sense of belonging to the local unit, and to feed back on local progress and successes.

With the weakening of central control over the format and content of team briefings, individual areas start to make changes. Now, as autonomous units with clear responsibilities for producing visible results, local managers want to involve their people in making a greater contribution, in greater productivity, more effective cost control and better service to customers. However, the team briefing practices they inherit are too focused on corporate information, which takes up valuable time and is a diversion from the local issues which are now much more important. Team briefing is too passive and is seen as too much of a one-way flow, a talking shop, where the staff put up with hearing news of little immediate relevance to their work.

Local units have now developed their own identities, and anything from the corporate centre is not welcomed. Units are now being charged for the services of the central corporate communications department. Local managers become increasingly restive about paying for the dubious privilege of bringing their people together, again at a cost, to be bored by irrelevant information. They believe they should be asking their employees more about issues which they see arising, and that time could be better spent talking about areas more immediately relevant to the staff.

The corporate messages are seen to conflict with local priorities, and the style of language and its tone seem increasingly at odds with what local managers are trying to achieve. Attempts to wed the information style received from above to that developed locally is increasingly felt to be confusing employees with mixed messages. Thus, now freed to take autonomous action, the local management team decides to re-cast the team briefing system as a two-way forum for updating its staff on local issues, progress on performance and problems that need to be addressed. It re-names this forum team meeting, not team briefing, to emphasize the different approach being taken, and to signal to its people the desire for two-way conversation and contribution.

Corporate messages are now, in effect, competing for time and attention, and with no local manager willing or able to translate corporate issues into local relevance, the corporate overlay of communication is left to atrophy while the local focus swells to fill employees' horizons. The corporate centre now has little control over the standards of communication, and since the business strategy now clearly states that local managers must manage their own people, communication is seen to be a local responsibility.

The clear message is that the local division now has the delegated autonomy to get on with the job, unshackled from corporate bureaucracy. This brings with it a promise from the local management team that it will listen to feedback and address any problems which are raised.

The main difference between team meetings and traditional team briefing is that people will have a greater opportunity to get involved and contribute ideas.

The aim is to develop an organization where there is a free flow of information and ideas, and those who are actually at the sharp end get all the information and support they need to do their job. Team meetings allow downward communication of information and upward feedback of ideas or issues that need to be resolved to improve effectiveness.

Team meetings are designed to be run in order to get contributions and ideas on service, quality, efficiency and cost from the group attending. In some organizations the aim of these sessions is to draw out ideas and suggestions from the teams themselves and to agree action which is practical and achievable.

Characteristics

- Local division originates brief, with little corporate input
- Focus is on improving performance and highlighting failures
- Meeting includes feedback on production faults, customer complaints, sales opportunities
- Questions and comments are fed back up to the local management team.

The creation of separate businesses from the monolithic British Rail in 1992 was a classic example of how a newly created, decentralized organization shifted the team briefing system inherited from its earlier stage of development.

InterCity became the flagship passenger business of British Rail, with a staff of around 30 000. Like the other discrete businesses created with it, InterCity owned its assets and was accountable for achieving its own financial targets.

InterCity shifted from a traditional focus on operational efficiency to a focus on closeness to the customer. It aimed at providing a high quality of personal service, with time and attention devoted to providing service face-to-face with customers. Since passengers' quality of experience depends on how staff deal with them, it was important that employees understood how they affected passengers and colleagues alike. The company also had to ensure that everyone working for it understood what their role was in the new company, its importance and how they fitted into the company, and played their part fully.

Historically, British Rail had talked with its staff through a formal consultation procedure and a variety of mailings, videos and written briefs. It had also used a conventional team briefing system, with limited success. To get message down the line, face-to-face, would take 16 weeks.

The sheer scale of the organization, in terms of job type and geographical spread, worked against staff having any sense of their role in the business. In such a huge organization the messages seen as important to the top management were frequently seen as totally irrelevant at the front line. Moreover, local managers felt bypassed by these information channels as senior management at headquarters tried to address the front line directly.

The process often demoralized briefers as they were used as a conduit for passing on messages, with little opportunity to discuss them. With little ownership of the message or process, naturally they resented having to pass on messages that they did not understand.

People identified with their local team, and this was seen as the way to connect them to the business as a whole. InterCity needed to concentrate fully on developing meaningful face-to-face meetings between teams and their leaders.

On board the train, it was important to create a sense of team across the different functions that together made up the passenger's experience of the journey. The senior conductor, on-board services catering staff and the train driver needed to work together as one team. Different members of the team used to have different reporting lines, with the senior conductor reporting in to operations. Now the whole team has the same reporting line, and although the senior conductor has the primary role of ensuring the train's safety, he no longer reports through operations.

A senior conductor described how life had changed both for him and the passengers. Given the time, the power and the technology, he thought that he was making life much better for customers and was gaining much greater job satisfaction for himself.

The train now carries mobile phones enabling the staff to obtain information about what is happening on the track and, where there are problems, to organize solutions. Staff feel more in control and better able to take the initiative if they have more information. When they do not have that information they can do little else but bustle past irate passengers, and take whatever complaints are levelled at them.

Pagers alert the conductors to news, delays at destinations, or security alerts at stations. The conductor reported that using the public announcement system on the train deflated 75 per cent of the complaints of lateness. Most people's irritation in the past had simply been because they did not know what was going on and no one had the courtesy to inform them. Now that the on-board team had the information themselves, they could allay concerns and improve the service they provided.

Being empowered to take whatever action was required to solve customers' problems was the single greatest change. The senior conductor now has the power 'within reason' to spend money on solutions. Recently a train had been significantly late, and he had been able to phone ahead to order 120 taxis for passengers. Typically, the senior conductor would offer refreshments if things were running late, and would alert stations to connection difficulties that passengers might have.

The on-board team is just the most visible team to the passenger, and other functions are similarly organized into teams. The logical extension of this when trying to provide better customer service is the Customer Action Team. If the train is running more than an hour late, the senior conductor will phone ahead to a station who will then board booking clerks and station staff onto the train to act as additional ticket collectors and problem solvers.

InterCity faced the communication needs created by the structural shift from centralization to decentralization. It not only had to reorganize its communication around a new identity and a new sense of belonging; it also had to organize itself to reflect its chosen strategy of leading with the quality of its customer service.

While InterCity restructured its team communication to suit its then stage of development and chosen strategy, other organizations go on to find that nothing stands still, and that any solution carries the seeds of the next set of problems.

Their decentralization seems to go too far. Different local management teams increasingly go their own way. Employees see little of the corporate group, and are encouraged to keep their eyes on the local scene. Different formats for team meetings start to appear within the same business, as individual departments take up the autonomous right to run their own meetings as they see most appropriate to their own teams.

Unease about communication begins to increase. At the corporate centre, all synergies of corporate membership seem to have disappeared – there is no apparent advantage to being part of a group, and local negotiation of pay and benefits becomes very price sensitive.

Inside the local businesses, different departments begin to complain of different approaches to communication. There is no common agreement on treatment of confidential information, and one area's junior managers know more than another's senior managers. Individual directors are seen to be giving different messages, and internal competition is fuelled.

Functions that are involved with internal customers across the company, such as personnel, finance and IT staff, begin to complain about the very different messages coming out of each area. There is increasingly a lack of knowledge or understanding about what other areas are doing, a reluctance to cooperate or collaborate, and an over-emphasis on local parochial interests.

Team meetings spend too much time focusing on the achievements of their own area, and complaining about the failure of other areas to support them properly. Colleagues from other departments who share the same lateral process are called in to account for their failures and given a hard time that does little to foster future cooperation.

Individual teams elect to drop the update on the organization as a whole, preferring to spend more time on their own problems and finding solutions to them.

The local management team begins to complain that the messages that it wants passed to the employees are being filtered out, and that it is receiving no feedback. It resolves to restructure the team meeting process to give itself more voice in the meetings, and begins to investigate how colleagues in other divisions have approached the problem.

Central coordination

As part of the corporate centre reasserting influence, the corporate communications department looks at creating a structure for team meetings that will meet both corporate and local business needs. The issue is not one of control, or of policing uniform meetings and formats, but is one of creating frameworks that allow for individual tailoring.

The main drive behind team meetings is to halt the fragmentation of the company, both at group and local level, and to knit together different parts of the company to create a more cohesive whole. Since the way team meetings have been run to date has aggravated fragmentation, they are now seen as a way of engineering relationships, and as a source of 'corporate glue' to help bring together the wider organization more effectively.

To this end, new levels of team meetings are created, making the local management teams members of teams that include colleagues from other businesses and colleagues from the corporate centre. These are held quarterly, as are the new team meetings for colleagues drawn from the same functions within the business, particularly marketing, finance, IT and personnel. Quarterly team meetings are also held between the account directors responsible for customers who buy, or could buy, from a number of businesses within the group, to create greater coordination and to explore further cross-selling. New product development (NPD) opportunities form the focus of NPD team meetings, where teams with NPD responsibility in the businesses come together.

Each local unit identifies a manager with responsibility for team meetings, and a network is formed to manage the communication flow through team meetings. Responsibilities are negotiated between the centre and the local business on the principle of what employees need to feel they belong to and what information they need. The role of the centre becomes one of monitoring standards and outputs, and of providing information in an accessible way.

It is agreed that local board directors and senior managers should see themselves as part of the corporate family, and their team meetings should include information from the centre, on group developments, and updates on specific issues within other sister businesses.

Within the businesses, local managers are allowed to develop agreed ways of running their meetings, with, for example, white-collar meetings being run differently from blue-collar meetings, and within a given time period. The areas of information relevant to each level and function are agreed and signed off by the local management team, and a communication policy on issues such as openness, confidentiality and areas of information is agreed and communicated.

Characteristics

- Restructure of team meetings to pull the organization together and consolidate the business
- Creation of senior managers' team meetings across divisions, and functional team meetings which pull dispersed functional colleagues together
- Creation of product development team meetings and customer team meetings
- Individual divisions tailor team meeting to local needs within a common framework and consistent standards
- Team meetings aim to create involvement and a greater sense of belonging to the whole organization
- Content includes updates on other divisions and corporate activities for senior managers within the businesses
- Tracking research is used to measure effectiveness.

NETWORKING

As customers become more demanding, and competition stiffens, the ability to respond to individual needs increases. The organization aims to devolve decision-making power to the level closest to the customer, and this requires greater sharing of resources, pooling of ideas and cooperation between local units. Information, knowledge and ideas become the currency of the business. Familiarity with the customer's industry and market becomes vital to tailoring a solution, and sharing knowledge of competitors' products internally among colleagues becomes increasingly important. The value of employees' expertise and knowledge is recognized, as the depth of knowledge and the ability to identify customer needs and relate them to the company's capabilities become competitive differentiators.

As knowledge and skills are recognized as valuable assets, the networking of knowledge among employees, and the sharing of experience and ideas is pursued as the way to build the business.

As it becomes less and less easy to capture the variety of information needed to deal with customers, or to apply existing expertise to new areas, the sharing of knowledge has to be done more and more through bringing people together. Cross-functional project teams are established to solve particular customer problems. The functional specialists in each unit start to get together to share ideas, pool resources, and explore more efficient cooperation. Individuals find themselves in a range of team meetings – new product teams, customer teams and project teams. In addition to coming into regional or corporate headquarters, they find themselves invited to additional team meetings hosted by colleagues in other units.

The reporting lines into headquarters become weaker as clusters of units start cooperating together on a regional basis. A cluster manager is appointed, to coordinate and lead the cluster's activities. The unit managers begin to specialize in functional areas, to provide stronger local expertise, and a more balanced cluster management team. Cluster manager teams are created, and meetings are established where cluster managers can mix and exchange ideas and best practice.

From the comparative stability of the past, the organization becomes more fluid, with individuals moving between teams according to the need of the day, and the temporary role they fulfil. Team meetings are far more frequent, and more fluid. As teams come together for relatively short periods, and have to cooperate early in their short lives, it becomes more important for members to share similar values and attitudes before they meet each other.

The role of the team leader is one of facilitator, helping the team members explore and resolve issues. The team may well include customers, suppliers and intermediaries, as well as external specialists and advisers. The leadership of the session may be rotated between members, and a team member in one team has to be ready to act as team leader in another. Skills become vital, as these teams demand the ability to help the group identify and analyse problems, and develop creative solutions.

Characteristics
- Shift is towards problem solving and innovation
- Team leader is a facilitator
- Structure is a matrix of teams
- Team meetings used for discussing issues and ideas generation
- Customers and suppliers attend meetings and are part of the team
- Senior managers attend to find out what is going on in the market
- Teams meet in more informal, social settings
- Individuals will be temporary members of many teams at different times.

The Automobile Association

The Automobile Association set out to create a team ethos among its people and then further developed its use of teams and team meetings. When the AA reorganized in 1989, it reduced the number of supervisory and management levels from 10 to 4, to produce a flatter structure, and focused on the team concept and the team leader as the main channel for communication. With so many field-based staff, the only way it could ensure face-to-face communication was to introduce a team concept.

All 5500 staff in Roadside Services were formed into teams, and a massive team-building exercise entitled STAR (Successful Teams Achieve Results), was undertaken for managers and team leaders, with follow-up local events for managers' teams of patrols and telephone operators.

The organization went through a phased approach to creating a team ethos, with the belief that the first-line supervisor would be the hero of the 1990s. Once the organization had been delayered to give shorter chains of command and communication, the next step was to begin creating teams from among the loners inside the organization.

Patrols were formed into teams of around 25, led by a team leader who became responsible for the performance, motivation and well-being of the team. Similarly, in the emergency operations centres, a team culture was established and was then rolled out throughout the organization.

Incentive schemes and payment systems also had to be re-designed to encourage people to start thinking and operating as a team.

The AA took a conscious decision to use the team leader as the pivot for both upward and downward communication. But devolving the ownership of communication to the front line also means that account-ability has to be devolved too. Team leaders had to be empowered to act directly on some of the messages from team briefing, to initiate ideas themselves without fear of retribution.

The initial focus of team briefing was simply to overcome some of the logistical difficulties. Patrols are by nature loners, out on the road on their own in their patrol vehicles, linked to an operations centre by data terminal. The creation of a team ethos and better communications have become all the more important since voice contact over the radio is much less frequent as jobs and instructions are generated via the data terminal printout. Since many patrols are not natural team players, the AA had to carefully integrate them into a team culture that did not threaten the personal qualities needed by someone who works largely alone.

Team meetings were held at a variety of locations, some at motorway service stations, others in the cab of a relay transporter pulled off the roadside. They are run by the team leader, who, in a reflection of the traditional culture, is called an inspector.

Keeping team briefing concise and relevant has also been critical to its success. The AA's experience indicates that the briefing should cover only key issues for information or debate, and that the content should be at least 50 per cent local, with the local team leader, rather than head office, being seen as the driving force. However, to give team leaders a national input, they do initiate team briefing sheets every two weeks which contain short national messages.

The next stage was to make team briefing a more two-way, interactive process. The teams received information about what was going on elsewhere in the organization, but used the opportunity of their team meeting to identify issues that could be addressed to improve their working life. This could include, for example, the kinds of tools and spares which patrols carried, and the best mix of vehicles that should be in the team.

A further development was the introduction of a process which built on team problem solving. The AA introduced what it called 'Teams in Action' where teams spent time, as a group, tackling their own problems. Inevitably their own problems – what worried them, annoyed them and stopped them from giving service – were problems for the organization too.

This aimed to take the amount of time spent on local problem solving much further. Teams are encouraged to feed questions, queries, complaints and solutions up the line. Queries are answered within 24 hours, and solutions and best practice that could benefit other teams are communicated on a national basis. Using Teams in Action techniques, teams have solved problems from 'How can shifts and annual leave be scheduled?', to 'What's stopping us from doing our job better?' They report that nine out of ten problems are resolved locally, and that the director of operations knows what the front line are saying and thinking within six days, rather than six months.

Teams in Action is a problem-solving technique employed by the whole team, facilitated by the team leader. Whereas team briefing had relied on the presentation skills of the inspector, there was a much greater demand for facilitation skills to focus the team on effective problem solving.

In order to introduce the programme, 250 team leaders participated in a three-day training course on how to facilitate group problem solving and discussion.

Having provided the structure and the skills to cooperate in teams, the AA moved to ensure they were not rewarding individually selfish behaviour.

An existing incentive scheme was not serving the needs of the new organization. Under this system local managers received a bonus based on monthly cost savings on the budget in their area, to share with their staff. However, the reward scheme ran counter to the objectives of the organization since in busy months, when patrols were busy rescuing members, they used up their budget and were penalized, while in easy months, when there was less to do, they built up more savings. The reward was not geared to the effort, and the incentive was to do less, not more. A staff opinion survey demonstrated that people valued recognition for their contribution as much as they valued the money. Alongside the existing 'Patrol of the Year Award' there is now a 'Patrol Team of the Year Award'.

Senior managers were keen that the incentive should be shared by the teams in which people now worked. Under a system called 'Team Work Pays', most people were rewarded on the *overall* performance of the organization as well as on a set of local performance measures on which teams competed in leagues.

The system demanded a lot of regular feedback to the team in terms of their performance. Each team had to be told every month whether it had met the criteria laid down.

The AA's drive to use teams when people are working alone is unusual. The aim is to create team spirit, and use it to enhance each individual's work. Rather than the team leader alone having to motivate people individually, team spirit and team pressure help team members to motivate each other.

Lyons Tetley

Lyons Tetley introduced team meetings into the company to address some of the communication issues identified by its research. Although individual parts of the business were already running some form of team briefing, and other areas had experimented with and then dropped them, there was no company-wide process with consistent practices or standards. Communication tended to be dependent on individual areas and individual personalities. The aim behind the team meetings was that they would be regular, structured meetings which, although they had a common style and needed to take place within a common time period, could be tailored to suit individual areas and individual needs of the company.

The objective was to create a company-wide system with meetings being run in roughly the same week, so that once the process was established team members could 'swop' meetings and attend those of their internal customers and suppliers, and their colleagues in turn could do likewise.

Rather than following the cascade process of team meetings, the process was designed to build on the strengths of local management communication and to make the local manager the hero of communication. The aim was that the local management team would receive information from above (from the board) would get feedback from internal customers and colleagues laterally, and would get feedback from the teams below them. All of these taken together would help them to form the content for their local communication.

Another key principle behind the team meetings was that it was a circular process, so that communication did not just happen for a single period over a month but was continuous, so that continuous communication would support continuous improvement.

Different teams used their meetings for different purposes. Some used them to exchange information, others to identify problems that were getting in the way of the team's work and to find some way of solving them.

The communication skills training that was given to the majority of senior managers was then extended to middle managers, supervisors and charge hands in operational areas.

Designing the team meeting process

Areas of information were developed at the centre, and individual formats for running team meetings were then developed with local management teams. This led in some areas to the development of the 'buddy system'. This was aimed at the specific problem of ensuring that the communication chain was not broken as it went from level to level. There were worries that individuals down the chain would bend, filter or block out certain messages, while there were also concerns by individuals on the chain that they would not be able to translate information coming from above well enough into a local context. In addition, some team leaders were nervous of taking up a more ambitious, facilitating role. In order to deal with all these problems it was decided to run sessions in pairs rather than as individuals. Thus someone who acted as a junior 'buddy' at one team meeting would go down to the next level and act as the senior 'buddy'. Each individual was assigned a specific role, either in terms of presenting information or leading discussion, and while one led the discussion the other had the responsibility of tracking actions and logging views.

As well as helping to build teams, and to position the team leader more strongly, Lyons Tetley also aimed to provide a local problem-solving session.

The final aim of the company was to organize team meetings laterally, whereby key business processes became the line along which communication ran. The first step was to ensure that information from the board flowed downwards, while local management teams developed more two-way communication with their people.

Customer-focused teams

The flaw in any team briefing process is that it perpetuates the hierarchical approach to communication, keeps people within their boxes and prevents lateral communication – which is increasingly what organizations need. Companies who established team briefing are now building on the system and changing it to a two-way process, where downward communication on objectives and direction meets upward feedback on what needs to be changed.

Membership of a team is one way of getting people out of their own immediate interests and taking a wider view of others' needs. A way of increasing commitment is to change the structure of teams. Instead of retaining the old way of organizing for the organization's convenience, companies create teams out of groups of people connected by a work flow, because, by definition, that comprises a chain of internal customers.

InterCity's creation of the on-board team is an example of this, as was British Airways' move to bring the flight crew together prior to boarding the aircraft. Traditionally, individual crew members assembled for an individual flight might only meet for the first time on board, as they were serving passengers. As part of increasing customer service, British Airways began assembling the flight crew as a team on the ground before the flight.

If teams are organized by the customer, they will have the customer in common, and communication will centre around the customer and external issues. If teams are hierarchically-based, what people have in common is their function, and the rest of the organization. Their internal problems and problems caused by other areas are likely to be the focus for conversation, reinforcing the 'us and them' syndrome.

Southern Electric used team briefing and their 600 team leaders to ask and then feed back on answers to the question, 'What are three things that drive customers mad?'

In the face of all the pressures facing both the NHS and the private health sector, the creation of GP fund-holders, and changes in the pattern of clinical care, healthcare providers cannot afford to continue in the way they have done historically. Now, with an increasingly complex environment, hospitals need to scrutinize their costs and change working practices to provide quality care.

BUPA Health Services has introduced extensive quality programmes in both its hospitals and its homes for the elderly. It conducts regular quarterly feedback research with patients and residents to track how well it is satisfying their needs and expectations, and to identify what other needs it can address.

Traditionally, in a hospital different areas were organized vertically for operational efficiency. Nurses looked after nursing, focused their communication primarily within the wards and concentrated on the well-being of the patients. Theatre staff concentrated on ensuring sterile, safe and successful operations in the theatres, and catering staff concentrated on producing attractive and nutritious food. Each area focused on its own task and concentrated on its own definition of operational excellence. Teams were organized around their functional and operational tasks, and more communication took place within those teams than between them.

Things were naturally different from the patients' point of view. They travelled through the hands of everyone in the hospital, and from their beds saw the housekeepers cleaning their rooms, and catering assistants delivering food to the ward, while the nurses moved about providing medical care.

In the continued effort to provide quality of care not just to their own professional standards but to the standards of each patient, the hospitals began to organize themselves to reflect the patient's experience. The definition of the team, and the relationships between the teams, also shifted.

In the hospitals, the emphasis on care for the patient has meant creating lateral rather than vertical teams of nurses to focus on patients. The introduction of team nursing means that a patient will be cared for by a team that combines a nurse from the ward, one from theatre and another from outpatients, the three clinical areas a patient will typically pass through. This builds better bridges between the ward, theatre and outpatients to smooth the patient's way and to ensure better cooperation and coordination throughout the process.

The teams will look at ways of improving the experience for the patient, and from the patient's point of view. At the changeover of shifts, where the outgoing nurse briefs the incoming one, the handover is now done at the bedside, so that the patient can join in the discussion and add or correct any of the briefing. Patient records are not retained by the nurses but are deemed to belong to the patient and are kept in the patient's room, locked up if preferred.

Nurses are central to providing service both to consultants and to patients. Nurses' training emphasizes the importance of communication, not simply for the smooth running of the ward but also to understand other areas within the hospital. Nursing is one part of a process of care in which the patient is involved; therefore there is a need for nurses, and others in the process, to understand how it all fits together.

The catering staff – ward hostesses and chefs – are also in continual contact with the patient and see themselves increasingly as ambassadors for the hospital. They need to be aware of the other factors affecting the

249

patient's well-being. Therefore there is a similar shift in this area from organizing for operational efficiency alone to finding ways of changing practices to accommodate the patient's requirements. Patients used to receive a tick-list menu on which they indicated their preferences for meals. When the catering staff discovered that patients believed their choice was limited only to what was on the menu, the catering manager started taking the menus around and using them as a prompt list of only some of the options available, finding out individually what each person wanted.

It is difficult for a patient to predict on the night before an operation how his or her appetite is going to be on the following day. As catering managers travelled the wards, they could spot the mismatch between food ordered the night before and the appetite of the patient who had placed the order. The practice of circulating menus to gather meal orders the night before was stopped.

Team nursing, and continuing communication between everyone who comes into contact with patients, or affects them, is aimed at continually improving the patient's experience and quality of care. It is not enough that each area individually provides a good service; how they all come together is at least as important. Team communication, both within the small teams and within the hospital or home for the elderly as a whole, is therefore all the more important.

There is a formal structure of sisters' meetings and ward meetings which ensure regular vertical communication, as do monthly departmental meetings within the unit. Using top-down communication alone, however, would not address the important issue of lateral communication which is needed for raising the quality of service, and in addition to monthly downward communication, and nurse team meetings, quarterly meetings put information and initiatives in a wider context and provide a channel for upward feedback. Some hospitals and homes unit managers run quarterly meetings for mixed groups of staff, to respond to feedback and reactions to initiatives that have happened over the preceding quarter or are imminent in the coming quarter. The advantage of a quarterly staff meeting is that it allows the manager to ensure that information is cascaded, allows time to put the task-focused department meetings into a wider context and gives staff from different areas the chance to meet up.

Matrons and their teams also ensure that 'bank staff' (regular, temporary staff) are kept feeling as part of the family, and informed of developments. Since patients do not discriminate between who is temporary and who is permanent, it is important to keep everyone involved.

There are a number of practical problems around cascading information. The clinical areas have a problem with scheduling, given the hectic pace. Catering and housekeeping areas suffer from similar constraints. Both sectors work in small groups and are on duty at different times of the day. They are busy all the time they are on site, and need to get away promptly at the end of their shift.

Some hospitals have solved the problem of organizing evening meetings, where updates are woven into a fairly informal setting where wine and nibbles are offered. This has the advantage of giving staff a chance to spend some unpressured time together, and to give nursing teams a chance actually to see each other and build some team spirit. It also means that there is plenty of chance for informal feedback about specific issues, as people feel comfortable enough to say what they think.

There are thus a number of lessons to be drawn from this use of team meetings: reorganizing into customer-focused teams; organizing communication laterally; coping with timing problems and shift patterns; and involving temporary or flexitime staff.

Organizations are increasingly fragmenting their workforce. Nearly a quarter of the workforce is now part-time, with 80 per cent of part-timers being women, juggling child care and domestic arrangements. It has been estimated that, on current trends, half the workforce will be part-time by 2003. The use of people for short shifts, job sharing, teleworking and staffing to match capacity to peaks and troughs in demand means that the traditional office setting where everyone is in the workplace at the same time is changing. Bringing people together will be logistically more difficult, and is likely to occur in some staff's own time. People value their own time more and more, and there will have to be an attractive reason to come in to work during this time.

There will be a shift towards the more informal, social team meetings for a number of reasons:

1 Organizations which, like General Electric, are looking to create a small business feel within large organizations, will shift towards the team meeting formats found in growth organizations.
2 The separation of task and relationship, and the concentration on the task, has worked against using the energies and creativity of teams. People's creativity tends to be freed up by the warmth of social acceptance and a lack of formality.
3 People like having fun, and will actually show up at meetings if they enjoy them. Ben & Jerry's fancy-dress days may be an advanced example of this, but even British human resource departments, hoping to attract attendees to their presentations, have started offering door prizes and raffles.
4 Business is about creating relationships and bonds. Social entertaining has long been a way of doing business at senior levels, and as the whole organization and everyone within it becomes part of the marketing and the competitive edge, more social events for staff will follow.

Team ownership of a segment of a chain of customers tends to give rise to team problem solving and team suggestions. However, there is a real danger in simply accepting that those closest to the problem know best how to solve it. They need to be given training in how to break down the symptoms of problems to discover the underlying cause, before going on to brainstorm possible solutions.

Equally, managers and team leaders need to be trained in how to facilitate the group so as to avoid the complaints about a problem deteriorating into a blaming session.

THE ROLE OF THE TEAM LEADER IN TEAM MEETINGS

Giving the direct line manager the responsibility for communication is a two-edged sword. Once the responsibility is devolved from some central function to the team leader, the organization is in the hands of that team leader – first, actually to run the briefing session when he or she is supposed to, and then to do it as well as possible. How well it is done naturally depends upon the individual skills of the manager. Those with good interpersonal skills and a good relationship with their staff take to it easily, but it is those most in need of improving their relationships with their people who tend to have to struggle most and are apt to cool off about conducting briefings.

Some companies address this issue by making the briefings as 'manager-proof' as possible. Briefing notes, if not complete scripts, are provided. Some companies even provide prepared overheads or videos. The good thing about these support materials is that they ensure a 'safety net' of communication quality below which the managers conveying information cannot fall. The unfortunate thing about using video, however, is that it tends to undermine the interactive intention of the briefing and the feedback process.

As a minimum, the provision of support media ensures consistency of message and a greater flow of information to employees. However, it does not solve the problem of the line manager's own skills and management style which continue to have a direct impact on the briefing session. The dilemma of providing support material is that the intention is often to minimize the impact of a poorly skilled manager, but in doing so it tends to undermine the manager's central role. At worst, this can result in a manager acting as a kind of cinema usherette, getting people in to watch the video and then ushering them out again.

The role of the team leader, and the extent of the skills he or she needs to possess, will depend upon which model of team meeting is adopted, and how ambitious the organization is in putting its teams to work.

There is no substitute for training of managers in briefing or broader communication skills. This does not simply mean training them in how to put on a video and conduct a question and answer session afterwards, but actually involves acknowledging the manager's wider role as a facilitator of the group. People need to be trained to run team meetings. These meetings represent a different game with different skills, and therefore require different skills in the player. Where these meetings often fail is that the players are applying old skills and old rules to a new game.

If the purpose of the meeting is primarily passing on information, then the ability to write succinctly, be able to chart up information, present clearly and use audio-visual equipment will be necessary. If the purpose of the meeting is to involve team members in innovative problem solving, more advanced skills will be needed. What does not work is launching out on the most fundamental form of team briefing without preparation and training, or intending to use team meetings for creative idea generation or problem solving and only providing team leaders with a three-hour training on the use of an overhead projector. A typical amount of initial training for anything beyond the role of highlighting the implications of data would be three days, with follow-up coaching and development of team leaders.

Figure 7.3 shows the range of skills that are needed at each step in the development of team meetings, which team leaders have to add to their repertoire as they develop:

- Present information
- Translate relevance
- Highlight implications of data
- Invite internal suppliers/internal customers
- Lead discussion of issues
- Clarify thinking
- Help to identify the real problem
- Facilitate problem solving
- Stimulate brainstorming.

Presenting information

Written and verbal presentation skills will help managers to translate and present the core brief in a way that is meaningful for their staff and to add relevant information that creates the context. Written information skills

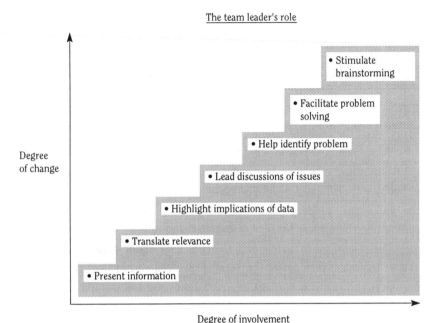

FIGURE 7.3 The range of skills needed by a team leader

allow much clearer formulation of core and local messages. Presentation skills will help to improve briefers' individual styles.

Using team meetings to encourage involvement, suggestions and a greater emotional commitment to the organization means creating a clearer understanding of the organization and the employee's role in it, but it also comes from generating a sense of ownership. That ownership requires the employee's greater sense of participation and involvement.

In terms of the skills needed to get the most out of meetings, there are three critical areas which are needed to avoid common pitfalls.

Leading the discussion of issues

Working with groups, who are traditionally used to being told what is happening and what to do, may be difficult at first. People will be familiar with, and understand, the rules of the old system. While they may want to be involved and to put forward ideas, they may be reluctant to do so for fear of saying the wrong thing, looking stupid in front of others or damaging their appraisal/job or career prospects. Their reluctance to get involved can only be overcome if they feel comfortable and at ease. The role of the facilitator is to allow the members of the group to feel safe to speak and to believe that they will be listened to.

Team members fear looking stupid: where they are not used to asking questions, they may fear being the first to do so. Managers may have difficulty in persuading people to make a contribution. When the 'rules of the game' are suddenly changed, people may be very cautious about committing themselves for fear of overstepping the mark.

The role of the team leader is to act as a facilitator during this time to ensure that each member of the team is involved and to elicit from his or her ideas and responses to issues which he or she has identified.

Clarifying thinking

A key point about running these meetings is that they should focus on resolving mainly *local* issues, and not becoming a complaints session about others elsewhere in the company or further up the hierarchy. Team leaders have to feel comfortable enough to help the team identify which issues affect the whole team and on which issues time can be best spent.

Facilitating a meeting means creating safety and comfort for members of the group to put forward their ideas. It involves making sure that everyone gets a chance to speak without fear of being put down, put right, damaging their job prospects or being made to look stupid in front of their friends and colleagues. Getting it wrong will mean some people will switch off, feel demotivated or lose confidence.

Underlying many meetings is a negotiation process in which each side advances and retreats from positions that are struck, and where, in the absence of agreed solutions, the person with the greatest hierarchical power forces through his or her position. To get the most out of the meeting the team leader needs to be able to create a sense of common purpose, as a basis for addressing real areas of disagreement and resolving conflict.

Team leaders can be uncomfortable in their role, and at the outset, before the team warms up, that discomfort can cause them to do precisely that which they know will cause conflict or switch people off. While they know they should be asking open questions to create involvement, under pressure they use closed questions.

Closed questions are posed often unconsciously to confirm the leader's position on a subject. These closed questions are seen as a manipulative attempt to force others into agreement. Ironically, having spotted, it believes, where the manager is trying to push it, the group then deliberately adopts positions and gives unexpected answers to foil the attempt at manipulation.

From the manager's point of view this simply looks like perversity and a refusal to cooperate productively. No wonder that meetings where people are allowed to give views and solutions have been described as 'herding cats'.

Team meetings can be extremely productive, however, once the causes of frustration have been identified. Managers who complain about how their own managers conduct meetings with them almost invariably reproduce precisely the same problems in their own meetings. More often than not these are due to lack of skills and awareness.

Helping to identify the real problem

The temptation in team meetings is to highlight problems and then invite the group to throw apparent solutions at it. The difficulty often lies in defining what the problem is. This is the vital step that is often missed. A group is not taken through the causes of problems, nor does it separate out symptoms and causes. Having identified that there is dissatisfaction, the team then throws solutions at its symptoms and apparent cause.

The net result is that poorly facilitated meetings generate shopping lists of demands and apparent solutions which, even if they are implemented, are unlikely to solve the problem that has been identified.

257

These lists of solutions are then fed up the organization to land on a senior manager's desk. The senior manager reviews these poorly thought through demands, and in frustration sends back the simple answer 'No' without any explanation. This in turn is interpreted by the team as a capricious rejection of a good idea, and proves yet again that despite the management rhetoric the team's involvement and ideas are not actually welcome.

The crucial point about making such a system work is the facilitation skills of the person running the session. It is in that meeting that the clear identification of a problem, and the suggestion and evaluation of a possible solution has to take place. The temptation, once the ideas are flowing, is to write them all up on a flipchart, thank the participants for their suggestions, ask them to 'Leave it with me', and then send the list off to the appropriate department. Managers who complain that they do not receive feedback on the team's ideas will often cheerfully admit that they knew at the time that the ideas they charted up were unfeasible and would never be implemented.

Organizations are learning to develop team meetings and find more productive ways of using valuable time. Team briefing can face competition from more exciting team meetings where people meet colleagues for more challenging and productive sessions.

Team briefing cascades communication monthly over a period of 48 hours. Organizations pursuing continuous improvement find this to be too infrequent and too unsuited to learning lessons quickly. Spreading information around the organization requires more frequent and more active contact.

Team briefing has been used to provide information on the progress of the company and of the team. Increasingly, team meetings provide this information, and then include discussion of issues and problems raised by the team.

In a further development, information about the company and the team's performance is circulated before the meeting, together with any administration and operational notices. The team meeting is used not to distribute information but to understand and discuss the implications of the information. Internal customers and suppliers attend, to lend their perspective, and the meeting is used to identify problems and agree actions to be taken.

Other organizations use both weekly and monthly team meetings for different purposes. Weekly team meetings focus on day-to-day operational issues, and on performance information and its implications. Monthly team meetings then focus on analysing trends shown by performance data, creative brainstorming and problem solving, with both external and internal customers and suppliers attending.

The change of the manager's role into that of a team leader, and the creation of team leader as an increasingly popular job title, reflects the sheer number of teams of which an individual might be a member – task teams, customer teams, project teams, key process teams, key supplier teams. Teams are one of the key ways in which a company mobilizes its people's talents to address change. However, they bring with them their own problems. Their sheer number, their competing claims on the individual's time resources and loyalty, the intertwining and competing lines of communication that link teams across the network, all work towards greater fragmentation and complexity.

Networks of teams can be used to their best advantage when there is a coherent management of communication that links the teams together. The next chapter looks at the need to manage communication differently in order to cope with increasing complexity.

Orchestrating communication

Organizations and individuals alike are beset with complexity, bombarded with information, inundated with initiatives and unnerved by uncertainty. The growing volume of information competing for employees' attention is confusing rather than clarifying, and frustration with how communication is managed is on the increase.

As the need for better communication increases at an accelerating rate, the problems that beset it multiply. The changing attitudes of the consumer, and the fragmentation of media, will have a major impact on how companies communicate with people at work.

Writing in the *Sunday Times* of 25 July 1993, Martin Jacques predicts the decline of the influence of television in day-to-day life with the phrase 'more channels, more choice – and less and less influence'.

> ... in the 1950s came television, the most powerful medium invented. It has dominated our culture for more than 40 years. But now, at the very peak of its powers, we can detect the signs of its decline.

Television symbolizes the idea of a mass, rather than individualized, society. The audiences are large and relatively undifferentiated. The viewer is a passive figure. Schedulers and programme makers are a powerful elite, determining the viewing habits of millions. Mass television is a hierarchical medium. But these are metaphors for how society was and not what it is becoming. Television is the leisure equivalent of the assembly line.

Time is at a growing premium: people will become steadily more choosy about how they use it.

The consumer is also becoming steadily more critical, more active, more independent, more discriminating, more powerful. There will be a growing premium on a more active relationship with the media. The spread of cable during the next decade will provide the conditions for interactive television. The distinctions between computers, telephone and televisions will blur, as these are hybridized to bring information into the home, whether as videos delivered down the telephone line, or children's books played via a compact disc onto the screen. The distinction between working and leisure time will narrow, and as a result people's use of time will become more complex and discerning.

People are increasingly becoming the target of a growing number of attempts by an increasing number of channels to communicate with them as consumers. The fragmentation of media, and the increasing bombardment by sellers using narrowly focused casting, will start to turn people off. People are desperately juggling different aspects of their lives – and a drive to simplify and get away from complexity will mean that they start to switch off to communication.

In order to make the necessary impression on customers, more people in more departments will want to communicate more ways through more media. With the media and technology becoming increasingly available, this is likely to turn any information super-highway into a communications traffic jam.

While society, and organizations within it, may be becoming less hierarchical, it is also becoming more segmented and individualized. Increasing amounts of information, products and services are creating greater complexity, while individuals seek greater control and simplicity.

Since consumers are employees, these pressures will be felt inside organizations. The increasing complexity of environments that organizations face, the increasing range of information with which they need to

261

educate their people, the wider range of criteria and enquiries that have to be satisfied among employees, the more diverse and segmented the audiences within the workforce, will all demand far more flexible and interactive media for communication.

While the role communication has to fulfil is becoming more complex, the environment in which it has to operate is itself becoming more complicated. A better understanding of the options open to organizations is all the more vital, if they are not to drown in their own proliferating messages.

People have higher expectations of communication, and as both consumers and employees they have greater access to the technology that allows them to select information. Power is shifting from the producer of communication to the consumer of information. The old models of communication do not help, and may hinder. A new model is needed, including:

- a different communication contract between employees
- greater cooperation between communicators
- the greater orchestration of communication
- the repositioning of the role of the communicator.

INFORMATION OVERLOAD

As the importance of internal communication is recognized, the danger of overload looms large. External marketing is increasingly about creating long-term relationships, not simply about broadcasting messages. As internal communication rises in importance, it threatens to inundate the employee.

Employees will be the targets for increasing amounts of communication competing for their time and attention. Each time a new product is launched, or a new business unit is formed, the amount of communication needed to keep everyone informed increases at what seems a geometric rate.

The strategy and implementation of internal communication seen from the producer's perspective masks the problems seen from the internal customer's viewpoint. While individual distributors of information see the employee as a finely identified target, the employee's experience is that he or she is under fire from all directions.

Fraternal Finance is a European financial services business, consisting of a network of branches, organized by region and with a central corporate headquarters. Employees within the company have been confronted on all sides by change. They feel themselves to be part of a successful organization and are optimistic about the future. However, the sheer number of initiatives happening around them is giving them 'initiative indigestion'. Employee attitude research shows that people have close links with their immediate team and with their immediate manager, but are more interested in getting on with the job in front of them than in taking an interest in the wider issues within the business.

Over the last couple of years the company has decentralized, with regional offices taking on a greater degree of autonomy in managing their local branches. Management teams have evolved at regional offices, and each region is responsible for its own personnel practices and training.

While there is a central corporate communications department, there are in effect a whole range of internal communicators competing with each other. The corporate communications department handles press relations, as well as the internal newspaper, the production of the corporate video, the organizing of the management conferences and the electronic mail network. However, at a regional level, there are team meetings, area newsletters and local training events.

The marketing department is also active in its production of information. Information on new marketing initiatives and new products is continually being fed to the branches.

Branch managers meanwhile complain of being swamped with information. All these individual communication initiatives which are separate and uncoordinated come together on the manager's desk. Each of the communicators is competing for the brainspace of the manager and his or her staff.

Confronted with over an hour each day of sorting through various amounts of paper, of being tasked with running team meetings with their people, showing them videos and explaining the corporate strategy, managers have to prioritize their time in order to fulfil all their tasks.

While they might be interested in the wider view of what is going on in the company, managers' immediate interest is in getting their job done. Their immediate loyalty, and more frequent contact, is with managers at the regional office, and so they tend to pay most attention to communication coming from them.

The manager sorts communication issues into three piles – one which must be dealt with immediately, which tends to be operational issues coming from the regional office; marketing information which provides an update of initiatives in other regions but which may also provide useful ideas; and updates on what is going on at the corporate level, copies of the corporate video and text of the chief executive's speeches. This final pile is kept for the manager's more leisurely moments, which are so few and far between that this is tantamount to binning the lot immediately.

From the internal customer's viewpoint, communication seems to be overwhelming and uncoordinated. Each of the regions is busily producing information which it is feeding into the communication channels. The marketing department is adding its information into the mix, and product areas are also feeding in information, requesting feedback on customer responses and ideas for new products. Added to this, the product managers are engaging in 'vanity publishing' – producing updates on their latest achievements and promoting their own favourite initiatives.

While the corporate communications department and the marketing department may have their budgets scrutinized in terms of how much they are spending on the production of information, operational areas have free rein to feed information into the network. While the cost of production may not immediately be visible, there is an obvious cost of consumption in terms of time at branch level.

The net result of this is information overkill at a local level, with communicators jockeying for attention and time, and creating an ever increasing clutter of electronic information and videos and brochures.

A common complaint is that operating units are on the receiving end of communication sent direct to them, without first being coordinated with other functional departments. This lack of co-ordination produces mixed signals, lack of coherence and competition for attention.

Departments at head office tend to be more isolated and less familiar with each other. The operating unit is the place where the component parts of the organization come together. In a relatively small space, where people are in constant contact, information between different areas is readily exchanged. At head office, functions tend to be more separate and focused on their own activities to the exclusion of other departments.

The assumption in the field is that departments at head office surely must be talking to each other, and that the lack of coordination they see day-to-day seems therefore baffling.

The first place where all the individual functional threads come together is on a manager's desk (see Fig. 8.1.), and it is his or her job to make sense of them. If the claims they make on his or her time, or the priorities they set, are competing or contradictory, the manager is the one who has to prioritize them and make them fit together. Managers may be unwilling to pass on information since it appears that not only do the

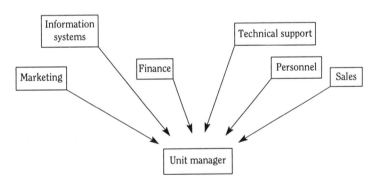

Where is the point of coordination?

FIGURE 8.1 Different strands of communication only come together when they reach the recipient

messages not match each other, but they have plainly been developed in isolation from each other. What they need is someone further up the line management chain to coordinate and match the communication so that it hangs together.

In an organization where information is closely guarded and where there are few communication channels, communication is simply transferred from the formal channels to the grapevine. Over-controlled, regulated communication stimulates the grapevine.

With deregulation, on the other hand, where there are many people with the means to communicate doing so, the result is clutter and competition for attention. If communication is not coordinated and orchestrated, the individual has to edit down the clutter to manageable levels using his or her own priorities. Those priorities are unlikely to match those of the organisation as a whole, and what passes through the editing process may not be what is most important to the organization.

Getting those functions who communicate together is important to avoid competition and clutter.

Why is communication uncoordinated?

Responsibility for managing communication is often scattered. Team briefing may be the responsibility of personnel, together with communications on pensions and hygiene and safety. The finance director may be responsible for producing the employee annual report, and marketing may be responsible for producing the in-house video and journal. Production may be championing a supplier quality programme, personnel may be spearheading an equal opportunities drive, while marketing and sales are launching new products or customer service initiatives. This is an inevitable result of having an organization divided into boxes, but one way of pulling them together is to have a group representing line areas and functions whose role is to integrate and ensure that initiatives are consistent.

The responsibility for all or part of internal communication can lie with corporate communications departments, personnel departments, marketing departments, IT departments, even the financial and legal departments, depending on the kind of organization and the status and recognized importance of communication. Sometimes this is simply an accident of history, sometimes the result of a carefully thought through strategy. It has been a popular pastime over the past few years for departments to argue over who should be responsible, or whether an entirely new department is needed.

It is worth remembering what happened to the central data processing department which housed the priests of the company's mainframe computer, and acted as the acolytes of computing power. The arrival of the desktop machine, and the networking of computing power, meant they had to become advisers and supporters to their internal customers, moving from control to customer service.

THE COMMUNICATOR'S ROLE

The need to orchestrate communication more will involve a redefinition of the communicator's role.

The typical corporate communications department has a number of people on its team operating at different levels. The director will act as a counsellor to the chief executive and to the chairman. The managers will act as technical advisers, craftspeople and distributors of information and messages through the organization. The department may be responsible for employee research, the internal newsletter, management conferences and the corporate video.

The production line approach to communication meant that the communications department was viewed as a department of production engineers – skilled craftspeople and wordsmiths who could turn out beautifully crafted messages on their communication lathes and then distribute them efficiently. The new demands on communication will mean that these same people will have to act as advisers and internal consultants, providing advice and setting standards for the range of internal communicators within the company. They will have to act as partners in the formulation of the business strategy, and counsellors in the translation of strategy into attitudes and actions.

For the moment, the corporate communications department is only one source of communication – and while there is a need for the management and orchestration of communication, no-one is currently fulfilling that role.

ORCHESTRATING COMMUNICATION

The debate about where the management of communication is best placed misses an important point – communication is already everywhere. It also misses a major threat – we are moving from a regulated communication environment to a deregulated one, where almost anyone can feed information into the system.

The debates about who should communicate with the employee rested on the assumption that there was a megaphone trained on the employee, and the only question was who should wield it. Controlling communication is largely a thing of the past. During the protests of Tiananmen Square, and the suppression of the Chinese students there, the students had fax machines with which they kept the West informed. The authorities might have been able to secure the radio stations, but they could not control individual fax machines. With the proliferation of media, and of competing communicators, the issue is not one of controlling communication but of orchestrating it to get the best result. There is a need for a communication air traffic control, which has an overview of communication activities and can advise on how best to avoid initiatives crashing into each other.

In a world where the ability and the need to communicate is proliferating, control is not the issue, nor is ownership of the function. The real issues is agreeing roles and responsibilities among internal communicators – choosing either self-regulation or confusing clutter. In a world of competing communication and clutter, where time and patience are at a premium, cleverer orchestration is needed. Collaboration between communicators is important not only to orchestrate communication, but also to share understanding about the agreed role of communication in the organization.

Wherever the formal responsibility lies, there will be no shortage of influences on communication from other parts of the organization. If internal communication looks uncoordinated from the customer's viewpoint, then for the person nominally in charge of communication the situation can be frustrating for different reasons.

Essential Service is a 24-hour computer services and support business, divided into three divisions, which are run autonomously by business directors within a strategic framework. There is a corporate centre which includes support directorates of finance and legal, personnel, corporate communications, and planning.

Logistically, internal communications is difficult. The organization has a flat structure, and people tend to work in teams, at customer sites and at different hours of the day. Staff are dispersed across a number of sites, and while involved on specific projects may not come into any of the offices or sites for weeks, if not months, at a time. Different teams of people are brought together for a particular project, and they will serve temporarily for that project under a different manager. There is therefore no easy or automatic cascade process by which line managers communicate with their people.

While internal communication has recently become the responsibility of the personnel director, it used to be the responsibility of the director of public affairs. She was very successful in raising the external profile of the company, particularly at a time when it was renewing, or tendering for a number of important contracts. She regarded internal communication as an outcrop of external public affairs, and her focus was on sending a continual flow of information out to employees.

She was particularly keen on using technology, and introduced a telextext system, using monitors in public areas and on some employees' desks. She also introduced update boards which were systematically changed weekly. An internal newspaper was created, with 8–10 issues a year. This carried a number of external news items which gave the company a high profile. Employees were given information on developments in the company and on new developments in products and technology.

Internal communication concentrated on the efficient distribution of information. The managing director and the directors sent out information about issues which interested and excited them but which were of little immediate interest to people at the bottom of the organization. The focus was on telling people what management thought they ought to know, rather than what they were actually interested in.

The director of personnel then took on the responsibility for communication, and saw a far greater need to use internal communication to help change the culture. While the company had been doing well, industry-wide over-capacity meant that the future was likely to be tough. Anticipating this, the company intended to reduce its cost base. The aim was to have teams looking closely at costs and at ways of working more efficiently and effectively together.

The personnel director believed that people who did not understand the wider picture would become resistant and disillusioned. He believed that there was a need for informed and committed staff who would take responsibility for their own areas. However, his approach was not characteristic of the rest of the board. They had different priorities and tended to be much more task-focused in their management style. They did not see communication as an investment, but as a burden. Communication on wider issues was seen as the heavy and interfering hand of the corporate centre.

Each business head had been given his own degree of autonomy. Financial considerations apart, each had been given the freedom to run his own ship as he saw fit. This meant that each business had hired its own personnel manager and its own external communications manager, believing that since their business was so unique only someone close to it could communicate about it effectively.

The personnel director was frustrated that while he had been given the mandate to improve communication, his chief executive clearly did not share his values, his understanding of what communication entails and the importance of getting it right. Each time he preached the importance of communication, the board tended to humour him and encouraged him simply to get on with the job. The chief executive relied on the personnel director to win round his colleagues on the board and to gain their approval to introduce communications systems into their autonomous businesses.

It is likely that, under a projected reorganization, new teams would be formed, and existing teams would take on new responsibilities or share responsibilities. In these cases, there would be a need to create and bond teams, to help them to move more quickly up the learning curve of their responsibilities and to increase goodwill and cooperation between teams across shared responsibilities. All of these would be hard business issues with cost implications, and all of which could be helped by improving their knowledge of each other and communication between them.

The personnel director believed that the central communication role should be one of coordination, ensuring the best linkage between the corporate communication channels and local communication initiatives. The centre's role should be to support, advise and equip managers to communicate more effectively. The shift should be from a model of the Public Affairs Director producing and disseminating information, to the communications manager as a facilitator and improver of the communication process.

The problems encountered by this organization are typical:

1 Communication is seen as the right of the business unit head. There is strong resistance to the idea of the corporate centre bypassing the business unit head to speak to his or people.

2 There are widely differing views about the role of communication and the responsibilities of communicators.

3 There are major shifts in the technology of communication which will affect the ability to manage it effectively.

4 Focusing on the employee as a customer means providing him or her not simply with the information the company wants to issue, but to making available a range of information which employees may access as they need it. This is a shift from a supply-driven approach to communication to a demand-led approach.

5 The shift from organizing functionally to organizing along key processes

is leading to viewing communication as a key process, and to organizing it to serve other processes.

6 The way people work within companies is changing, with more teleworking, and less contact with their office base or with an immediate line manager.

7 The creation of ad hoc teams, who work together for the span of a project before dispersing, is a trend which is increasing.

Negotiating responsibilities

Organizations are beginning to realize that information overkill is consuming precious time, creating clutter, creating mixed messages and exacerbating the media attack on the individual. Realizing the danger that their own employees will turn off, they will have to start managing the flows of information within the organization more sensitively. Organizations will have to orchestrate communication, to shift from having individuals competing in their communication to collaborating.

This is already being driven by the realization that time and patience to consume and understand information is at a premium, and that scarce resources need careful management. However, there is also the realization that individuals need different levels of communication at different times. They need both information to do their job and a sense of relationship with a wider whole. Communication includes elements of both information and relationship, and there is a role for a number of different communicators in different roles to fulfil the employee's spectrum of needs.

People need the day-to-day operational information to allow them to get on with their job, but they also need the wider context of where the organization is going, how trends in their industry are developing and how these may affect them in the future.

Equally, people like different kinds of contact, from the time-efficient meeting that allows them to complete a task, through to a relaxed social event that allows them to meet and talk to other people inside the organization. People have different levels of identification and loyalty – they feel part of their operational team at the local site – but also like getting together with colleagues from other divisions which form part of the same group. Putting these different factors together demands that all those with communication responsibility or access to employees get their act together to get the most from their efforts, and to get the most out of the time their employees give them.

Traditionally the barrier to this orchestration is the insistence by local managers that their staff need to know only local information in order to be able to get on with their job. However, as change starts to bite, and people start looking for a wider context and a greater sense of values, local managers find themselves wishing their people knew the wider context.

There is a communication role for each level of the management structure. While each employee might focus on local issues of interest to him or her there is a general need to identify with the organization as a whole, and to know where it is going. Dividing communication responsibilities means, for example, that the chief executive can create awareness of the strategy via a management conference. Understanding of the strategy, and creating support for it, could be taken up by the heads of the individual businesses working in management seminars to flesh out the implications of the strategy for the company. They could conduct their own conferences and stage roadshows and small group seminars for employees.

All of this would be supported by the corporate centre which would integrate the internal newspaper and the teletext service, both to flag up headline issues and to encourage employees to ask their line manager for further details. The IT function would provide database conferences for the discussion of the strategy implications, and the chief executive would log on and join the debate with his or staff.

Figure 8.2 shows the division of responsibilities among different levels of management, each of whom take responsibility for specific communication objectives and specific communication channels.

The negotiation of roles in a communication strategy needs to shift from arguing who has the right to communicate with whom, to what the business strategy requires, and how communication should be organized to support it.

273

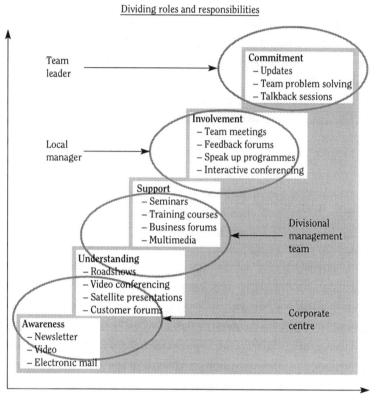

Dividing roles and responsibilities

FIGURE 8.2   To move employees up the communication escalator, different levels of management should divide the job into complementary roles and responsibilities

The way organizations currently manage communications

The way organizations currently manage communications often reflects their underlying priorities, together with:

● the stage of development of the organization
● the nature of the corporate identity
● the proposition the organization makes to the customer.

A US-based multinational pharmaceutical company organized communication on the underlying assumption that it was a centralized organization with a monolithic brand, and required national subsidiaries to market products developed and proven in the home market.

The centre's communication responsibility was focused on providing tools, promoting awareness and communication about the global organization, and on communication about the brand. The corporate headquarters was responsible for worldwide communication on policy, issues, research and development and environmental concerns, and for informing countries about each others' developments and activities. It provided the countries' communication departments with communication media: video/audio briefing packs which were to be adapted and tailored to local needs.

In the division of communication responsibility, the national subsidiary was responsible for local communication, for creating face-to-face communication forums and for developing team meetings. The corporate centre provided frameworks and guidelines for face-to-face communication, and provided training courses for managers at international headquarters.

The management of communication made sense in the context of the business strategy. The company was focused on offering leading products, and gaining operational efficiencies in its production and marketing. Its philosophy was largely to reproduce successful formulae in all areas of its operations.

A multinational oil company with a well recognized, similarly monolithic brand, but with a decentralized structure, evolved its split of responsibilities differently.

This oil company had a monolithic brand which was well recognized by its retail customers, as well as its corporate ones. It was organized by line of business, and operational units tended to be decentralized with a high degree of autonomy. It also involved a matrix structure, where reporting was both by country and by line of business with weaker functional reporting lines. The key responsibility for communication rested with line managers. However, within each business unit there were Human

Resources managers and communication managers who together had the responsibility for supporting the line manager.

At national level there was a corporate communications department whose functions included communication with the City and with analysts, responsibility for environmental issues and community affairs, and responsibility for providing corporate communication tools such as corporate videos and employee annual reports. It was also responsible for translating and adapting any materials sent to it from the communications department at international headquarters.

In terms of responsibilities each unit focused on different audiences with different objectives.

The *worldwide communications department* focused on only the top management teams of national subsidiaries. It organized and coordinated management exchanges and secondments, and developed strategic conferences on particular issues to which the country leadership groups and functional specialists were invited.

The *national communications department* had responsibility for the national corporate publications and for producing the corporate video. It was also responsible for managing the electronic communication system, including electronic mail and voice messaging, as well as for providing the news text service offered via electronic mail.

In the *business units*, the communication department was responsible for developing conferences, the team briefing process and business unit publications.

In both the organizations described above, the way responsibilities for communication are split reflect the stage of development and the business strategy. What happens when the strategy changes, the offer to the customer alters, the corporate identify shifts and the organisation moves to another stage of development?

BET is a conglomerate of business ranging from hand towels to cranes. It has grown largely by acquisition, and businesses have usually developed their own strong brand identities in their individual markets. In the late 1980s BET changed the proposition it made to its different customers. There was a logic that linked the portfolio of businesses which it owned. They all dealt with areas of support services – providing hygiene and towels in the washroom, security for the office building, scaffolding for renovation – that an office building manager would have to organize. The offer BET made was that in one place that manager could find a one-stop shop for all the services he needed. The offer was one of operational efficiency: Get all your services in one coordinated package, with one call – 'Your chore services are our core services.'

To deliver on that proposition, BET had to have a portfolio of services which were closely linked, and staff from each area who would work better and more coordinately than would separate contractors picked from the Yellow Pages.

BET had been a name known to the City, but unknown to some of its employees in the individual businesses. Now that promises were being made in BET's name to business customers and consumers alike, employees needed to understand and to see beyond the immediate concerns of their own business unit.

At the heart of the offer was the promise of greater central coordination of a federation of businesses, and a need to create a stronger central communication function. To encourage that cohesion and cooperation, BET raised the profile of the corporate brand internally, as well as in an external advertising campaign. The corporate 'starburst' was attached to individual business brand names, and staff were encouraged to identify with the wider corporate aims of BET as a whole.

The offer to the customer dictated the need for greater central coordination, and the need to present a single face involved the creation of a central communications department to manage the process. This worked closely with managers in the individual businesses, who knew more about their own staff, and a network of communication and personnel managers were used to coordinate communication and negotiate the best means of implementation.

While BET needed to communicate all the way down to the employees who were in contact with the customers, other organizations may have different requirements.

The Turnover Engines Group operates in eight countries in Europe on 60 sites. It is respected for its engineering skills and for the technical excellence of its products. Operational sites carry different brand and product names, which are a legacy of acquisition, and sporadic new product development. Some operations are clustered into product areas; others are organized by market sector. There has traditionally been a great deal of autonomy granted to local units to encourage them to get on with producing technically good products. More recently, however, the need to tender for Europe-wide business, and the pressure from customers to develop new products for collaborative European aviation projects, has driven a need for greater internal coordination and collaboration.

The people who have to collaborate are at relatively senior levels in the company. They are becoming more interested in career progression in other parts of the group as units come up with interesting innovations, and as competition for development funds intensifies.

As a first step to creating a greater feeling of 'group-ness', an employee communication manager was added to the centre, solely to create links between the business units. He sets up twice-yearly meetings for the most senior managers across the organization, to meet face-to-face. This cuts across all divisional, departmental and country boundaries. The purpose of these meetings is to improve communications at the most senior level, and to begin spinning a network of informal contacts which can be drawn on later.

The role of employee communications manager at the corporate centre is as a central focus for communication across 'the federation'. He is not seen as the communicator – that job belongs to the line manager and the supervisor. He acts as adviser and coach on communication.

As a way of tackling communication across geographically separated and dispersed sites, Turnover has also adopted a system of 'key communicators'. This system identifies people who are vital in the communications chain, and who are not necessarily line managers. It crosses boundaries, and includes not only managers responsible for large groups of people, but also specialists such as researchers, or financial or legal managers who have contacts within their own functions and with internal customers.

These key communicators all receive special training in communications as they need not only to pass information on, but listen for feedback as well. Ensuring consistency of style is as important as ensuring consistency of messages.

Creating the greater feeling of 'groupness' was not just the desire of the centre to exert influence over the units. It also stemmed from the need to be more innovative and collabortive to respond to customers, and to maintain product leadership.

The examples above are of decentralized federations, in pursuit of greater operational efficiency and product leadership. Greater central coordination through more communication from the centre helped them.

A strategy for becoming closer to the customer can cause fragmentation, as business decentralize, pushing information and authority as close as possible to the customer. Here communication has to be orchestrated to help create new 'corporate glue'. However, communication also has to be managed at local levels. Using central communication to communicate the virtues of decentralization and empowerment risks undermining the message.

In addition to using the line management chain initially to communicate face-to-face, First Direct also has a communications coordinator in each department. The internal communications manager uses the communication coordinators as an additional network, and individual coordinators tend to network with each other.

Formal face-to-face briefings are done via the line management, but coordinators do what they call 'mystery shopping' – going round checking that people understand and have received communication, expanding where necessary, and updating any people who were absent from the meetings. The aim is to ensure that communication is flowing around the organization, with the recognition that it does not simply have to go up and down vertical line management chains.

While organizations may want to devolve decision-making power to the level closest to the customer, there is usually the accompanying concern that this will lead to the reinvention of the wheel, the waste of resources and the failure to share learning and best practice.

Branches, hospitals, car dealerships, etc. compete in overlapping local areas for business and guard their business advantages and experience from each other. One approach to this is to cluster these activities in local networks. Instead of having each unit duplicating exactly the functions of the others, specialists in a discipline live in one unit and form part of the network, available to all the units in the local network. Now the focus can be concentrated on beating the competition rather than beating each other.

This means that good ideas found to work in one location can be tried in a neighbouring unit's area. Someone who is found to be skilled in a needed area – selling an insurance policy, recognising particular customer profiles, fixing a car – can be loaned to colleague units. This allows for greater sharing of resources, pooling of ideas and cooperation.

Sharing resources and having fewer experts, with deeper knowledge and being more available to more staff, enables everyone else to focus on the customer and develop their skills in understanding and serving them.

It also allows better coordinated local marketing, tailored to regional and local differences rather than national standards, and removes the need for every unit to offer every capability and service. In a cluster, each unit can specialize, if necessary, with the cluster as a whole representing a full portfolio of services and products.

Planning and targeting is thus based not on individual units' ability to place products with customers, but on the cluster as a whole, and its success in deepening relationships with customers. For this to work, it has to be supported by communication. Staff have to have a clear picture of the customers that they serve, the similarities between customers in their neighbouring locations, and their idiosyncracies.

They also have to identify not with their own individual unit, but with the network, or the cluster of which they are part. The unit manager does not therefore own the employees' loyalty, but has to create familiarity and trust among colleagues across the cluster. Staff have to focus not on the unit, but on what the cluster is doing, how it is performing and what its priorities are.

Staff need to have contact with other members of the cluster, especially where trust needs to be built in specialists living in another unit. The business strategy therefore calls for the focus of communication to be at cluster level, with one team member being responsible for the management of information and the creation of relationships.

However, to ensure that all the clusters feel part of one organization, and to ensure flows of ideas between clusters, the corporate centre will use communication about the rest of the organization and its overall aims and values, as a way of holding the network together. The shift towards customer-focused clusters will mean managing communication on the model of a network.

As it becomes more and more difficult to contain in an instruction manual the infinite variations of circumstance that may face customer-contact people, sharing of knowledge has to be done more and more through bringing people together. Contact between individuals creates familiarity, and familiarity creates a relationship and trust. Individuals constantly report that the most valuable time they spend together is in the bar in the evening during training courses and at conferences. There are frequent anecdotal reports about discovering that colleagues are doing the same projects and have valuable lessons to offer.

Creating structures to communicate knowledge and create relationships will involve the intelligent orchestration of networks through induction programmes, mixing people on training courses and then organizing regular reunions of participants. Some events will need to be organized at the local cluster level, but it is important for staff to keep the rest of the organization in view. So the cluster cannot be the sole focus of communication. Contact with others in the organization will be orchestrated by establishing special cross-functional project teams to solve particular customer problems, mixing colleagues from different regions on business seminars to foster greater mutual trust, and connecting networks of professionals on electronic mail, teleconferencing and telephone, to debate issues before coming together to resolve them.

To achieve this requires the technology to distribute information to the lowest point where it is needed. The technology allows the separating out of the strands of information distribution and relationship intertwined within communication. The two have to be balanced, as information technology without the balance of relationship leads to the instance quoted of one user of electronic mail sending a welcome back email to a colleague who had been off sick. The colleague was sitting in the next office.

Use of technology

To network people effectively means giving them the information they need and using technology to do so. Employees, especially the young, are increasingly computer-literate, and accustomed to using technology as customers. Technology will pervade every aspect of their working and leisure time in the future. It is cost-effective and efficient in transferring information.

The types of technology being used for communication include:
- electronic mail
- electronic reference library
- electronic daily news service
- news monitor screens within offices and at public access points
- electronic conferencing, allowing employees to open a discussion on an issue that interests them, wholly owned by employees and not by management
- business television, with networks linking offices and sites nationally and worldwide
- videoconferencing, with two-way audio and video communications link
- multi-media, with the capability to mix text, image and sound, and allow for different levels of detail and interest.

The use of technology carries its own dangers, especially the 'M25 effect'. When the M25 was built, it promised a way of moving traffic swiftly around and out of London. Now it has become virtually a circular car park, and it has been claimed that the creation of the road created its own traffic jams. Knowing that they had the M25, people moved further out of London, or chose schools for their children on the other side of London, relying on the new capability for fast travel. The benefit of smoother traffic never materialized – instead, the benefit has been taken in different patterns of commuting.

The spread of camcorders has stimulated a vast increase in video footage, with debatable levels of quality. Desktop publishing has allowed almost anyone to start up a newsletter. In electronic communication, the capability to copy a memo to senior executives worldwide stimulates 'vanity publishing', as ambitious managers copy the world on the progress of their work. In one high-tech company, the clutter on screen became so great that managers would print off their messages onto paper, take them home and throw them in the bin there.

One organization that looked at the match between people and technology was Apple Computers. It grew fast on the back of an innovative product and missionary zeal in its development and sales. The organisation was strongly decentralized, and with a culture of independent 'empowered' individuals, there was a cultural resistance towards central direction and control.

However, with the need to become a serious competitor in both the personal and business markets, there was a need for greater worldwide coordination and for the local implementation of a global strategy. The need to reduce selling prices to become more competitive had had a serious effect on the gross margin of products, calling for a significant reduction in the cost base, less spending and more belt-tightening. As a result, the organization shifted to a stage of greater central coordination.

Regional headquarters had dedicated 'organization communication managers', whose role it was to take a more strategic approach to communication. Respecting the tradition of national autonomy, there was a network of national communicators who adapted centrally provided tools to local conditions.

In Apple everyone had a machine on their desk. This allowed them to use the screen as the main vehicle for communication, and there was a heavy use of electronic communication. Part of the culture was the love affair with the technology, and it was recognized that this had to be offset by face-to-face communication.

A series of conferences for different management tiers were designed, with high investment in face-to-face forums and conferences to create understanding and ownership of the new strategy.

There was a worldwide publication, and worldwide videos are regularly produced as both a means of education and communication, and following a management conference interactive CD-ROM packages were developed as tools for managers to communicate with their employees.

Within the countries, national communication was based on regular face-to-face briefings, the use of a national publication and cross-functional communication meetings. Resource centres and libraries of video, text and software were available to anyone who wanted to know more about specific areas of information.

During one of its major periods of change, Apple opened a debate on screen into changes going on. What was most impressive about it was not the technology, but the openness of the debate and the no-holds-barred nature of the discussion. John Sculley, the then chief executive, would also periodically join the discussion, replying to points made and clarifying points of information.

Here was an example where technical capability met the willingness to discuss issues openly, and the combination was a powerful one.

The attraction of satellite broadcasting, business television and teleconferencing is that they put people in touch across geographically separated locations, and offer the opportunity for dialogue. Technology supports communication; it is not a substitute for it. Having the technical capability, and being unwilling to use it to say much of substance, is like using a racing car to deliver milk.

The IT function needs to be a member of the communication team, working with human resources and corporate communications, rather than being left to spread the technological capability without the understanding to make it work to best effect. Communication includes both information and relationships. Technology is a useful way of making information available, but it still requires face-to-face contact to build relationships.

REWRITING THE COMMUNICATION CONTRACT

There needs to be a redefinition of the implicit communication contract that prevails within the organization. In a meeting someone says, pointedly, 'I was not aware of that'. He does not mean that he has not availed himself of the information which was readily available, he means that someone has failed to bring it to his attention. Communicating information to him is solely someone else's responsibility.

This expectation, this implicit 'communication contract' has been based on the old assumption that knowledge was in the heads of those at the top of the hierarchy, and decisions had to be made about how much to distribute to the rest of the organization. There was an implicit promise that people would be kept informed, on a need to know basis, in a timely, relevant and appropriate manner.

Organizations cannot deliver on that promise now. In a relatively stable environment, with little change, it might have been possible. Now it is impossible. No one can predict all the information that will be needed.

Employee research continually shows dissatisfaction with internal communication, in part because the responsibility to communicate is felt to lie with management. Poor ratings of management's ability to identify individual needs, and to meet them in a timely and appropriate way, are like a diner's poor rating of a restaurant waiter who has not been able to predict the customer's individual food preferences, choose his favourite wine or know his food allergies.

It is impossible to provide a full service communication restaurant, but it is possible to provide a cafeteria. Here information is available, on display and easily accessible, and the choice is made by the individual.

This needs a shift in the appreciation of who is responsible for information. In an organization where employees' relationship with management is one of a child with its parent, it is the manager's responsibility alone to feed the children with the appropriate information. When someone feels he or she did not know something, it is blamed on a failure of management. Management feel their role is to communicate at employees; while staff feel it is someone else's job to inject them with communication, and someone else's fault if they do not know something.

In a bureaucracy where information is the currency, status is gained from hoarding it. In an open environment information is widely available, and individuals have the responsibility to access it for themselves. Information systems exist that make the wide distribution and accessibility of information possible. What prevents the full use of them is the clinging to an old contract of communication.

It is the manager's role to communicate, but that does not mean he or she has to be the conduit for all information. The communication channels that exist, and the time people have, will be overwhelmed by the information that needs to be passed through. To free up time for better use, face-to-face time is better spent discussing and solving issues, using the chemistry of the team and harnessing its creativity.

In an adult organization, it is the individual's responsibility to be nosy, and his colleagues' responsibility to put information where it can be readily accessed. People should not expect to be made well informed, they should have the opportunity to become well informed. Effective communication depends upon people feeling and accepting that responsibility, as Peter Drucker (1991) points out:

> The other requirement of an information based organisation is that everyone take information responsibility ...
>
> The key to such a system is that everyone asks: Who in this organisation depends on me for what information? and on whom, in turn, do I depend?
>
> Information responsibility to others is increasingly understood, especially in middle sized companies. But information responsibility to one's self is still largely neglected. That is, everyone in an organization should constantly be thinking through what information he or she needs to do the job and to make a contribution.

Some organizations have developed communication charters which tell employees what to expect of communication. They serve as a basis for a communication contract, and let people know what the company will provide and what employees should seek for themselves.

Seeking for yourself requires you to know what the company is trying to achieve, and what your role is in relation to that. People need to be clear about what they are supposed to be doing, and once they know their own role, they can seek the information they need to perform it. Without a clear sense of individual purpose, use of an information cafeteria simply becomes 'grazing', tasting a little of this and a little of that for interest and entertainment.

It is tempting to be drawn into the intricacies of technology and media, focusing on execution rather than the soundness of strategy, and the appropriateness of methods being used. The communication expertise needed for the future will include technical know-how about production tools, but it will certainly demand the ability to identify how communication can help achieve the business strategy, and a knowledge of the variables that affect communication within the organization. The internal communicator will need to be both a consultant in the communication process and an expert scout familiar with the cultural terrain of the business.

John Naisbitt (1990), tracker of mega-trends, described the need to balance high-tech' with 'high-touch', putting a human face to technology. In all this discussion of communication, it is worth remembering the heartfelt plea of one individual, responding to a communication survey, who offered the following advice:

Stop communicating with me, talk to me.

References

Drucker P.F. *Post Capitalist Society*. Boston: Harvard Business School Publishing

Drucker P.F. (1991). *The Coming of the New Organisation*. Boston: Harvard Business School Publishing

Hampden-Turner, Charles (1990). *Corporate Culture for Competitive Edge*. London: The *Economist* Intelligence Unit

Ingersoll Engineers (1993). *Creating Confidence: Communication, Planning and Successful Change*, Ingersoll Engineers Ltd.

Jacques, M. (1993). *The Sunday Times*. London

Katzenbach, J.R. and Smith D.K. (1993). *The Wisdom of Teams*. Boston: Harvard Business School Press, Boston

MacDonald, M. (1993). 'Inside Business', *The Independent on Sunday*, 23rd May. London

Martin, R. (1993). *Changing the Mind of the Corporation*. Boston: Harvard Business School Publishing

McGregor, D. (1960). *The Human Side of Enterprise*. New York: McGraw-Hill

Moss Kanter, R. (1991). *The New Managerial Work*. Boston: Harvard Business School Publishing

Naisbitt, J. and Aburdene, P. (1990). *Megatrends 2000*. London: Sedgwick and Jackson

People in Business (1991). *Managing Change in the 1990s*. London: People in Business

Popcorn, F. (1991). *The Popcorn Report*, London: Random House

The Economist, June 1993

The Price Waterhouse Cranfield Survey. (1991). Project Annual Report, Cranfield: Cranfield Press

Tracey, M. and Wiersema, F. (1993). *Choosing Disciplines or Choosing Customers*. Boston: Harvard Business School Publishing

Trompenaars, F. (1993). *Riding the Waves of Culture*. London: The Economist Books

Vandermerwe, S. (1993). *From Tin Soldiers to Russian Dolls*. London: Butterworth Heinemann

Wriston, W.B. (1991). *The State of American Management*. Boston: Harvard Business School Publishing

Index